Community Seed Banks

Community seed banks first appeared towards the end of the 1980s, established with the support of international and national nongovernmental organizations. This book is the first to provide a global review of their development and includes a wide range of case studies.

Countries that pioneered various types of community seed banks include Bangladesh, Brazil, Ethiopia, India, Nepal, Nicaragua, the Philippines and Zimbabwe. In the Global North, a particular type of community seed bank emerged known as a seed-savers network. Such networks were first established in Australia, Canada, the UK and the USA before spreading to other countries. Over time, the number and diversity of seed banks have grown. In Nepal, for example, there are now more than 100 self-described community seed banks whose functions range from pure conservation to commercial seed production. In Brazil, community seed banks operate in various regions of the country.

Surprisingly, despite 25 years of history and the rapid growth in number, organizational diversity and geographical coverage of community seed banks, recognition of their roles and contributions have remained scanty. This book reviews their history, evolution, experiences, successes and failures (and reasons why), challenges and prospects. It fills a significant gap in the literature on agricultural biodiversity and conservation, and their contribution to food sovereignty and security.

Ronnie Vernooy is a Genetic Resources Policy Specialist at Bioversity International, Rome, Italy.

Pitambar Shrestha is a Program Officer with Local Initiatives for Biodiversity, Research and Development (LI-BIRD), Pokhara, Nepal.

Bhuwon Sthapit is a Senior Scientist and Regional Project Coordinator for Bioversity International, based in Pokhara, Nepal.

Issues in Agricultural Biodiversity
Series editors: Michael Halewood and Danny Hunter

This series of books is published by Earthscan in association with Bioversity International. The aim of the series is to review the current state of knowledge in topical issues associated with agricultural biodiversity, to identify gaps in our knowledge base, to synthesize lessons learned and to propose future research and development actions. The overall objective is to increase the sustainable use of biodiversity in improving people's well-being and food and nutrition security. The series' scope is all aspects of agricultural biodiversity, ranging from conservation biology of genetic resources through social sciences to policy and legal aspects. It also covers the fields of research, education, communication and coordination, information management and knowledge sharing.

Published titles:

Crop Wild Relatives
A Manual of *in situ* Conservation
Edited by Danny Hunter and Vernon Heywood

The Economics of Managing Crop Diversity On-Farm
Case Studies from the Genetic Resources Policy Initiative
Edited by Edilegnaw Wale, Adam Drucker and Kerstin Zander

Plant Genetic Resources and Food Security
Stakeholder Perspectives on the International Treaty on Plant Genetic Resources for Food and Agriculture
Edited by Christine Frison, Francisco López and José T. Esquinas

Crop Genetic Resources as a Global Commons
Challenges in International Law and Governance
Edited by Michael Halewood, Isabel López Noriega and Selim Louafi

Community Biodiversity Management
Promoting Resilience and the Conservation of Plant Genetic Resources
Edited by Walter S. de Boef, Abishkar Subedi, Nivaldo Peroni and Marja Thijssen

Diversifying Food and Diets
Using Agricultural Biodiversity to Improve Nutrition and Health
Edited by Jessica Fanzo, Danny Hunter, Teresa Borelli and Federico Mattei

Community Seed Banks
Origins, Evolution and Prospects
Edited by Ronnie Vernooy, Pitambar Shrestha and Bhuwon Sthapit

Community Seed Banks
Origins, Evolution and Prospects

Edited by
Ronnie Vernooy,
Pitambar Shrestha and
Bhuwon Sthapit

Routledge
Taylor & Francis Group

LONDON AND NEW YORK

from Routledge

First published 2015
by Routledge
2 Park Square, Milton Park, Abingdon, Oxon OX14 4RN

and by Routledge
711 Third Avenue, New York, NY 10017

Routledge is an imprint of the Taylor & Francis Group, an informa business

© 2015 Bioversity International

British Library Cataloguing-in-Publication Data
A catalogue record for this book is available from the British Library

Library of Congress Cataloging in Publication Data
Community seed banks : origins, evolution, and prospects / edited by Ronnie Vernooy, Pitambar Shrestha, and Bhuwon Sthapit.
    pages cm. — (Issues in agricultural biodiversity)
    Includes bibliographical references and index.
    1. Seeds—Collection and preservation—Citizen participation.
    2. Germplasm resources, Plant.   3. Germplasm resources
    conservation—Citizen participation.   I. Vernooy, Ronnie, 1963–
    SB123.3.C63 2015
    631.5'21—dc23   2014042159

ISBN: 978-0-415-70805-0 (hbk)
ISBN: 978-0-415-70806-7 (pbk)
ISBN: 978-1-315-88632-9 (ebk)

Typeset in Bembo
by Keystroke, Station Road, Codsall, Wolverhampton

Printed and bound in the United States of America by Publishers Graphics, LLC on sustainably sourced paper.

Contents

Notes on contributors

A. Xinxiang, MsD, is involved in rice breeding and research on genetic resources at the Yunnan Academy of Agricultural Sciences, China.

Joyce Adokorach, MSc (environment and natural resources), is a research officer/ ethnobotanist with the National Agricultural Research Organisation in Uganda.

Anna Crystina Alvarenga, MSc (agro-ecology), is an agronomist and a researcher at the Centre for Alternative Agriculture of the North of Minas, Brazil.

Carlos Antonio Ávila Andino is an agronomist and regional project coordinator with Fundación para la Investigación Participativa con Agricultores de Honduras (FIPAH) at Vallecillo.

Irajá Ferreira Antunes, PhD (agro-biodiversity and plant breeding), does research on common bean landraces at Empresa Brasileira de Pesquisa Agropecuária (EMBRAPA), Rio Grande do Sul, Brazil.

Flavio Aragón-Cuevas, BSc, MSc (genetics), is a researcher at the Instituto Nacional de Investigaciones Forestales, Agrícolas y Pecuarias. He is in charge of the germplasm bank of native species, as well as community seed banks in Oaxaca, Mexico.

Bai Keyu, PhD (ecology), is a scientist and associate coordinator at Bioversity International's subregional office for East Asia in Beijing. She has a special interest in grassland ecology and resource management and the conservation and utilization of agricultural biodiversity.

Brendan Behrmann, MLIS, is the chief librarian and a cultivator at the Toronto Seed Library, Canada. He is also an avid seed saver, camper and alternative library advocate.

Katie Berger, MES candidate, is a sustainable food systems researcher, writer and advocate. She is an anti-capitalist community organizer, and a cultivator with the Toronto Seed Library, Canada.

Gilberto A. P. Bevilaqua, PhD (seed technology), is an agronomist in the temperate climate section of Empresa Brasileira de Pesquisa Agropecuária (EMBRAPA), Brazil.

Bharat Bhandari, MSc (management of biological diversity), is a senior agricultural specialist with USC Canada based in Nepal. He is working in eco-agricultural development.

Satie Boodoo is project manager at SJ Seed Savers, Trinidad.

Paul Bordoni (agro-biodiversity and knowledge management), is a research fellow with Bioversity International. He is investigating formal and informal seed and knowledge systems at the University of Cape Town, South Africa.

Hamadoun Bore is a smallholder farmer and manager of the community seed/ gene bank in the village of Boré, Douentza district, Mopti region, Mali.

Marvin Joel Gómez Cerna is an agronomist and regional project coordinator with Fundación para la Investigación Participativa con Agricultores de Honduras (FIPAH) at Yoro.

Pashupati Chaudhary, PhD (environmental science), is the programme director for Local Initiatives for Biodiversity, Research and Development (LI-BIRD), Nepal.

Rabiul Islam Chunnu has a degree in social science and is engaged in policy research for development alternatives in Bangladesh.

Dai Luyuan, PhD, is vice-president of the Yunnan Association for Science & Technology. He is studying wild rice and other rice resources in Yunnan, China.

Sarah Paule Dalle, PhD, is a programme manager with USC Canada's Seeds of Survival programme in Ethiopia and provides leadership in the development and implementation of USC Canada's planning, monitoring and evaluation systems.

Carlos Alberto Dayrell, MSc (agro-ecology and sustainable rural development), is a researcher at the Centre for Alternative Agriculture of the North of Minas, Brazil.

Rachana Devkota, MSc (agriculture economics), is a programme coordinator with Local Initiatives for Biodiversity, Research and Development (LI-BIRD), Nepal.

Lucien D'Hooghe, BSc (construction and public works), is a project manager and country representative with Welthungerhilfe in Uganda and Burundi.

Terezinha Aparecia Borges Dias, MSc (ecology), is an agronomist with the genetic resources and biotechnology section of Empresa Brasileira de Pesquisa Agropecuária (EMBRAPA), Brazil.

Mabjang Angeline Dibiloane, Dipl. (animal science), BTech (agricultural management), is the senior technical information officer in the Food Import and Export Standards directorate at the Department of Agriculture, Forestry and Fisheries, Republic of South Africa.

Ada Hamadoun Dicko, MA (rural development and management), is responsible for the development, monitoring and evaluation of the agro-biodiversity strategies for USC Canada's Seeds of Survival programme in Mali.

Dong Chao, MsD, is interested in the valuation and identification of rice germplasm at Bulang in Yunnan province. He is with the Yunnan Academy of Agricultural Sciences, China.

Nadi Rabelo dos Santos is an agro-ecologist working as a research assistant at Empresa Brasileira de Pesquisa Agropecuária (EMBRAPA), Brazil.

Gaylong Dukpa is the agriculture officer for the Bumthang administrative district in Bhutan.

Leonidas Dusengemungu, MSc (agriculture extension/education), is a socio-economist in charge of agricultural innovation platforms at the Rwanda Agriculture Board. He works with community seed banks under a Bioversity International project on linking farmers with multilateral systems.

Carlo Fadda, PhD (evolutionary biology and zoology), is based at Bioversity International in Kenya. His research focusses on the complexity of conservation efforts in the context of agricultural development.

Cristiane Tavares Feijó, MSc (indigenous biodiversity and ethnology), is a geographer and anthropologist. She researches Mbya Guarani biodiversity management at the Universidade Federal de Pelotas, Brazil.

Juan Carlos Hernández Fonseca is an agronomist in the Bean Program at the National Institute of Agricultural Technology Innovation and Transfer, Costa Rica.

Fabio de Oliveira Freitas, PhD (genetics and plant breeding), is an agronomist with Empresa Brasileira de Pesquisa Agropecuária (EMBRAPA), Brazil.

Gea Galluzzi, PhD (agricultural biodiversity), collaborates with Bioversity International on research on the conservation and sustainable use of agricultural biodiversity in Latin America.

Jean Rwihaniza Gapusi, MSc (biodiversity conservation), is a project officer with the Eastern Africa Plant Genetic Resources Network at the Association for Strengthening Agricultural Research in Eastern and Central Africa, Uganda.

Abdrahamane Goïta is a rural engineer and director at the USC Canada Seeds of Survival programme in Mali.

Orvill Omar Gallardo Guzmán is an agronomist and regional research coordinator at the Fundación para la Investigación Participativa con Agricultores de Honduras (FIPAH).

Mainor Guillermo Pavón Hernández, BSc (agricultural management), is a plant breeder and coordinator at the socioeconomic development programme of the Programa de Reconstrucción Rural (PRR) in Honduras.

Toby Hodgkin is coordinator at the Platform for Agrobiodiversity Research (PAR) and an honorary research fellow for Bioversity International. He works on the conservation and use of agro-biodiversity.

Teshome Hunduma, MSc (natural resource management and sustainable agriculture), is the agro-biodiversity policy advisor for the Development Fund, Oslo, Norway.

Devra I. Jarvis, PhD (botany), is the principal scientist at Bioversity International, Rome, and is currently leading a number of projects on the conservation and use of crop genetic diversity in various countries around the world.

Dilli Jimi is a farmer-leader, who manages the community seed bank in Tamaphok, Sankhuwasabha, Nepal.

Manisha Jimi is a member of the community seed bank in Tamaphok, Sankhuwasabha, Nepal.

Jahangir Alam Jony is a researcher in the field of biodiversity based farming with Unnayan Bikalper Nitinirdharoni Gobeshona, Bangladesh.

Patrick Kasasa, BSc (agriculture), MPhil (legume agronomy), leads the Agricultural Biodiversity Program at the Community Technology Development Trust (CTDT), Zimbabwe.

Jacob Kearey-Moreland, BA (sociology and philosophy), is a journalist, public speaker and systems designer. He is also a seed farmer and a cultivator with the Toronto Seed Library, Canada.

Kamal Khadka, MSc (plant breeding), is a programme coordinator with Local Initiatives for Biodiversity, Research and Development (LI-BIRD), Nepal.

E. D. Israel Oliver King, PhD (botany), is a principal scientist (biodiversity) at the M. S. Swaminathan Research Foundation in Chennai, India. He specializes in sacred forests, millets and community biodiversity management.

Catherine Kiwuka, MSc (botany), is an in-situ conservationist/research officer with the National Agriculture Research Organization (NARO) in Entebbe, Uganda.

N. Kumar, MPhil (economics), is a senior research fellow (biodiversity) at the M. S. Swaminathan Research Foundation in Chennai, India. He specializes in millets, community biodiversity management, agro-forestry and animal husbandry economics.

K. M. G. P. Kumarasinghe is a young farmer, a maths teacher and the field coordinator at the Kanthale site of the community-based biodiversity management project in Sri Lanka.

Marjorie Kyomugisha is a research officer with the Mbarara Zonal Agriculture Research and Development Institute at the Uganda National Agriculture Research Organization (NARO), Uganda.

Isabel Lapeña, MSc (environmental policy), is a lawyer specializing in genetic resources policies and legislation. She is currently working as a consultant at Bioversity International participating in the project 'Strengthening national capacities to implement the International Treaty on Plant Genetic Resources for Food and Agriculture'.

Fahima Khatun Liza has a degree in social science and is engaged in on-farm seed conservation and selection of crop varieties in Bangladesh.

Marcia Maciel, PhD (agronomy and ethnobotany), is a biologist and independent environmental consultant in the area of on-farm conservation in Brazil.

Nkat Lettie Maluleke, BSc (botany), is the plant collection officer at the National Plant Genetic Resources Centre, Republic of South Africa. She is responsible for the planning and collection of all plant genetic resources for food and agriculture from all ecological zones.

Thomas Marx, MSc (human geography), MA (international humanitarian assistance), is a desk officer at Welthungerhilfe headquarters, Bonn, Germany.

Hilton Mbozi is an agronomist in the Biodiversity Program at Community Technology Development Trust (CTDT) in Zimbabwe.

Tovhowani Mukoma, BTech (agriculture management and horticulture), is the in-situ conservation officer overseeing the national in-situ and on-farm conservation programme at the National Plant Genetic Resources Centre, Republic of South Africa.

Andrew T. Mushita works on issues related to seeds, and farmers' rights to agricultural biodiversity and local knowledge systems. He is the executive director of the Community Technology Development Trust (CTDT) in Zimbabwe.

Rose Nankya is a conservation biologist with Bioversity International in the Agricultural Biodiversity and Ecosystem Services Program, based in Uganda.

Theophile Ndacyayisenga, MSc (plant breeding and seed systems), is a scientist working on potato breeding at the Rwanda Agriculture Board (RAB), Rwanda.

Sognigbe N'Danikou, MSc (ethnobotany and natural resources management), has studied cucurbits and leafy vegetables in West Africa and developed propagation methods for *Vitex doniana* domestication.

Christian Ngendabanka, MSc (environmental planning), is a food security coordinator with Welthungerhilfe in Burundi.

Godefroid Niyonkuru, MSc (agricultural engineering), is a project coordinator and specialist in monitoring and evaluation for Welthungerhilfe in Burundi.

Antoine Ruzindana Nyirigira, MSc (biostatistics), is a biostatistician with the Rwanda Agriculture Board (RAB) and head of the biometrics programme and curator of the Rwanda National Genebank.

Rosalba Ortiz, MSc (ecological economics), is programme coordinator for the Development Fund, Oslo, Norway.

Gloria Otieno, MSc, is an agricultural economist specializing in genetic resources and food security policy at Bioversity International based in Uganda.

Mariam Sy Ouologueme is a rural development professional. Until 2013, she worked with the USC Canada programme in Mali as a community organizer in health, waste management and farmer organization.

Stefano Padulosi, PhD (biological sciences), is an agronomist specializing in plant genetic resources and their sustainable conservation and enhanced use. He leads the Marketing Diversity Research Theme at Bioversity International, Rome, Italy.

Milton Pinto, MSc (genetic resources and plant biotechnology), an agronomist, is head of Agricultural Biodiversity at the Fundación para la Promoción e Investigación de Productos Andinos's (PROINPA) Altiplano office in Bolivia.

Ubiratan Piovezan, PhD (ecology), is a zoologist with Empresa Brasileira de Pesquisa Agropecuária (EMBRAPA), Brazil.

Flor Ivette Elizondo Porras, a social anthropologist and business administrator, is the coordinator at the Bean Research and Agricultural Technology Transfer Program, Ministry of Agriculture and Livestock, Costa Rica.

G. Rajshekar, PhD (agriculture extension), is with the Centre for Sustainable Agriculture in India. He is working on establishing community seed banks and reviving traditional crop varieties.

G. V. Ramanjaneyulu, PhD (agriculture extension), is with the Centre for Sustainable Agriculture in India. He is currently working on open-source seed systems and community-managed seed enterprises.

Marleni Ramirez, PhD, is a biologist and physical anthropologist. She is the regional director for the Americas at Bioversity International, serving the region out of its offices in Cali, Colombia.

K. Radha Rani, PhD (horticulture), a scientist at Dr. YSR Horticultural University, is working on vegetable breeding and volunteering with the Centre for Sustainable Agriculture in India on seed-related work.

Wilfredo Rojas, MSc (crop science), is an agronomist specializing in genetic resources. He is currently the coordinator at the Altiplano regional office of the Fundación para la Promoción e Investigación de Productos Andinos (PROINPA) in Bolivia.

Karina Sandibel Vera Sánchez, a biologist, is the technical evaluator of conservation, use and sustainable management projects for the 11 vegetable and fruit networks of the Sistema Nacional de Recursos Fitogenéticos para la Alimentación y la Agricultura, Mexico.

Krishna Sanjel, BA, is a teacher in Dalchowki, where he is a volunteer member of the Dalchowki Development Committee and secretary of the seed bank committee, Nepal.

Juliana Santilli, PhD (environmental law), is a lawyer and researcher. She is a federal prosecutor in Brazil, specializing in environmental and cultural heritage law and public policy.

Rosalinda González Santos, MSc (botany), is a biologist with over five years of experience in coordinating the Sistema Nacional de Recursos Fitogenéticos para la Alimentación y la Agricultura, Mexico.

Chris Schmidt, PhD, is interim executive director and former director of conservation at Native Seeds/SEARCH, USA.

Pitambar Shrestha, MA (rural development), is a programme officer with Local Initiatives for Biodiversity, Research and Development (LI-BIRD), Nepal.

Pratap Shrestha, PhD (traditional knowledge systems), is the regional representative and scientific advisor for USC Canada's Asia office based in Nepal.

Amadou Sidibe, MSc (seed industry), is the plant genetic resource programme manager at the Institut d'Economie Rurale in Mali. He has contributed to the development of the national seed production system and regional seed regulation in West Africa.

M. A. Sobhan, PhD (botany), specializes in plant breeding and conservation of plant genetic resources in Bangladesh.

Bhuwon Sthapit, PhD (plant biology), is a senior scientist/regional project coordinator at Bioversity International's Nepal office. His work focusses on community-led biodiversity management, participatory tools and methods of on-farm diversity assessment, community seed banks and participatory plant breeding.

Sajal Sthapit, MSc (sustainable development conservation biology), is a programme coordinator with Local Initiatives for Biodiversity, Research and Development (LI-BIRD).

Asta Tamang is the principal biodiversity officer at the National Biodiversity Centre (NBC), Serbithang, Thimphu, Bhutan.

Tang Cuifeng, MsD, is engaged in rice breeding and genetic resource conservation at the Yunnan Academy of Agricultural Sciences, China.

Jaeson Teeluck is the manager and seedsman at SJ Seed Savers, manager of Agro Plus 2007 Ltd and president of the Broomage Agricultural Cooperative Society, Trinidad.

Surya Thapa, BSc (agriculture), is a project officer for Helping Hands, Nepal, and is responsible for implementing the Local Initiatives for Food Security Transformation project in South Lalitpur.

Evert Thomas is an associated scientist at Bioversity International, dedicated to promoting the conservation and sustainable use of forest genetic resources in Latin America and the Caribbean.

Juana Flores Ticona, agronomist, is a field technician in the area of agricultural biodiversity at the Fundación para la Promoción e Investigación de Productos Andinos's (PROINPA) Altiplano office in Bolivia.

Thabo Tjikana, MSc (conservation and sustainable use of plant genetic resources), began work at South Africa's gene bank as the plant collection officer; he is now curator at the gene bank.

Karolina Martínez Umaña is an agricultural economist and independent consultant, who was part of the Costa Rican team for the Food and Agriculture Organization (FAO)'s Seeds for Development project.

Deepak Upadhyay, MSc (agriculture economics), is a programme officer with Local Initiatives for Biodiversity, Research and Development (LI-BIRD), Nepal.

Jacob van Etten is a researcher at Bioversity International. His work is focussed on how to harness biological and environmental diversity in agriculture to adapt to variable and shifting climatic conditions.

Maarten van Zonneveld, PhD (applied biological sciences), is an associate scientist with Diversity for Conservation and Use at Bioversity International, based in Costa Rica.

Ronnie Vernooy, PhD (rural development sociology), has a long record of involvement in agricultural biodiversity and natural resource management. Currently, he is genetic resources policy specialist at Bioversity International in Rome, Italy.

Rodolfo Araya Villalobos, a specialist in bean breeding and seed production, is editor of the journal *Revista Agronomía Mesoamerica* and a professor at the University of Costa Rica.

Raymond S. Vodouhe, PhD (genetics and plant breeding), an agronomist, has bred Asian rice varieties for resistance to blast and drought and develops crop diversity and seed systems for sustainable production in adverse climate conditions in West Africa.

C. L. K. Wakkumbure is the project manager for the community-based biodiversity management project under the Green Movement of Sri Lanka.

Susan Walsh, PhD, is the executive director at USC Canada, a development cooperation organization focussed on seed security and food sovereignty in the Global South and Canada.

Mulumba John Wasswa, PhD, is a senior principal research officer with the National Agriculture Research Organization (NARO) and head of the Plant Genetic Resources Centre in Entebbe, Uganda.

Xu Furong, PhD, is engaged in the collection and conservation of medicinal herb germplasm at the College of Traditional Chinese Medicine, Yunnan University of Traditional Chinese Medicine, China.

Yang Yayun, PhD, is engaged in the collection, conservation and use of traditional rice germplasm at the Biotechnology and Genetic Resources Institute, Yunnan Academy of Agricultural Sciences, China.

Jorge Iran Vásquez Zeledón, MSc, is a forestry engineer. He is an advisor for the Farmer to Farmer programme (PCaC) of the National Farmers' and Ranchers' Union (UNAG) in Nicaragua.

Zhang Enlai, MsD, is engaged in research into genetic diversity and resistance to drought of rice resources in Yunnan province. He works at the Yunnan Academy of Agricultural Sciences, China.

Zhang Feifei, MsD, is exploring the physiology of plant stress and cell signal transduction at the Yunnan Academy of Agricultural Sciences, China.

Acknowledgements

Our journey across the globe in search of community seed banks and their stories was made possible thanks to the commitment and time of many colleagues and friends. We appreciate their various contributions to this book – from discussion of the original idea to finalization of the manuscript.

Elsa Andrieux and Gea Galluzzi joined us on the first part of the journey when we developed the rationale of the book, designed the case studies, drafted the analytical framework for the analysis of functions and services and collected the first reference materials. Gea also co-authored three of the case studies.

Herman Adams, Kamalesh Adhikari, Lucia Jane Beltrame, Walter de Boef, Manuel Delafoulhouze, Dimary Libreros, Francesca Gampieri, Maria Garruccio, Helga Gruberg, Yang Huan, Sally Humphries, Lise Latremouille, Lorenzo Maggioni, Marleni Ramirez, Zachary Rootes, Laurent Serrure, Fredy Sierra, Bell Batta Torheim, Valerie S. Tuia, Camilla Zanzanaini and Nancy Zinyemba searched for and sent us many useful references and contacted people in their networks who knew someone or something useful for the book.

Eliseu Bettencourt, Grace Delobel, Claudine Piq and Alexandra Walter translated several of the case studies from French, Portuguese and Spanish into English. Margarita Baena, Arwen Bailey, Nicolle Browne, Evelyn Clancy, Maria Gehring, Maninder Kaur and Maria Ximena Ocampo assisted with communications, reporting and administration. Michael Halewood, Danny Hunter, Isabel López-Noriega and Gloria Otieno provided technical and moral support all along the way. Emile Frison, former director general of Bioversity International, and Balaram Thapa, executive director of Local Initiatives for Biodiversity, Research and Development (LI-BIRD), strongly endorsed the book and gave us space to carry out our long journey as part of our busy schedules.

Dieter Nill (Deutsche Gesellschaft für Internationale Zusammenarbeit or GIZ) offered not only technical advice but also financial support. Alberto Camacho-Henriquez (also at GIZ), who inherited the book file from Dieter, critically reviewed the comparative analysis chapters and a number of the case studies. Tim Hardwick and Ashley Wright steered the publication process in the right direction. Sandra Garland skillfully edited the whole book, in particular succeeding in 'harmonizing' the many and diverse case studies.

Our special thanks go to the more than 100 authors of the case studies and the larger communities of farmers they represent in far-away and often little-known places around the world. Finally, the smiles of Tara Jimi, Sabina Jimi, Kamala Jimi, Manisha Jimi, Shanta Jimi, Bhim Kumari Jimi and Bina Jimi of the Tamaphok community seed bank in Nepal embellish the cover of our book. We thank all seven for their permission to portray them on the front page.

Ronnie Vernooy
Pitambar Shrestha
Bhuwon Sthapit

GIZ
An innovative partner for the global challenges of tomorrow

The wide range of services offered by the Deutsche Gesellschaft für Internationale Zusammenarbeit (GIZ) GmbH is based on a wealth of regional and technical expertise and on tried and tested management know-how. We are a German federal enterprise and offer workable, sustainable and effective solutions in political, economic and social change processes.

Most of our work is commissioned by the German Federal Ministry for Economic Cooperation and Development (BMZ). However, GIZ also operates on behalf of other German ministries and public and private bodies in Germany and abroad. These include governments of other countries, European Union institutions, such as the European Commission, the United Nations and the World Bank. We are equally committed to helping our clients in the private sector attain their goals.

Facts and figures

GIZ operates throughout Germany and in more than 130 countries worldwide. Our registered offices are in Bonn and Eschborn. We have 16,510 staff members around the globe, almost 70% of whom are employed locally as national personnel. GIZ's business volume was over EUR 1.9 billion as at 31 December 2013.

(Figures as at 31 December 2013)

1 The rich but little known chronicles of community seed banks

Ronnie Vernooy, Pitambar Shrestha and Bhuwon Sthapit

Thirty years of experience and still growing

Community level seed-saving initiatives have been around for about 30 years. They have been designed and implemented to conserve, restore, revitalize, strengthen and improve local seed systems, especially, but not solely, focussed on local varieties. These efforts have taken various forms and names: community gene bank, farmer seed house, seed hut, seed wealth centre, seed-savers group, association or network, community seed reserve, seed library and community seed bank. They handle major crops, minor crops and so-called neglected and underused species. The multiple initiatives have sought to regain, maintain and increase the control of farmers and local communities over seeds and to strengthen or establish dynamic forms of cooperation among farmers and between farmers and others involved in the conservation and sustainable use of agricultural biodiversity.

The initiatives include establishing and supporting multiple activities, such as community gene banks and seed banks, local farmer research groups or committees, participatory plant breeding teams, farmer and community agricultural biodiversity committees, seed-saver clubs and networks, seed exchange networks, seed production cooperatives and networks of custodian farmers. In this book, we focus on community seed banks – locally governed and managed, mostly informal, institutions whose core function is to maintain seeds for local use (Development Fund, 2011; Shrestha et al., 2012; Sthapit, 2013). Beyond this core conservation function, community seed banks have a broad range of additional purposes and vary significantly in scope, size, governance and management models, infrastructure and technical aspects, e.g. seed collection, seed storage and conservation, documentation and administration (Vernooy, 2013).

The drivers underlying their establishment, evolution and sustainability over time vary considerably. Some were set up following a famine, drought or flood and the loss of local seed supplies. Others were initiated following participatory crop improvement efforts that resulted in the availability of new cultivars and new skills to locally maintain healthy and genetically pure seed. Still others were established because farmers were far removed from a reliable source of quality seed. In developed countries, community seed banks often arose when hobby farmers and gardeners started to conserve and exchange their seeds in their neighbourhoods (Nabhan, 2013). Depending on management capabilities, governance modality and type, and level and duration of external support, community seed banks withered rapidly or endured.

This books aims to fill a gap in the scientific literature about community seed banks. Despite 30 years of existence and growth, no book has been published that reviews their history, evolution, experiences, successes, challenges and prospects. We believe this book is unique in bringing together a rich compilation of 35 diverse case studies from around the world and an in-depth comparative analysis of the key aspects of the operations and viability of community seed banks. Case studies were based on a common framework and include individual community seed banks (23 cases from 19 countries), organizations that support community seed banks (seven cases) and countries with policies in support of community seed banks (five cases).

Brief review of the literature

Most written information about community seed banks has been empirical and can be found in the grey literature or in reports or briefs of the nongovernmental organizations (NGOs) that assist farmers in conservation and sustainable use of local crops and landraces (Vernooy, 2013). A small number of references to community seed banks can be found in the literature on seed systems and the management of agricultural biodiversity (e.g. Almekinders and de Boef, 2000; CIP-UPWARD, 2003; de Boef et al., 2010, 2013; Shrestha et al., 2007, 2008; Sthapit et al., 2012). In this literature, community seed banks are treated as examples of local-level institutions that contribute to seed conservation, in particular of farmer varieties, countering erosion of crop diversity or its loss following natural disasters. Surprisingly, a major international publication, such as the FAO's (2010) *The Second Report on the State of the World's Plant Genetic Resources for Food and Agriculture*, does not make reference to community seed banks.

A working paper, 'A typology of community seed banks,' (Lewis and Mulvany, 1997) is, to our knowledge, the first and only attempt to characterize community seed banks globally. The authors focussed on the following distinguishing features: type of seed stored, seed-storage method and seed exchange and multiplication mechanisms. Based on these, the authors identified five types of community seed banks: de facto seed banks, community seed exchanges, organized seed banks, seed-savers' networks and ceremonial seed banks. Because of its focus on the type and management of the seeds, this work could be described as input centred and is a very useful early attempt to categorize the wide variation in community seed-saving efforts. However, it fails to fully address the diversity of functions and services provided by community seed banks and, as far as we know, it has not been brought up to date since it was published 18 years ago.

Jarvis et al. (2011) developed a framework to identify multiple ways of supporting the conservation and use of traditional crop varieties (key components of agricultural biodiversity) within agricultural production systems. They list grassroots seed-saver networks, community seed banks, community-based seed production groups and seed cooperatives as effective participatory mechanisms to improve the availability of plant genetic materials. This more recent framework integrates community seed banks with a broader perspective of conservation and use of plant genetic resources. It does not, however, elaborate what seed banks actually do, what functions they perform, what services they deliver and what factors influence their sustainability.

Sthapit (2013) proposes community seed banks as platforms of community-based management of agricultural biodiversity that can ensure effective implementation of farmers' rights through the recognition of their knowledge of local biodiversity, their participation in decision-making concerning its conservation, benefit-sharing and the existence of a supportive policy and regulatory framework. He argues that community seed banks can also provide an opportunity for interaction and integration of informal and formal seed systems, for the promotion of in-situ and ex-situ links to back up genetic resources locally as building blocks of crop improvement, food security and sustainable community development. Sthapit's careful attention to the political, institutional, socioeconomic and agro-ecological dimensions of community seed banks allows for the development of a coherent holistic framework. The framework we use in this book builds on his analysis.

Contents of this book

This book is divided into two major parts. Part I, Chapters 2–8, offers a comprehensive comparative analysis of key operational aspects of community seed banks. Part II contains the 35 case studies. The reading order of the two parts can be debated, as we did as editors: those who wish to view the bigger picture first are invited to follow the sequence as laid out. Those who prefer to read the detailed ground material first may jump forward to Part II. An epilogue aims to provide some food for thought concerning the future of community seed banks. Parts I and II are bridged by a collection of photos from the field representing diverse aspects of community seed banking around the world. The photos were selected from submissions received from the case study contributors and from the personal archives of the editors.

Part I: Comparative analysis of key aspects of community seed banks

Although most seed banks were created thanks to the financial and technical support of NGOs and the farming communities in which they are located, in recent years, a number of national governments have developed plans and mobilized some financial and technical resources for community seed banks. In search of self-support mechanisms, some of the more recently established community seed banks in developing countries have expanded their seed multiplication services, e.g. maize seed banks in Guatemala (FAO, 2011) and in the Philippines (Reyes, 2012). In Chapter 2, we describe the origins and evolution of community seed banks around the globe in more detail.

Community seed banks are examples of on-farm management of local crop diversity; they allow the processes of both natural and human selection to continue as part of the agricultural production system (Brush, 2000; Frankel et al., 1975). But, perhaps surprisingly, community seed banks have rarely been the subject of systematic scientific enquiry. In Chapter 3, we propose a framework for filling this knowledge gap. It allows a comprehensive analysis of the multiple facets, functions and services of local seed-saving experiences that can be united under the common definition of community seed bank. The elaboration of this framework is based on a combination of a comprehensive review of the global literature carried out by the book editors, an analysis of the case studies brought together in this book and our own field research experiences working with community seed banks in diverse settings around the world.

Chapter 4 looks at how community seed banks are dealing with governance and aspects of management, including costs. What has gone well and not so well? What key issues have emerged? We present a typology to categorize the various forms of governance that can be found among the case studies. We highlight the active roles and contributions of women, as custodians and caretakers of seeds in many countries, in the day-to-day functioning of many community seed banks. Across the case studies, considerable variety exists in terms of exactly how governance and management tasks are executed. Although most seed banks pay attention to these factors, variance can be observed in the rigour and regularity of their execution.

Chapter 5 discusses the minimum set of technical criteria and the issues that must be addressed by those who wish to operate community seed banks. To some degree, the technical issues depend on the type of seed bank in operation, but many are relevant to all seed banks. Technical issues emerge throughout the cycle of seed management, from the early stage of selecting which crop species and varieties to keep (and that selection may change over time) to the documentation of the collection and its use. Our findings indicate that, among the case studies, a number of community seed banks are highly competent and functioning well in terms of collection, documentation, regeneration, storage, distribution and marketing of seeds of diverse local and improved varieties. However, the overall picture is not that positive. We observe that community seed banks in most of the case study countries have work to do in such areas as applying scientific methods to the collection, storage and regeneration of seeds; documenting information and traditional knowledge; and introducing the latest technologies and management innovations into community seed bank management.

Community seed banks are usually small-scale organizations that store seed on a short-term basis and serve individual communities or several communities in surrounding villages. However, such local efforts can have a multiplier effect if the seed banks cultivate partnerships and engage in networking and sharing of information and seeds with other informal and formal seed system actors. Small community seed banks can, thus, sometimes become large ones, or a network of small community seed banks with considerable scope and depth can emerge. Chapter 6 offers some insights into the kinds of networks and the roles of the networks in which community seed banks become involved. We have grouped the case studies into two categories: light (few linkages) versus dense (multiple linkages) webs. Unfortunately, the case studies do not allow for an in-depth sociological assessment of how the nature of these networks affects performance and sustainability.

Across the world, community seed banks operate in countries with diverse political regimes and policy and legal contexts. Our review of the literature indicated that very little attention has been paid to analyzing the policy and legal environment in which community seed banks operate. Chapter 7 aims to fill that gap. The case studies offer a wide array of ways in which current policies and laws affect community seed banks, both positively and negatively. It is interesting and encouraging to note that, in recent years, promising changes have been taking place in a number of countries. This trend seems to confirm the (untapped) potential of community seed banks as well as the increasing awareness of this potential among key decision-makers and their interest in integrating community seed banks into a broader framework of policies, strategies and programmes.

The comparative analyses of key operational aspects of community seed banks in Chapters 2–7 feed into Chapter 8 where we discuss sustainability or long-term organizational viability. This is the greatest challenge facing community seed banks. What capacities must community seed banks have to be and remain effective in the long run? Our case studies suggest that a number of conditions must be met: legal recognition and protection, options for financial viability, members with adequate technical knowledge and effective operational mechanisms. Careful and systematic planning right from the start is another important factor. In this chapter, we elaborate on some aspects of sustainability of community seed banks, namely, human and social capital, economic empowerment, policy and legal environment and operational modality.

Part II: Case studies from around the world

Based on a review of the literature and enriched by the experience of the editors of this book with community seed banks over the last 20 years, we sent 50 invitations to a diverse group of people directly engaged with community seed banks in various parts of the world to contribute case studies to this book. We received 35 positive responses. Although the 35 case studies describe a considerable diversity of experiences, they do not pretend to cover in a statistically significant way the number of community seed banks per country, or region or continent. They do, however, all address key aspects of the operations and factors that influence the viability of community seed banks:

origin and history, functions and activities, governance and management, technical issues, support and networking, policy and legal environment and sustainability. The 35 case studies illustrate the rich but little known chronicles of community seed banks. Contributors include community leaders, custodian farmers, NGO staff, researchers and research managers. Case study countries include Bangladesh, Bhutan, Bolivia, Brazil, Burundi, Canada, China, Costa Rica, Guatemala, Honduras, India, Malaysia, Mali, Mexico, Nepal, Nicaragua, Norway, Rwanda, South Africa, Spain, Sri Lanka, Trinidad, Uganda, the United States of America and Zimbabwe. One case study covers Central America as a region.

We hope that the detailed comparative analysis of Part I and the narratives of Part II together will appeal to researchers, practitioners and decision-makers working on the conservation and sustainable use of plant genetic resources, seed systems, agricultural biodiversity and seed and food sovereignty.

References

Almekinders, C. and de Boef, W. (eds) (2000) *Encouraging Diversity: Conservation and Development of Plant Genetic Resources*, Intermediate Technology Publications, London, UK

Brush, S. B. (ed.) (2000) *Genes in the Field: On-farm Conservation of Crop Diversity*, Lewis Publishers, Boca Raton, Florida, USA; International Development Research Centre, Ottawa, Canada; International Plant Genetic Resources Institute, Rome, Italy

CIP-UPWARD (2003) *Conservation and Sustainable Use of Agricultural Biodiversity: A Sourcebook*, CIP-UPWARD, Laguna, Philippines

de Boef, W. S., Dempewolf, H., Byakweli, J. M. and Engels, J. M. M. (2010) 'Integrating genetic resource conservation and sustainable development into strategies to increase the robustness of seed systems,' *Journal of Sustainable Agriculture* vol 34, no 5, pp504–531

de Boef, W. S., Subedi, A., Peroni, N., Thijssen, M. and O'Keeffe, E. (eds) (2013) *Community Biodiversity Management: Promoting Resilience and the Conservation of Plant Genetic Resources*, Earthscan from Routledge, London, UK

Development Fund (2011) *Banking for the Future: Savings, Security and Seeds*, Development Fund, Oslo, Norway, www.planttreaty.org/sites/default/files/banking_ future.pdf, accessed 3 September 2014

FAO (Food and Agriculture Organization) (2010) *The Second Report on the State of the World's Plant Genetic Resources for Food and Agriculture*, FAO, Rome, Italy

—— (2011) *Agricultores mejoradores de su propia semilla: fortalecimiento de la producción de maíz a través del fitomejoramiento participativo en comunidades de Sololá*, FAO, Guatemala City, Guatemala

Frankel, O. H., Brown, A. H. D. and Burdon, J. J. (1975) *The Conservation of Plant Biodiversity*, Cambridge University Press, Boston, Massachusetts, USA

Jarvis, D. I., Hodgkin, T., Sthapit, B., Fadda, C. and López-Noriega, I. (2011) 'An heuristic framework for identifying multiple ways of supporting the conservation and use of traditional crop varieties within the agricultural production system,' *Critical Reviews in Plant Sciences* vol 30, nos 1–2, pp115–176

Lewis, V. and Mulvany, P. M. (1997) *A Typology of Seed Banks*, Natural Resources Institute, Chatham Maritime, UK

Nabhan, G. P. (2013) 'Seeds on seeds on seeds: why more biodiversity means more food security,' *Grist*, 2 November, www.grist.org/food/seeds-on-seeds-on-seeds-why-more-biodiversity-means-more-food-security/, accessed 3 September 2014

Reyes, L. C. (2012) 'Farmers have more access to good quality seeds through community seedbanks,' *Rice Today* vol 11, no 2, pp16–19

Shrestha, P., Sthapit, B., Shrestha, P., Upadhyay, M. and Yadav, M. (2008) 'Community seedbanks: experiences from Nepal,' in M. H. Thijssen, Z. Bishaw, A. Beshir and W. S. de Boef (eds) *Farmers, Seeds and Varieties: Supporting Informal Seed Supply in Ethiopia*, Wageningen International, Wageningen, The Netherlands, pp103–108

Shrestha, P., Sthapit, B., Subedi, A., Poudel, D., Shrestha, P. Upadhyay, M. and Joshi, B. (2007) 'Community seed bank: good practice for on-farm conservation of agricultural biodiversity,' in B. Sthapit, D. Gauchan, A. Subedi and D. Jarvis (eds) *On-farm Management of Agricultural Diversity in Nepal: Lessons Learned*, Bioversity International, Rome, Italy, pp112–120

Shrestha, P., Sthapit, S., Devkota, R. and Vernooy, R. (2012) 'Workshop summary report: national workshop on community seedbanks, 14–15 June 2012, Pokhara, Nepal,' Local Initiatives for Biodiversity, Research and Development, Pokhara, Nepal

Sthapit, B. (2013) 'Emerging theory and practice: community seed banks, seed system resilience and food security,' in P. Shrestha, R. Vernooy and P. Chaudhary (eds) *Community Seedbanks in Nepal: Past, Present, Future. Proceedings of a National Workshop, 14–15 June 2012, Pokhara, Nepal*. Local Initiatives for Biodiversity, Research and Development, Pokhara, Nepal, and Bioversity International, Rome, Italy, pp16–40

Sthapit, B., Shrestha, P. and Upadhyay, M. (eds) (2012) *On-farm Management of Agricultural Biodiversity in Nepal: Good Practices* (revised edition), Bioversity International, Rome, Italy; Local Initiatives for Biodiversity, Research and Development, Pokhara, Nepal; Nepal Agricultural Research Council, Khumaltar, Nepal

Vernooy, R. (2013) 'In the hands of many: a review of community gene and seedbanks around the world,' in P. Shrestha, R. Vernooy and P. Chaudhary (eds) *Community Seedbanks in Nepal: Past, Present, Future. Proceedings of a National Workshop, 14–15 June 2012, Pokhara, Nepal*. Local Initiatives for Biodiversity, Research and Development, Pokhara, Nepal, and Bioversity International, Rome, Italy, pp3–15

Part I

Comparative analysis of key aspects of community seed banks

2   Origins and evolution

Ronnie Vernooy, Pitambar Shrestha and Bhuwon Sthapit

Community seed banks have been around for about 30 years. As this book illustrates, they can be found across the globe. Their forms and functions are diverse, and their histories differ. Some countries, such as Brazil, India, Nepal and Nicaragua, have a relatively large number of them – from about 100 to several hundred, although exact numbers are hard to determine. Other countries, such as Bhutan, Bolivia, Burkina Faso, China, Guatemala, Rwanda and Uganda, have only a few nascent ones. Colleagues in some regions of the world suggest that no community seed banks have been established yet in central Asia, eastern Europe or the Middle East, but we have not carried out an in-depth search. There are community seed banks in the Pacific, but no case studies could be obtained for this book.

It is difficult to pinpoint the origin of community gene banks or seed banks, but nongovernmental organizations (NGOs) have played a key role and continue to do so in many countries. In recent years, government agencies at the national or state level in a number of countries have become interested in establishing and supporting community seed banks, often as part of a national in-situ or on-farm conservation strategy. Examples include Bhutan, Bolivia, Brazil, South Africa and the countries of Mesoamerica (see the case studies in Part II).

In this chapter, we summarize what we have learned about the origins of community seed banks based on a review of the mostly grey literature and the case studies we have collected. We then present a schematic timeline of their evolution, based solely on the case studies.

Roots

In the Global South, NGOs have set up community gene or seed banks most of all to conserve local or 'farmer' varieties and rare varieties before this genetic diversity was lost because of societal pressures (commercialization of agriculture, expansion of the industrial food sector, monopolization of seed production) or recurring natural disasters (most notably droughts, floods and hurricanes).

Among the founders of community seed banks are the Rural Advancement Foundation International (RAFI), now known as ETC Group or Action

Group on Erosion, Technology and Concentration. In 1986, RAFI produced a 'community seed bank kit', as far as we know, the first how-to guide for establishing a local gene or seed bank.

In the case study on the work of USC Canada (Chapter 37), the authors describe how the idea of community seed banks emerged as a component of an ambitious programme called Seeds of Survival (see www.usc-canada.org/what-we-do/seeds-of-survival). As a response to the disastrous drought and subsequent famine in Ethiopia, this programme, launched in 1989, began to work in partnership with farmers to rebuild the local systems that had been seriously affected by the drought. Scientists from Ethiopia's Plant Genetic Resource Centre of Ethiopia (now the Institute of Biodiversity Conservation), a government agency, worked in the regions most affected by drought to multiply, on farm, as many varieties as possible of sorghum, wheat and locally adapted maize (Worede and Mekbib, 1993; Feyissa, 2000; Feyissa et al., 2013). These varieties were then re-integrated into the local seed systems by participating farmers and distributed to thousands of other farmers. Community seed banks were initiated to guarantee local stocks of these varieties. USC Canada, based in Ottawa, with partner NGOs around the world continues to run the Seeds of Survival programme (Green, 2012; see Chapter 37).

Inspired by RAFI, in 1992, the Southeast Asia Regional Initiatives for Community Empowerment (SEARICE) assisted another Philippine NGO, CONSERVE, to set up a community gene bank (Bertuso et al., 2000). In Latin America, the Chile-based Centro de Educación y Tecnología (CET) began to establish community seed banks in a number of Latin American countries. In Brazil, a diversity of community seed bank initiatives emerged throughout the country, some of them local, others connected to international NGOs (see Chapters 12, 13, 39). Other examples include Unnayan Bikalper Nitinirdharoni Gobeshona (UBINIG) in Bangladesh where the impetus was flooding and a cyclone in the late 1980s (Mazhar, 1996; see Chapter 9), the Relief Society of Tigray (in 1988) and Ethio-Organic Seed Action in Ethiopia (Feyissa et al., 2013).

In Zimbabwe, a pioneer was the Community Technology Development Trust (CTDT), which established the first community seed bank in 1992 following severe drought (Mujaju et al., 2003; see Chapter 38). In India, several NGOs took the lead, including the GREEN Foundation (starting in 1992), the Academy of Development Sciences (in 1994; see Khedkar, 1996), the Deccan Development Society (Satheesh, 1996), the MS Swaminathan Research Foundation (in 2000; see Chapter 18) and Gene Campaign (in 2000). In Nepal (Shrestha et al., 2013b), there were USC Canada Asia (in 1996; see Chapter 24) and Local Initiatives for Biodiversity, Research and Development (LI-BIRD, in 2003; see Chapter 34); in Nicaragua, the Centro Intereclesial de Estudios Teológicos y Sociales (CIEETS) and the Programa Campesino a Campesino (PCaC, Farmer to Farmer program) (SIMAS, 2012; see Chapter 26).

The Norwegian Development Fund, which is active in several countries around the world, has been another continuous supporter of community seed banks (Development Fund, 2011; see Chapter 35). Other international NGOs that have supported community seed banks include ActionAid and OXFAM. Bioversity International has pioneered and supported the establishment of community seed banks in a number of countries (e.g. Bolivia, Burkina Faso, China, Ethiopia, India, Malaysia, Nepal, Rwanda, South Africa and Uganda) as part of its research on the conservation and sustainable use of agricultural biodiversity and, more recently, on adaptation to climate change.

Partly preceding and partly in parallel with establishment of seed banks in the Global South, many 'seed-saver' groups, associations and networks have formed in Western nations. These are made up mostly of hobby farmers, breeders and gardeners, often thousands of miles apart, who share a common interest in keeping traditional and local crop diversity alive. These seed savers form a community of practice more than a geographic community.

The USA-based Seed Savers Exchange, a not-for-profit, member-supported organization, was established in 1975 by Diane Ott Whealy and Kent Whealy (see www.seedsavers.org/). Its aim is to preserve heirloom seeds by building a network of committed people who collect, save and share seeds and plants. Heirloom seeds are passed on from generation to generation. In the North American context, many of these seeds were carried by settlers from European countries. The organization is based at a 360ha heritage farm in Iowa, where seeds are reproduced, catalogued and disseminated and where educational activities take place. The farm operations give continuity to the network's efforts.

In 1986, inspired by the example of the USA, the Australian Seed Savers was set up by Michel and Jude Fanton. First established nation-wide without government support, it has since developed into a network of local networks spread out across the country (Fanton and Fanton, 1993; Seed Savers' Network and Ogata, 2003). Since 1995, the Australian network has been supporting the establishment and strengthening of such groups in almost 40 countries, including Afghanistan, Bosnia, Cambodia, Croatia, Cuba, Italy, Japan, Kenya, Palau, Portugal, Serbia, Solomon Islands, South Africa, Spain, Taiwan and Tonga (see www.seedsavers.net/).

In Canada, Seeds of Diversity operates as a charitable organization dedicated to the conservation, documentation and use of public-domain, non-hybrid plants of Canadian significance. The 1,400 members grow, propagate and distribute over 2,900 varieties of vegetables, fruit, grains, flowers and herbs. The seed network, first established in 1984, describes itself as 'a living gene bank'. Each year, Seeds of Diversity produces a Member Seed Directory which allows members to obtain samples of the seeds and plants offered by other members in exchange for return postage (see www.seeds.ca/).

In Europe, a large number of seed-saver groups and associations vary considerably in membership and scope of activities; these organizations exist in Austria, France, Germany, Greece, Holland, Ireland, Italy, Spain and the UK.

Evolution and emerging trends

Increasing scope and function

Based on the experiences described in the case studies, a number of trends can be discerned. One has been a broadening of the functions and scope of community seed banks, mainly a result of a natural learning-by-doing process. Although many community seed banks were initially set up for the purpose of conservation, over time additional functions were added: providing access to and availability of seeds, operating as a platform for community development and contributing to seed and food sovereignty. In some cases, this happened as a result of successful conservation efforts and a growing demand among local farmers or farmers from other communities for materials maintained in the seed banks. In other cases, it was a result of the difficulties faced by community seed banks in dealing primarily with conservation, most notably lack of incentives to keep up the work.

The experiences of two international NGOs that pioneered support for community seed banks are illustrative. USC Canada's support for strengthening community seed supply systems has grown from a seed recovery programme responding to drought and genetic erosion in Ethiopia into a global programme focussed on promoting food security and food sovereignty through the sustainable use of agricultural biodiversity. Community seed banks have grown into centres for experimentation and innovation around seeds that can handle the vagaries and extremes of climate change and have become facilitators to help farm communities organize around their rights and interests in production that is affordable, productive and respectful of the integrity of their landscapes and plant genetic resources (see Chapter 37). Community seed banks supported by the Development Fund have evolved from seed restoration and rehabilitation centres, supported by participatory plant breeding, into organized seed grower associations for local seed production and marketing (see Chapter 35). The sole case study from the Caribbean region, in Trinidad (Chapter 29), describes the evolution of a small seed supply unit into an advanced storage facility with land for carrying out trials and seed selection. The facilitators of the seed bank also set up farmers' groups who connect with each other through Facebook. In addition, the seed bank established links with a civil society foundation working with communities on such projects as backyard gardening for households.

Other examples of growth come from Bolivia (Chapter 11) and Honduras (Chapter 33), where the original efforts in participatory variety improvement gradually evolved into a broader programme that includes the conservation and use of agricultural biodiversity. In Bolivia, community seed banks moved from quinoa and cañihua storage banks to agricultural biodiversity community banks. Apart from conservation, new areas of interest have developed, such as seed health, soil fertility, increased yields and commercialization of agricultural biodiversity products. In Honduras, when farmers and the NGOs working with them began to realize the importance of conserving and documenting the local materials they were collecting, they decided to conserve seed at the community and regional levels.

Connecting on a higher level

A second trend can be seen in efforts to reach levels higher than the local community. This has resulted in the formation of networks or associations of community seed banks supported by facilitated reflection on past experiences, targeted training in organizational development and technical cooperation with other institutions. In Nepal, at a first national workshop on community seed banks held in 2012, participants concluded that although Nepal has a large number of seed banks, sharing and learning among them has not taken place, except for a few exchange visits by farmers' groups and practitioners (Shrestha et al., 2013a). In a follow-up workshop in March 2013, farmers and groups involved in managing community seed banks formed an ad hoc committee to establish a national network to be a platform for learning and sharing among community seed banks, to facilitate exchange of seeds and planting materials, to prepare a national catalogue of genetic resources conserved by community seed banks, to facilitate a process of linking community seed banks with the national gene bank, to represent community seed banks in national fora when necessary and to facilitate incorporation of the conservation of plant genetic resources into community seed banks where it has not yet been done (Chapter 34). Note also that community seed banks in Nepal are supported by Bioversity International, the Development Fund of Norway, the Department of Agriculture of the government of Nepal, OXFAM and USC Canada. In Brazil, community seed banks have become part of regional movements. For example, so-called regional seed houses represent a conservation strategy that combines various elements of conservation and sustainable use put into practice by peasant farmers, organizations and social movements in the field of agro-ecology and by federal institutions of teaching and research (Chapter 13).

Increasing numbers

Another trend has been the multiplication of efforts by a supporting agency or other organization based on success and experience accumulated in one area of a country or inspired by examples from other countries. In Mali, eight community banks in an area in the north of the country have formed a network that works in partnership with community seed banks in southern Mali to carry out key activities to enhance the value of and conserve farmers' seeds: seed fairs, multiplication of seeds in the south that are unsuited to conditions in the north, seed exchanges and advice to improve the productivity of different varieties.

In Burundi, Welthungerhilfe of Germany developed a plan and training programme for the construction and management of seed stores, a particular type of community seed bank (Chapter 32). Later, the plan and approach inspired other organizations, such as the Alliance 2015 partner of Welthungerhilfe,

Concern International, the Belgian Technical Cooperation and the support programme of the European Union in Burundi (Programme Post-Conflit de Développement Rural) to also invest in this kind of seed store. The local government is now starting a support programme for all seed stores. In the USA, the pioneering work of Native Seeds/SEARCH has provided an example of a regional seed model that has inspired efforts elsewhere and brought the importance of crop diversity to public attention in the southwest USA and beyond (Chapter 31).

Bioversity International's most recent efforts to establish and support community seed banks in China, Rwanda and Uganda have been inspired by previous experiences in other countries, such as Burkina Faso, Ethiopia and Mali. USC Canada, the Development Fund and LI-BIRD have benefitted from similar learning tracks. In Bhutan and South Africa, the lead government agencies supporting the establishment of community seed banks have learned from past experience to take a cautious approach: first set up a small number of community seed banks and monitor their development before expanding the programme.

A caveat is necessary here. Good examples cannot always be adopted and adapted. The Malaysia case study (Chapter 20) indicates that cultural issues can prevent people from reaching a shared agreement about how best to set up a community seed bank. This case also highlights the need to consider the availability of enough capable people to dedicate time to the efforts required to set up and run a community seed bank. In the context of urban migration, labour constraints have become common in many rural areas of the world.

Government support

A fourth trend is the emerging interest of national and state governments in establishing and supporting community seed banks. Examples in this book include case studies from Bhutan, Bolivia, Burundi, the Central American countries, Mexico, Nepal and South Africa. This trend might be partly the outcome of longer-term efforts of community seed banks and their supporting organizations to raise awareness of the roles and achievements of community seed banks, including their role as a mechanism to implement farmers' rights. Another likely factor is the increased preoccupation of governments with strengthening national capacity to respond to climate change. In Central America, community seed banks have also gained recognition as effective organizations to respond to natural disasters and related problems (hurricanes in particular often leading to landslides and flooding and the resulting loss of seeds).

Over the last years, three Brazilian states (Paraíba, Alagoas and Minas Gerais) have approved laws aimed at providing a legal framework for existing community seed banks created and maintained by small-scale farmers' associations with the support of NGOs and sometimes local governments. A provision has been made to include seeds produced by community seed banks in regular extension programmes. Four other states (Bahia, Pernambuco, Santa Catarina and São Paulo) have similar legal bills being discussed in their legislative assemblies (Chapter 39).

In Nepal, Seed Vision 2025 is a major policy document with a clear statement about community seed banks, gene banks, community-based seed production and capacity building among seed producers and other producer groups to promote production and access to high-quality seeds (earlier, the government published a community seed bank implementation guideline, but it was not widely circulated). The government document also envisions identifying, mapping and developing seed production pockets within the country and emphasizes investment by the private sector. The government of Nepal has started to provide technical and financial support to a small number of community seed banks in the country (Chapter 41). In 2013, the government of South Africa started a similar effort with support from Bioversity International (Chapter 43).

Evaluation

A fifth trend, also recent, is the carrying out of evaluative research and impact assessments to better understand and document the factors that contribute to long-term sustainability of community seed banks. Several organizations supporting community seed banks are taking the lead in this kind of research and assessment: ActionAid, Bioversity International, Development Fund, LI-BIRD, OXFAM-Nepal and USC Canada. A number of review studies have been produced in recent years (Development Fund, 2011; SIMAS, 2012; Sthapit, 2013; Vernooy, 2013), and this book is another example of critical reflection on the functions of community seed banks and their prospects for the future. This work is combined with the design and implementation of specific strategies to develop organizational and financial sustainability of community seed banks.

One such strategy deployed by several community seed banks across the world is the acquisition of formal organizational status, in particular as a cooperative. This is already taking place, for example, in Burundi (Chapter 32), Mali (Chapter 22) and Nepal (Chapter 24) and is envisioned in Mexico where producer cooperatives would sell not only seeds but also traditional products made with native plant varieties conserved by the network of community seed banks (Chapter 42). In the Kolli Hills of India, community seed banks have evolved into village millet resource centres that not only deal with conservation but also with technology and value-chain development (Chapter 18). In Oaxaca, a federal state of Mexico, community seed banks are being transformed into private limited rural production companies. This legal status allows farmers access to resources from the municipal, state or federal government (Chapter 23).

If and how the trends outlined above will evolve in the future is discussed in the final chapter.

References

Bertuso, A., Ginogaling, G. and Salazar, R. (2000) 'Community genebanks: the experience of CONSERVE in the Philippines,' in C. J. M. Almekinders and W. S. de Boef (eds) *Encouraging Diversity: Conservation and Development of Plant Genetic Resources*, Intermediate Technology, London, UK, pp117–133

Development Fund (2011) *Banking for the Future: Savings, Security and Seeds*, Development Fund, Oslo, Norway, www.planttreaty.org/sites/default/files/banking_future.pdf, accessed 3 September 2014

Fanton, M. and Fanton, J. (1993) *The Seed Savers' Handbook*, Seed Savers Foundation, Byron Bay, Australia

Feyissa, R. (2000) 'Community seedbanks and seed exchange in Ethiopia: a farmer-led approach,' in E. Friis-Hansen and B. Sthapit (eds) *Participatory Approaches to the Conservation and Use of Plant Genetic Resources*, International Plant Genetic Resources Institute, Rome, Italy, pp142–148

Feyissa, R., Gezu, G., Tsegaye, B. and Desalegn, T. (2013) 'On-farm management of plant genetic resources through community seed banks in Ethiopia,' in W. S. de Boef, A. Subedi, N. Peroni, M. Thijssen and E. O'Keeffe (eds) *Community Biodiversity Management: Promoting Resilience and the Conservation of Plant Genetic Resources*, Earthscan from Routledge, London, UK, pp26–31

Green, K. (2012) 'Community seedbanks: international experience,' *Seeding* vol 25, no 1, pp1–4

Khedkar, R. (1996) 'The Academy of Development Sciences rice project: need for decentralized community genebank to strengthen on-farm conservation,' in L. Sperling and M. Loevinsohn (eds), *Using Diversity: Enhancing and Maintaining Genetic Resources On-farm*, International Development Research Centre, New Delhi, India, pp50–254

Mazhar, F. (1996) '*Nayakrishi Andolon*: an initiative of the Bangladesh peasants for a better living,' in L. Sperling and M. Loevinsohn (eds) *Using Diversity: Enhancing and Maintaining Genetic Resources On-farm*, International Development Research Centre, New Delhi, India, pp255–267

Mujaju, C., Zinhanga, F. and Rusike, E. (2003) 'Community seed banks for semi-arid agriculture in Zimbabwe,' in *Conservation and Sustainable Use of Agricultural Biodiversity: A Sourcebook*, CIP-UPWARD, Laguna, Philippines, pp294–301

Satheesh, P.V. (1996) 'Genes, gender and biodiversity: Deccan Development Society's community seedbanks,' in L. Sperling and M. Loevinsohn (eds) *Using Diversity: Enhancing and Maintaining Genetic Resources On-farm*, International Development Research Centre, New Delhi, India, pp268–274

Seed Savers' Network and Ogata, M. (2003) 'Grassroots seed network preserves food crops diversity in Australia,' in *Conservation and Sustainable Use of Agricultural Biodiversity: A Sourcebook*, CIP-UPWARD, Laguna, Philippines, pp284–288

Shrestha, P., Gezu, G., Swain, S., Lassaigne, B., Subedi, A. and de Boef, W. (2013a) 'The community seedbank: a common driver for community biodiversity management,' in W. S. de Boef, A. Subedi, N. Peroni, M. Thijssen and E. O'Keeffe (eds) *Community Biodiversity Management: Promoting Resilience and the Conservation of Plant Genetic Resources*, Earthscan from Routledge, London, UK, pp109–117

Shrestha, P., Vernooy, R. and Chaudhary, P. (eds) (2013b) *Community seedbanks in Nepal: past, present, future. Proceedings of a national workshop, 14–15 June 2012, Pokhara, Nepal*. Local Initiatives for Biodiversity, Research and Development, Pokhara, Nepal, and

Bioversity International, Rome, Italy, www.bioversityinternational.org/uploads/tx_
news/Community_seed_banks_in_Nepal__past__present_and_future_1642.pdf,
accessed 3 September 2014

SIMAS (Servicio de Información sobre Agricultura Sostenible) (2012) *Bancos
comunitarios de semillas: siembra y comida*, SIMAS, Managua, Nicaragua

Sthapit, B. (2013) 'Emerging theory and practice: community seed banks, seed system
resilience and food security,' in P. Shrestha, R. Vernooy and P. Chaudhary (eds)
*Community Seedbanks in Nepal: Past, Present, Future. Proceedings of a National Workshop,
14–15 June 2012, Pokhara, Nepal.* Local Initiatives for Biodiversity, Research and
Development, Pokhara, Nepal, and Bioversity International, Rome, Italy, pp16–40

Vernooy, R. (2013) 'In the hands of many: a review of community gene and seedbanks
around the world,' in P. Shrestha, R. Vernooy and P. Chaudhary (eds) *Community
Seedbanks in Nepal: Past, Present, Future. Proceedings of a National Workshop, 14–15 June
2012, Pokhara, Nepal.* Local Initiatives for Biodiversity, Research and Development,
Pokhara, Nepal, and Bioversity International, Rome, Italy, pp3–15

Worede, M. and Mekbib, H. (1993) 'Linking genetic resource conservation to farmers
in Ethiopia,' in W. de Boef et al. (eds) *Cultivating Knowledge: Genetic Diversity, Farmer
Experimentation and Crop Research*, Intermediate Technology, London, UK,
pp78–84

3 Functions and activities

Pitambar Shrestha, Ronnie Vernooy
and Bhuwon Sthapit

A community seed bank is much more than a bank for money. It is a bank for
life-food.
— A woman farmer from Zimbabwe (Chapter 38)

A community seed bank can perform multiple functions. Depending on the
objectives set by its members, it might undertake raising awareness and education; documentation of traditional knowledge and information; the collection,
production, distribution and exchange of seeds; sharing of knowledge and
experience; promoting ecological agriculture; participatory crop improvement
experiments; income-generating activities for members; networking and policy
advocacy; and the development of other community enterprises. Apart from the
concrete results that these activities produce, farmers' involvement can contribute
to their empowerment as individuals and groups. Based on our global review of
community seed banks, we can conclude that some are highly focussed on
conservation of agricultural biodiversity including reviving lost local varieties,
while others give priority to both conservation and access and availability of
diverse types of seeds and planting materials suitable to various agro-ecological
domains, primarily for local farmers. In addition to these two main functions,
promoting seed and food sovereignty is another core element of some community
seed banks.

Based on the experiences collected in this book and other analyses (Sthapit,
2013; Vernooy, 2013), we have grouped the functions and activities of community seed banks into three core areas: conservation, access and availability,
and seed and food sovereignty. In theory, this could lead to seven possible
types of seed banks: three single function, three double functions and one that
would undertake all three functions. However, considering only the community seed banks described in the second part of this book, we have limited
our classification to four types (Table 3.1).

A focus on conservation

Conservation of local crop varieties is one of the most important functions of
community seed banks. In fact, except for a few cases, most community seed

Table 3.1 Classification of the community seed bank case studies based on functions

Functions*	Case study examples (Chapter)
Conservation	Bhutan (10), Malaysia (20), Mexico (23, 42), Rwanda (27)
Access and availability	Burundi (32), Canada (14), Costa Rica (16), Uganda (30)
Conservation; and Access and availability	Bolivia (11), Brazil (12, 13), China (15), Guatemala (17), Honduras (33), India (18, 19), Mali (21, 22), Nepal (24, 25, 34), Nicaragua (26), South Africa (43), Sri Lanka (28), United States (31), Trinidad (29), Zimbabwe (38)
Conservation; Access and availability; and Seed and food sovereignty	Bangladesh (9), Brazil (39), Spain (36)

*Conservation = conservation of local varieties, heirloom varieties and restoration of lost varieties from the area; Access and availability = platform offering access to multiple varieties at the community level, fostering exchange and seed production of participatory plant bred varieties; Seed and food sovereignty = local control over seed conservation, sharing of agricultural biodiversity knowledge and expertise and promoting ecological agriculture.

banks were established to stop the rapid loss of local varieties and rebuild local crop diversity through rescue and rehabilitation. A number of factors have contributed to the loss of crop diversity and, in many parts of the world, continue to do so. We can distinguish between social factors, such as farmers following what their neighbours do in terms of replacing local varieties with modern ones; political factors, where the public sector has promoted improved and hybrid varieties without considering loss of local varieties; natural factors, such as prolonged drought and devastating flood leading to the total destruction of local crops; and economic factors, such as the replacement of local varieties with improved and hybrid ones to increase production and household income. An additional factor is the lack of awareness among farming communities about the current value and future potential value of local varieties. In concrete terms, Nepalese farmers used to cultivate more than 2,500 local varieties of rice before the process of modernization of agriculture began; now it is estimated that only several hundred remain.

A community seed bank is based on the principle of conserving local varieties on farm, that is, in farmers' fields or home gardens. However, most community seed banks include a seed-storage facility collectively managed by the farming community. This represents a community-level ex-situ facility, similar to that of a national or international gene bank. In practice, except in a few cases, community seed banks store seeds only for one season and regenerate seeds each year through various mechanisms.

For example, the community seed bank in Bara, Nepal, establishes a diversity block of more than 80 local rice varieties in an appropriate area each year to characterize and multiply seeds for the next season (Chapter 34). At the same time, they also distribute seeds of each local variety to one or more members on a loan basis, so that the bank has two sources of new seeds each year. Such on-farm conservation efforts allow continued evolution through both natural and human selection. A recently established community seed bank in Bhutan is putting efforts into maintaining existing buckwheat varieties and restoring lost ones to enhance genetic diversity in the area, thereby strengthening farmers' capacity to adapt to changing climatic conditions (Chapter 10). Community seed banks in Mexico were established as part of a national strategy for in-situ and on-farm conservation. There, 25 community seed banks have formed a network that has been integrated into a National System of Plant Genetic Resources for Food and Agriculture. These community seed banks have focussed on conserving a large number of local varieties of maize, beans, squash and chili (Chapter 42). The community seed banks described in the case countries have more or less similar stories. The Quilinco community seed bank in Guatemala hosts about 657 accessions of maize. A large number of rice, cucurbit and other neglected and underutilized species can be found in community seed banks in Bangladesh and Nepal, and a diversity of beans, cowpeas and millets in Rwanda and Uganda. It is likely that many of these local varieties would have been lost in the absence of such community seed bank initiatives.

A focus on access and availability

Access to and availability of a large quantity of farmer-preferred varieties, local or improved or both, are the core business of some community seed banks. The goal of these banks is to make seed available to needy farmers when required. Depending on rules and regulations set by the farmers' organization operating the seed bank, it provides seed on a cash or loan basis. When community seed banks sell seeds, they always set a competitive price based on a service motive rather than to make a profit. In the case of seed loans, the borrower must return 50–100 per cent more than the borrowed amount after harvesting his or her crop. For example, each year, the Kiziba community seed bank in Uganda provides common bean seeds to more than 200 farmers. Here, the borrowers have to return twice the amount they borrowed (Chapter 30). In Burundi, community seed banks have been integrated with a community granary to make seed available to farmers who lose seeds because of poor storage conditions, theft or because they sold their seed during a cash shortage. The community granary provides a secure space for farmers to store seeds for the next planting season (Chapter 32).

Involvement of community seed banks in participatory plant breeding activities, selection of farmer-preferred varieties and seed production on a commercial scale are other ways that contribute to increased access and availability of newly improved varieties. A community seed bank in southern Costa Rica produces more than 32t of bean seed each year, which is directly sold to the members of the Union of Seed Producers (Chapter 16). The community seed bank in Bara, Nepal, in collaboration with a local research organization, has developed a new rice variety named Kachorwa 4 using a participatory plant breeding method. This community seed bank now produces and sells 5–10t seeds of Kachorwa 4 each year and generates income to support the seed bank (Chapter 34). These quantities of seed are significant and indicate the potential for well-organized community seed banks to operate as bona fide seed suppliers. More technical and financial support would be of great help to further professionalize this function.

The Toronto Seed Library in Canada has a different approach to making seeds available to seed savers and gardeners, based on the principle of wanting to offer an alternative to the genetically modified seeds produced by large corporations. The seed library obtains seeds free of charge from individuals, seed companies and seed stores in and around Toronto and disseminates them to as many people as possible, also free of charge (Chapter 14).

In addition to making seeds available in these ways, many community seed banks also promote informal exchanges through seed or diversity fairs and participatory seed exchange events. The motto of these events is usually, the more seeds that circulate the better.

Combining conservation with access and availability

Most of the community seed banks that we surveyed perform both conservation and access functions. In many countries, community seed banks are a major source of local varieties guaranteeing farmers access to native seeds. These banks are engaged in on-farm conservation of a large number of local varieties and also make diverse types of high-quality seeds available to farmers through sales, loans or free of charge. Production of many seed varieties – from a few kilograms to several tonnes a season – as well as storage, cleaning, grading, packaging, distribution and selling are regular activities of such seed banks. In general, community seed banks give priority to local varieties, but some also include farmer-preferred improved varieties released or registered by the national system.

Several examples exist. Native Seed/SEARCH in the United States holds a collection of 1,900 accessions of domesticated crops, dominated by traditional and heirloom varieties of maize, beans, squash and wild relatives. At the same time, it distributes more than 50,000 packets of seeds of local varieties each year (Chapter 31). Three community seed banks in Zimbabwe, supported by the Community Technology Development Trust, have maintained, over time, 31–57 local varieties of mostly sorghum, pearl millet and cowpeas. Farmers associated with these community seed banks have developed links with seed companies and produce and sell more than 350t of improved varieties of sorghum, cowpea and pearl millet seeds each year (Chapter 38). In Nepal, 15 community seed banks have conserved 1,195 accessions of diverse crop species and nearly 2,000 farmers use seeds from these banks annually (Shrestha and Sthapit, 2014). Similar stories can be told about community seed banks in Brazil, Guatemala, India, Mali and Nicaragua. Combining conservation with access and availability, when managed well, gives community seed banks greater operational vitality, and this can contribute to sustainability.

Linking conservation, access and availability with seed and food sovereignty

Some community seed banks function beyond the scope of conservation of agricultural biodiversity and making seeds available to farmer communities. In addition, members of these seed banks are continuously working on relevant issues, such as empowerment of farming communities; promotion of ecological agriculture; implementation of participatory plant breeding and grassroots breeding activities; establishing farmers' rights over seeds; and development of fair community-level benefit-sharing mechanisms that may arise from the use of genetic resources. Although primarily facilitated by civil society organizations, this kind of community seed bank has developed seed autonomy to some extent. For example, in Bangladesh, the Nayakrishi seed huts and community seed wealth centres, which are supported by the nongovernmental organization (NGO) UBINIG, have been able to promote ecological agriculture among 300,000 farming households in the country (Chapter 9).

The Spanish Seed Network has also been conducting a campaign demanding a legal framework that: allows farmers to produce and sell their farm-saved seeds; promotes recovery of cultivated heritage; values small-scale farming and organic production including fighting against patents in agriculture; and mitigates the impact of genetically modified varieties (Chapter 36).

In Nepal, NGOs developed a community-based biodiversity management approach to empower communities to manage agricultural biodiversity on farm and enhance biodiversity-based livelihood strategies. Part of this approach is grassroots plant breeding. The local Nepali rice varieties called Kalonuniya and Tilki, which were disappearing from farms, have become common again thanks to this farmer-based plant breeding programme (Shrestha and Sthapit, 2014). Another element of the approach is the community biodiversity management fund, which has evolved as a key mechanism for the equitable sharing of benefits that may arise from the use of genetic resources (Shrestha et al., 2013). Such a fund contributes to the empowerment of farmers to manage biodiversity locally, by strengthening biodiversity-based livelihoods. As such, it can also contribute to the multiple objectives of a community seed bank (Chapter 34).

In the state of Minas Gerais, Brazil, the community seed banks known as regional seed houses represent a conservation strategy that complements other strategies and actions used by a network of male and female peasant farmers, organizations and social movements in the field of agro-ecology, and federal teaching and research institutions. The objective of the regional seed houses is to strengthen agricultural biodiversity as managed by communities, identifying the diversity, species density and varieties resistant to climate change; broadening the local diet; ensuring local and regional food security and sovereignty; and conserving traditional native seeds as well as the biodiversity of the region's agricultural systems (Chapter 13).

References

Shrestha, P. and Sthapit, S. (2014) 'Conservation by communities – the CBM approach,' *LEISA India*, vol 16, no 1, pp11–13

Shrestha, P., Sthapit, S., Subedi, A. and Sthapit, B. (2013) 'Community biodiversity management fund: promoting conservation through livelihood development in Nepal,' in W. S. de Boef, A. Subedi, N. Peroni, M. H. Thijssen and E. O'Keeffe (eds) *Community Biodiversity Management: Promoting Resilience and the Conservation of Plant Genetic Resources*, Earthscan from Routledge, London, UK, pp118–122

Sthapit, B. R. (2013) 'Emerging theory and practice: community seed banks, seed system resilience and food security,' in P. Shrestha, R. Vernooy and P. Chaudhary (eds) *Community Seedbanks in Nepal: Past, Present, Future. Proceedings of a National Workshop, 14–15 June 2012, Pokhara, Nepal*, Local Initiatives for Biodiversity, Research and Development, Pokhara, Nepal, and Bioversity International, Rome, Italy, pp16–40

Vernooy, R. (2013) 'In the hands of many: a review of community gene/seed banks around the world,' in P. Shrestha, R. Vernooy and P. Chaudhary (eds) *Community Seedbanks in Nepal: Past, Present, Future. Proceedings of a National Workshop, 14–15 June 2012, Pokhara, Nepal*, Local Initiatives for Biodiversity, Research and Development, Pokhara, Nepal, and Bioversity International, Rome, Italy, pp3–15

4 Governance and management

Bhuwon Sthapit, Ronnie Vernooy
and Pitambar Shrestha

In this chapter, we look at how community seed banks are dealing with governance and aspects of management, including costs; what has gone well and not so well; and what key issues have emerged. We present a governance typology to categorize the various forms that can be found among the case studies. Both governance and management are influenced by social and gender variables, and the case studies in Part II shed some light on how this takes place.

Governance is a process whereby a group of individuals works as a collective to assure the health of an organization. It usually includes moral, legal, political and financial aspects. The way in which accountability is dealt with is central to governance. A community seed bank, as defined in this book, represents a community-managed approach that comprises community-based practices of conservation and sustainable use of plant genetic resources from the level of household seed storage to the community (and sometimes beyond). The daily operations of community seed banks are expressions of collective action. The value of a community seed bank is that it is governed by local people based on rules and regulations that are locally developed. The very process of community seed banking builds social capital by mobilizing the local community, and this can lead to community empowerment. It also creates a learning platform for community-based management of agricultural biodiversity through use and conservation.

Management refers to the day-to-day coordination, execution and monitoring of key tasks required to maintain a community seed bank in the short and long term. It usually involves human resources, as well as technical, administrative, organizational and financial elements. In most countries, community seed banks are characterized by a high degree of voluntary effort, and this has a direct impact on the way management is organized.

Governance

Looking at the case studies in this book, only a small number have all the basic elements of governance and management structures. Some have detailed formalized rules and regulations; some have only general working principles; and many have mostly informal ways of organizing both governance and day-to-day management. The seed banks described in the case studies can be grouped into five categories of governance and management systems (Table 4.1). In many community seed banks, no matter which type, women play key roles, sometimes facilitated by outside intervention, but often because of

Table 4.1 Governance and management structures of community seed banks

Type	Basic elements of governance	Case study examples (Chapter)
Basic stage of implementation without key formal elements of governance	Run by external stakeholders, usually project managers, often a nongovernmental organization (NGO) or donor staff. Custodian farmers are encouraged to take a leadership role as they have an affinity with local crop diversity.	Bolivia (11), Rwanda (27)
Under strong control of a public-sector agency and managed as a kind of decentralized national gene bank	Operated by public-sector agency. Phytosanitary regulations in place. Technically driven operational plans for ensuring quality and genetic purity.	Bhutan (10), China (15)
Governed by a board of volunteers and managed as a seed network based on formal membership	Managed by small committees with both conservation and commercial arms. Support from private companies, membership fees and income from seed sales.	Brazil (13), Honduras (33), Mali (21, 22), Mexico (23, 42), Spain (36), Trinidad (29), United States (31)
Governed by elected committee (of men and women farmers) with transparent operational plans and guided by locally developed rules and regulatory framework	Executive committee (usually with balanced representation of women and men) has overall responsibility for collecting, cleaning, drying, storing, distributing and regenerating seed. Locally developed operation plans match technical requirements. Identified roles and responsibilities of committee members. Sometimes include an ex-situ backup system; a community biodiversity fund; and social auditing.	Bangladesh (9), Costa Rica (16), Nepal (24, 25, 34), Nicaragua (26), Zimbabwe (38)
Governed by ideology of free access, open source and seed sovereignty	Volunteer based (with varying degrees of formal management) or network of seed-saver groups. Some cases prefer the concept of seed library over seed bank as seed should not be privatized.	Canada (14); see also Kloppenburg (2010)

women's strong interest and leading role in seed management in the household and community.

A caveat on this typology is necessary. Most of these seed banks have evolved and continue to evolve through a 'learning by doing' approach. Over time, a clearer distinction between what is governance and what is management might emerge, rules and regulations will become more elaborate and formalized and, overall, the activities related to governance and management will become more complex. For example, in Mali, community seed banks have been formally registered as cooperative societies whose governance and management follow internal regulations. Each community seed bank has a general assembly, a board of directors and an oversight committee. The general assembly is the decision-making body and meets at least once a year, with additional meetings held on special occasions. The board of directors is in charge of implementing the decisions made by the general assembly while the oversight committee ensures that these decisions are applied correctly (Chapter 22). Surprisingly, many of the community seed banks documented here operate in a legal grey area. Only a few have been formally registered, for example, under a non-profit civil society organization umbrella (e.g. Sri Lanka) or as cooperatives (e.g. Burundi, Mali, Mexico and Nepal) or as seed enterprises (e.g. India). This aspect is discussed in more detail in Chapter 7, Policy and legal environment.

The issue of accountability, apart from proper management of infrastructure and finances, is most clearly expressed through the rules and regulations concerning the use of seeds maintained in community seed banks. All community seed banks have adopted a clear principle about this. Some examples are given in Box 4.1.

Box 4.1 Keeping seeds on the shelves (examples from the case studies)

Nicaragua

Seed loan requests are received in April, right before the first growing cycle (May to June). The management committee reviews these requests, considering whether the applicant farmer is known to be an honest person – an important factor taken into account to ensure that the community seed bank will recover its seed. On receiving a seed loan, the farmer signs a promissory note and a contract in which he or she agrees to return seed of the same quality that has been selected, weighed, cleaned, dried and is free of mould. Although community seed bank members have priority, non-members are also granted loans when enough seed is available. The interest rate is 50 per cent, i.e. when 100g is borrowed, 150g must be returned.

China

Farmers from various villages are encouraged, through crop seed diversity fairs and locally displayed posters, to store their seeds in the community gene bank. At farmers' field day activities, farmers are able to examine various species of rice, corn, etc. To obtain seeds of varieties other than his or her own, the farmer must deposit seeds in the community gene bank in a 1:1 ratio, i.e. 100g deposited allows the farmer to borrow 100g from the bank.

Management

Often a community elects a management committee to oversee the community seed bank, with formal distribution of tasks that include coordination and leadership, technical issues, finance, administration, communication and outreach. However, more often the roles and responsibilities of each member are not that well defined. The number of farmers making up the management committee varies, from three in the case of Oaxaca, Mexico, to six in Nicaragua. In a few cases, the committee is guided by a constitution drafted by the farmers (e.g. Nicaragua) or, in some cases, with external support from an NGO (e.g. Bara in Nepal and the community seed banks in Zimbabwe). In a few cases, both technical and management committees have been set up to undertake specialized functions and provide expertise (e.g. Bangladesh and Trinidad). Women, as custodians and caretakers of seeds in many countries, play an active role in the day-to-day functioning of community seed banks. In Nicaragua, several banks are run exclusively by women.

The technical committee is usually responsible for deciding on:

- collection methods (e.g. through seed fairs, on farm/in the field, household seed storage, collections maintained by custodian farmers, etc.);
- phytosanitary standards (e.g. keeping seed free of diseases and pests, removing weed seeds, sun drying, etc.);
- documentation methods (e.g. passport data sheets, variety catalogue, community biodiversity register, etc.);
- seed multiplication and evaluation (based on farmers' descriptors);
- storage methods (e.g. short versus long term, local storage structure or scientific approach);
- monitoring of seed samples (e.g. viability and vigour, initially and at planting time);
- rejuvenation (e.g. annual seed multiplication in diversity blocks, decision tools to determine which seeds should have priority, pollen control in open-pollinated crops, etc.);

- distribution (e.g. systems to improve access and availability; access for various categories of users: men or women, poor or rich, community or outsiders, researchers, private sector, etc.).

Across the case studies, considerable variety exists in terms of exactly how these tasks are executed. Although most seed banks pay attention to these factors, variation can be observed in the rigour and regularity of their execution.

Reviewing both governance and management, the case studies seem to offer evidence that a number of the NGO-supported community seed banks could benefit from strengthening the roles and capacities of technical committee members. The public-sector-run or gene-bank-facilitated community seed banks could benefit from improved governance so that the community plays a stronger role in leading the process. In these cases, the local community could build capacity through input from science and support from various sources so that the seed bank activities are long term, useful and sustainable. Both technical and management committees have to play a joint role in collection, multiplication and evaluation processes and in developing strategies for seed distribution to needy people.

Costs

How much does it cost to establish a community seed bank, and what are the annual operating costs? This kind of information is hard to obtain from the case studies. A better understanding of the roles played by community seed banks in the conservation and use of agricultural biodiversity and the costs involved in this work is important in terms of gaining recognition from formal seed sectors and policymakers who can provide technical and institutional support. Community seed banks combine in-situ and ex-situ conservation; they store species in seed containers, packets or a dedicated conservation field, but with the idea that those crop varieties are immediately available for local use. Physical structures, storage units and equipment needed for regeneration of seeds and day-to-day operations and care both in the field and at storage facilities are major costs.

Estimates of the cost of modern types of ex-situ conservation exist. In contrast, for most community seed banks, the physical structure, storage materials and equipment are often simple and low cost. Labour-intensive tasks are carried out by volunteers, although some community seed banks hire a local person to carry out day-to-day operations. Costs also vary depending on the extent of activities; some seed banks deal with a few local varieties and provide small quantities of seeds (e.g. Bhutan and China) while others deal with tonnes of seeds (e.g. Costa Rica and Zimbabwe). As far as we know, no thorough cost calculations have been carried out.

Some community seed banks started with a small seed fund of about US$1,000–2,000. Others received start-up funds ranging from US$5,000–10,000 to build social capital and initial physical infrastructure, including seed-storage units. Communities often mobilize local resources, such as construction materials, land (obtained sometimes from the local government) and labour. In parallel, external support agencies, through their regular project activities, also assume part of the cost of building social, human and physical capital from which community seed banks benefit. In a few cases, government agencies cover these expenditures.

When support organizations are associated with community seed banks over a long period, the total costs (including professional staff time, travel costs, costs of meetings, training, materials, etc.) will likely be higher by several hundred dollars a year per community seed bank. However, long-term capacity development is essential for building successful community seed banks. Investment in excellent and experienced community organizers to mobilize community members and support local leadership represents an important component of this process.

Community seed banks act as a central node where farmers can exchange seeds through their own networks or via social events such as seed fairs. They are also platforms for sharing seed-related skills and knowledge. They are a key source of good-quality local species, especially those not covered by commercial plant breeders and, thus, make an important contribution to agricultural biodiversity. Community seed banks are locally based and locally run (often by women) and located within reach of the communities that use them. Local practices, such as seed huts, seed fairs and seed exchanges, can overcome the expense of distributing seeds and make seeds easily available.

Key issues and challenges

Building legitimacy and a strong local institution

Community seed banks can be effective mechanisms, either in the absence of other local organizations or as another form of local organization, to mobilize existing social capital (trust, networks and customary practices). Either way, being recognized and supported as a legitimate form of organization is important. The more the establishment and development process is based on community-driven participation that integrates the new knowledge and practices with the local social system and local rules and norms, the greater the chance that the community seed bank will be effective in the short and long term (Sthapit et al., 2008a,b), even in an environment that is not fully supportive. To build and strengthen the social capital required to operate community seed banks, Local Initiatives for Biodiversity, Research and Development (LI-BIRD) has developed the following steps:

- sensitize the community;
- strengthen local institutions;
- develop rules and regulations;
- construct seed-storage facilities;

- receive seed deposits or collect local seeds;
- document community biodiversity using a register/inventory/passport data;
- mobilize a community biodiversity management fund for community development and conservation;
- multiply seeds;
- monitor seed transactions and impacts.

This approach, which is centred around institution building, has produced good results in Nepal (see Chapters 25 and 34) and has been followed by other organizations in other countries working with community seed banks, e.g. Sri Lanka (Chapter 28). The success and sustainability of community seed banks depend on how the technical knowledge and management capacity of the change agents are enhanced and how the bank is empowered to conduct a self-directed decision-making process. Similar experiences can be found in the cases from the Americas, such as Nicaragua (Chapter 26), Mexico (Chapter 23) and the United States (Chapter 31).

Recognition, access and benefit-sharing mechanisms

As the case studies indicate, community seed banks can be legitimate and effective community-based organizations to improve access and benefit sharing of locally important crop diversity, but in many countries they have yet to be formally recognized by the government. Recognition can take different forms: visits by local, national or foreign officials; awards for special efforts and achievements from the local or national government; invitations to participate in important policy events locally or nationally; funds from local or national government and international donor agencies; and publicity in the local, national or even international media (Sthapit, 2013).The case studies, with a few exceptions (Bangladesh and Nepal, Chapters 9 and 24), do not mention these forms of recognition, suggesting that much more work remains to be done.

Although recognition is important, the development of proper access and benefit-sharing mechanisms is equally important. Civil society organizations and the private sector have a common interest in good governance to ensure that the quality of seeds is maintained or enhanced and that reliable and useful genetic resources remain available. Community seed banks have to face the challenges of the technical superiority of hybrid and modern cultivars, on the one hand, and restrictions related to intellectual property rights on most of these cultivars, on the other. Thus, it is essential that community seed banks develop niche outlets for local landraces and farmer-improved cultivars and strengthen the marketing of locally produced or bred varieties. Such efforts are described in the case studies from Bolivia, Guatemala, Honduras, India (two case studies), Nicaragua and Nepal (Bara) (Chapters 11, 17, 33, 18, 19, 26 and 34, respectively).

Based on the diverse experiences and lessons of community seed banks, there is another way to conceptualize access and benefits: as an institutional platform for ensuring farmers' rights. Policymakers might consider community seed banks as a mechanism for ensuring the effective implementation of farmers' rights, in terms of recognition, participation in decision-making, benefit sharing and a supportive policy and seed regulatory framework. This also provides an opportunity for interaction and integration of informal and formal seed systems to address local problems; promotion of in-situ and ex-situ links to backup genetic resources locally (as a building block of crop improvement and food security); and ensuring community development in a sustainable way. This approach is highlighted in a few case studies, in particular the one about the Development Fund (Chapter 35) and the Community Technology Development Trust in Zimbabwe (Chapter 38). Bioversity International has been making a similar case (Vernooy, 2013), but recognizing and rewarding community seed banks as such takes time.

Starting a community seed bank requires a major effort, but keeping it alive over time has been a challenge for many, as the case studies demonstrate. The seed banks that are strongly dependent on outside resources and support have particularly struggled at times. This challenge is discussed in more detail in Chapter 8, Sustainability.

References

Kloppenburg, J. (2010) 'Seed sovereignty: the promise of open source biology,' in H. Wittman, A. A. Desmarais and A. Wiebe (eds) *Food Sovereignty: Reconnecting Food, Nature and Community*, Fernwood, Halifax, Canada, pp152–167

Sthapit, B. R. (2013) 'Emerging theory and practice: community seed banks, seed system resilience and food security,' in P. Shrestha, R. Vernooy and P. Chaudhary (eds) *Community Seed Banks in Nepal: Past, Present, Future: Proceedings of a National Workshop, 14–15 June 2012, Pokhara, Nepal*, Local Initiatives for Biodiversity, Research and Development, Pokhara, Nepal, pp16–40

Sthapit, B. R., Shrestha, P. K., Subedi, A., Shrestha, P., Upadhyay, M. P. and Eyzaguirre, P. E. (2008a) 'Mobilizing and empowering community in biodiversity management,' in M. H. Thijssen, Z. Bishaw, A. Beshir and W. S. de Boef (eds) *Farmer's Varieties and Seeds. Supporting Informal Seed Supply in Ethiopia*, Wageningen International, Wageningen, the Netherlands, pp160–166

Sthapit, B. R., Subedi, A., Shrestha, P., Shrestha, P. K. and Upadhyay, M. P. (2008b) 'Practices supporting community management of farmers' varieties,' in M. H. Thijssen, Z. Bishaw, A. Beshir and W. S. de Boef (eds) *Farmer's Varieties and Seeds. Supporting Informal Seed Supply in Ethiopia*, Wageningen International, Wageningen, the Netherlands, pp166–171

Vernooy, R. (2013) 'In the hands of many: a review of community gene/seed banks around the world,' in P. Shrestha, R. Vernooy and P. Chaudhary (eds) *Community Seed Banks in Nepal: Past, Present, Future: Proceedings of a National Workshop, 14–15 June 2012, Pokhara, Nepal*, Local Initiatives for Biodiversity, Research and Development, Pokhara, Nepal, pp3–15

5 Technical issues

*Pitambar Shrestha, Bhuwon Sthapit
and Ronnie Vernooy*

The recent popularity of community seed banks raises the question of whether they are able to address the technical issues inherent in their operations, considering the specific local contexts in which they are located. Community seed banks that are set up without a proper understanding of the complexities of seed management may have a short lifespan. In this chapter, we discuss the minimum set of technical criteria and the issues that must be addressed by those who wish to operate community seed banks. To some degree, the technical issues depend on the type of seed bank (see Chapter 3 for our classification framework), but many are relevant to all seed banks. Technical issues emerge throughout the cycle of seed management, from the early stage of selecting which crop species and varieties to keep (and that selection may change over time) to the documentation of the collection and its use. A number of guides offer useful knowledge and practices (e.g. Fanton and Fanton, 1993; Saad and Rao, 2001; Fanton et al., 2003; Seeds of Diversity, 2014), but we have found that few seed banks are aware of or make good use of these resources.

The basic requirements for seed management are: the seed should be physically and genetically pure; it should be free from diseases and pests; it should germinate and establish quickly; and it should be accompanied by useful information and knowledge. The case studies in this book describe a wide variety of ways in which community seed banks deal with technical issues. The technology used ranges from simple to complex. Some rely on local knowledge and expertise, while others involve expertise from outside the community (e.g. agronomists, plant breeders, gene bank managers, organizational experts). Costs vary considerably, and planning ranges from ad hoc to detailed. All together, the cases clearly indicate that technical issues remain a major challenge and that capacity development and stronger technical support could make these operations more robust, both in the short and long term.

Choosing crop species and varieties

The selection of crop species for conservation and management by a community seed bank is usually a matter of discussion among the farmers in charge, in a number of cases informed by interaction with outsiders, such as nongovernmental organizations (NGOs) or government research or extension staff. Most of the community seed banks in the case studies have focussed on local varieties of crop species that are of global significance and local importance and of which there is mainly traditional seed available locally (e.g. Bangladesh, India and Nepal). Some specialize in a few crops native to the area, such as maize and beans in Guatemala; maize, beans, squash and chili in Mexico and southwestern United States; potatoes in Bolivia; and sorghum, pearl millet and cowpeas in Zimbabwe. In other words, community seed banks tend to choose crop species that are locally important.

Some community seed banks have given priority to reviving traditional crops associated with local culture. For example, buckwheat in Bhutan used to be the staple crop, but because of government intervention, its diverse varieties were completely replaced by potato in the late 1970s (Chapter 10). Another example is the recovery of 'lost' crop varieties in Ethiopia, where, after repeated severe droughts and the complete failure of improved varieties of wheat, local wheat varieties that were still maintained by the national gene bank were restored to use (Chapter 37; Development Fund, 2011). In recent years, community seed banks have also given priority to the identification, multiplication and distribution of varieties that are tolerant to local stresses, such as heat, drought and flooding, and that are better adapted to poor soil conditions (for example, Chapters 9, 21, 27, 29 and 31). Community seed banks in Mexico have been rescuing wild species of maize and beans – other important crops.

An important factor related to choosing crop species and varieties is whether a community seed bank should limit its work to local varieties or include improved varieties. One can easily argue for or against these options, but what matters most is whether communities have made an informed decision. The community seed banks in Bangladesh (Chapter 9), Mexico (Chapter 23) and the United States (Chapter 31) have focussed primarily on conservation and promotion of local varieties, based on a situational analysis in which diversity loss is central. But a number of successful community seed banks also deal with both local and improved varieties, e.g. Costa Rica (Chapter 16), Nepal (Chapter 34), Trinidad (Chapter 29) and Zimbabwe (Chapter 38). The idea behind dealing with both local and improved varieties is to provide access to diverse seeds that farmers need at their doorsteps, at a reasonable cost and on time, as well as to generate some revenues to support conservation of local varieties and institutional sustainability through the sale of improved varieties. The broadening of functions thus leads to the broadening of the base of crops or varieties, which has direct consequences for all other technical issues.

Collecting seeds and planting material

The number of local varieties collected and conserved in each community seed bank varies, depending on many factors: the number of crop species grown locally and their availability; human and technical capacity, resources and strategies chosen to identify and collect in the community and surrounding areas; the level of awareness of the value of local genetic resources and their role in conservation; the energy to promote community seed banking efforts; and the nature of the enabling environment.

Several tools are at hand to help decide about selection. Participatory four-cell analysis facilitated by Local Initiatives for Biodiversity, Research and Development (LI-BIRD) and Bioversity International in Nepal helps communities understand on-farm diversity and whether varieties are localized or widespread, common, endangered, rare or lost. Organizers in Nepal held a diversity fair (Adhikari et al., 2012) to help locate rare materials and complete an inventory of available seeds and associated information in a community biodiversity register (Subedi et al., 2012) before establishing a community seed bank. On the one hand, this type of activity helps create awareness among a large number of people about the value of biodiversity and, on the other hand, helps identify custodians of rare, unique and valuable genetic resources. Thus, a broad resource base is created for collecting seeds and planting materials for a community seed bank. Other community seed banks form a committee of two or three members to locate interesting materials and areas of diversity and collect seeds on behalf of the seed bank. Community seed bank members usually also collect seeds via social networks of neighbours, friends, relatives and extension agents.

A critical factor to be considered while collecting seeds is how samples are taken and how to select disease-free material. No field guide is available to help with this process, but the best techniques include sampling from different parts of a field (not just one corner), collecting from a number of plants or panicles and avoiding those next to the road. Attention should also be paid to choosing disease-free plants, panicles or fruit. This should be done in the field to the extent possible, although material can be examined later.

The case studies reviewed seldom describe the scientifically based management practices of community seed banks, including information management, internal quarantine (to safeguard against seed-borne disease) and monitoring of seed germination, viability and vigour.

Documenting, sharing and communicating information

Community seed banks are not only repositories of large numbers of seeds and planting materials, but also places where traditional knowledge and associated information about local varieties can be found. This type of knowledge is usually documented with support from external agencies using a standard form. In general, such documentation includes the local name of the genetic resource, its specific use and value, current status, general characteristics, method of cultivation, related agro-ecology, the extent and distribution of its cultivation, its capacity to tolerate biotic and abiotic stresses in the field, perceived nutritional value and cultural and religious uses (if any).

To a large extent, such documentation depends on the practices and guidance provided by the facilitating organization. For example, in Nepal, community biodiversity registers and passport data have been maintained as basic documents since the establishment of the community seed banks. This information is further used for planning conservation and development activities that are part of a 'community biodiversity management plan'.

To promote ex-situ and in-situ linkages, LI-BIRD has adopted the standard format of passport data for the national gene bank so that transfer of information is error free (Chapter 34). Similarly, passport data, morphological characteristics and seed stock records are kept in Mexico (Chapter 23). The Spanish seed network has been recovering traditional and farmers' knowledge about local varieties and management practices by interviewing farmers (Chapter 36). The point is that every community seed bank should have, in some form, a sound mechanism for documenting basic data, associated information and farmers' knowledge, including farmers' descriptors related to the genetic resources they are conserving and promoting. Not all seed banks reviewed in this book have followed this good practice, however.

Sharing information and experiences among members, non-members and other stakeholders is another important role of community seed banks. Each community seed bank has its own way of doing things, using a variety of processes. In several of the case studies, banks make use of seed fairs and biodiversity fairs: for example, Costa Rica (Chapter 16), Mexico (Chapter 23), Nicaragua (Chapter 26) and Zimbabwe (Chapter 38). Such fairs provide an open and dynamic forum for farmers to learn and share knowledge and experiences. Seed fairs are also a simple way to assess the status of local crop diversity and monitor and collect rare and threatened genetic resources or collect information from custodians to plan future collection. They also allow farmers to convey the value of genetic resources through dancing, singing, poetry and other cultural activities.

In Nepal, some community seed banks organize seasonal participatory seed exchange programmes to share seed and associated knowledge (Shrestha et al., 2013). Community seed banks in Mexico organize seed fairs at local, state and national levels each year. The Mexican network of community seed banks envisions creating an electronic communication network as part of the national conservation strategy (Chapter 42). Field days, demonstrations, sharing at church events, community meetings, training events and community social reunions are some of the other tools used in several cases. Web-based information sharing and use of social media are also becoming common these days, mostly in developed countries, e.g. the Toronto case study (Chapter 14).

Storing seeds: structures and methods

To keep seeds clean, healthy and viable, proper storage equipment and methods are critical. The case studies offer a wide variety of seed-storage structures, depending on the goal, objectives and core values of the facilitating organiza-tions as well as the availability of resources. Some are temporary while others are permanent. Many donor-funded initiatives have invested in large-scale infrastructure that the community may not be able to handle, rather than building the social capital needed to sustain the facilities. Support for physical capital only *after* social and human capital have been built tends to result in an organization that is more self-sustaining. Some seed banks use mostly local materials, while others use 'imported' materials. Some are simple and small; others have multiple rooms or a second floor. Except in a few cases, however, most community seed banks do not have a mechanism for controlling temperature and humidity, which is key to maintaining genetic material over a long period.

Depending on the crop species, community seed banks usually follow traditional methods for storing seeds and planting material, not only to make management simple, but also because farmers are well acquainted with the traditional system and, thus, there are fewer chances of making mistakes in construction. They use mud, bamboo, straw, dried bottle gourds, etc. to make structures and equipment. They use the sun to dry seeds and cool them before storage in mud-sealed containers. In Bangladesh, the community seed bank consists of a storage area and a meeting room constructed using locally available materials; seeds are stored in traditional containers, such as earthen pots (Chapter 9). In most cases, community seed banks consist of just one room for everything, but some (in Zimbabwe and Nepal, for example) have separate rooms for local germplasm and bulk seed storage as well as office and meeting space.

To keep stored seeds healthy and viable, community seed banks are gradually replacing traditional storage structures with modern equipment, such as airtight, transparent plastic or glass jars, metal bins and even SuperGrain bags (multi-layer plastic bags that provide a gas and moisture barrier). These practices are becoming common in China, Guatemala, Mexico and Nepal. In Nepal, zeolites (aluminosilicate-based absorbents) have been introduced to control moisture levels. In the exceptional case of Native Seeds/SEARCH in the United States, seed banks have sophisticated storage facilities, such as cold rooms and freezers for short-term storage of their core collections.

Regenerating seeds: bulk seed production and quality assurance

In general, community seed banks hold a large number of local crop species and varieties and few commercial varieties. For the commercial varieties, it is easy to determine the amount to be produced each year based on demand at the local and regional levels. Community seed banks that collaborate with seed companies are producing and selling tonnes of seeds (e.g. in Zimbabwe and Costa Rica). To be able to produce large quantities of seeds, community seed banks require land, water, human resources, transport facilities and large processing and storage facilities. Moving to commercial seed production in such volumes could easily affect the conservation of local crop diversity and change the direction of the seed bank. This is something we have seen in the field, but it is not readily acknowledged by those operating seed banks.

Almost all community seed banks regenerate the seeds they conserve annually, although that practice is not universal. Some seed banks also produce and market local varieties of seed on a large scale. The area to be planted and the quantity of seed to be produced each year largely depend on local demand, but also on the ability and availability of resources within the seed banks. There are no technical guidelines available yet to provide a basis for determining the area needed to produce specific quantities of seed for each variety. The case studies show few commonalities.

In Nepal, the Bara seed bank, located in the central terai area, transplants more than 80 rice landraces in plots of 9m^2 that each produce about 5kg of seed, on average, every year. The small scale allows farmers to keep management costs low and operations under control. This practice also has great advantages in terms of evolutionary selection based on climate variation.

To ensure good-quality seed (free from disease, insects, weeds and inert materials and isolated from other varieties), community seed banks employ various measures. Some establish a small technical committee for this purpose (e.g. Bangladesh, Costa Rica and Uganda), while, in other cases, the bank's executive committee is responsible for seed quality in the field and in storage (e.g. Nepal). In Nepal, a local person is hired by the community to be in charge of materials and quality assurance in the seed bank. In Bangladesh, community seed banks supported by UBINIG have a Specialized Women's Seed Network responsible for day-to-day management and the annual regeneration of seeds.

On-farm characterization and assessment

Around the world, community seed banks are conserving and promoting thousands of globally significant crop genetic resources native to their areas and adapted to local climatic conditions. Many have documented information and traditional knowledge associated with those genetic resources in various forms and claim that they have conserved local varieties with invaluable traits, such as tolerance to drought, flooding, diseases and insects; good eating qualities; market-preferred traits; long fruiting period; religious and cultural importance, etc. Such documentation may provide the basis for further development of valuable traits through breeding and promotional activities.

However, very few community seed banks have characterized their accessions in detail using standard descriptors or published a diversity catalogue. They may need to collaborate closely with research organizations to carry out this type of work. Apart from traditional knowledge, the nutritional and medicinal properties of local varieties conserved in community seed banks are largely lacking.

Knowledge gaps

Among the case studies, some community seed banks are highly competent and functioning well in terms of collection, documentation, regeneration, storage, distribution and marketing of seeds of diverse local and improved varieties. To a large extent, seed banks are able to build the capacity of their members through training and other activities. Training sessions in quality seed selection and production, management, protecting seeds from insects and pests and enhancing conservation of local varieties are commonly held at most of the seed banks we reviewed. The communities tend to understand the value of conservation when farmers are directly involved in participatory plant breeding and develop their own varieties by crossing a local strain with a modern one. In Bara, Nepal, within a span of seven years, the community seed bank was able to develop a new rice variety (Kachorwa 4), begin seed multiplication and sell high-quality seed to other farming communities, thus earning income to support the seed bank and conservation of local varieties (Sthapit, 2013). In the process, the farming community not only realized the importance of maintaining landraces, but also gained knowledge in plant breeding, seed selection and marketing. This further motivated the community to mobilize social capital for collective action on community-based management of local crop diversity.

Monthly meetings are treated as a permanent forum where information is shared and issues are discussed. Exposure visits, within and between countries, are another way to empower farmers and bridge knowledge gaps. In Uganda, farmers are taught the life cycle of the weevil so that they can find ways to prevent the damage it can cause by timely harvesting and proper drying of bean seeds. Similarly, in Mali, the knowledge and skills of community seed bank members are enhanced in a field school, a place where local seeds are multiplied. Likewise, in Bangladesh, UBINIG organizes campaigns, advocacy work and training in the negative effects of conventional agriculture.

However, community seed banks in most of the case study countries have to think about how to bridge knowledge gaps in such areas as applying scientific methods to the collection, storage and regeneration of seeds; documenting information and traditional knowledge; and introducing the latest technologies and innovations into community seed bank management.

References

Adhikari A., Upadhyay, M. P., Joshi, B. K., Rijal, D., Chaudhary, P., Paudel, I., Baral, K., Pageni, P., Subedi, S. and Sthapit, B. (2012) 'Multiple approach to community sensitization,' in B. Sthapit, P. Shrestha and M. Upadhyay (eds) *On-farm Management of Agricultural Biodiversity in Nepal: Good Practices* (revised ed), Local Initiatives for Biodiversity Research and Development, Pokhara, Nepal, pp21–24, www.bioversityinternational.org/uploads/tx_news/On_farm_management_of_agricultural_biodivesity_in_Nepal_Good_Practices_revised_edition_2012_1222_.pdf, accessed 24 July 2014

Development Fund (2011) *Banking for the Future: Savings, Security and Seeds. A Short Study of Community Seed Banks in Bangladesh, Costa Rica, Ethiopia, Honduras, India, Nepal, Thailand, Zambia and Zimbabwe*, The Development Fund, Oslo, Norway

Fanton, M. and Fanton, J. (1993) *The Seed Savers' Handbook*, The Seed Savers' Network, Byron Bay, Australia

Fanton, J., Fanton, M. and Glastonbury, A. (2003) *Local Seed Network Manual*, The Seed Savers' Network, Byron Bay, Australia

Saad, M. S. and Rao, V. R. (eds) (2001) *Establishment and Management of Field Genebank. A Training Manual*. IPGRI-APO, Serdang, International Plant Genetic Resources Institute, Office for Asia, the Pacific and Oceania, Serdang, Malaysia, www.bioversityinternational.org/uploads/tx_news/Establishment_and_management_of_field_genebank_786.pdf, accessed 24 July 2014

Seeds of Diversity (2014) *Micro-seedbanking: A Primer on Setting Up and Running a Community Seed Bank*, Seeds of Diversity, Toronto, Canada, www.seeds.ca/int/doc/docpub.php?k=2f6ffc26420e3ea79473956419b097c700001004, accessed 24 July 2014

Shrestha P., Sthapit, S. and Paudel, I. (2013) 'Participatory seed exchange for enhancing access to seeds of local varieties' [in Nepali], Local Initiatives for Biodiversity, Research and Development, Pokhara, Nepal, www.libird.org/app/publication/view.aspx?record_id=109&origin=results&QS=QS&fl_4417=Pitambar+Shrestha&fl_4501=5&fl_4554=2013&union=AND&top_parent=221, accessed 24 July 2014

Sthapit, B. R. (2013) 'Emerging theory and practice: community seedbanks, seed system resilience and food security,' in P. Shrestha, R. Vernooy and P. Chaudhary (eds) *Community Seedbanks in Nepal: Past, Present, Future. Proceedings of a National Workshop, 14–15 June 2012, Pokhara, Nepal*, Local Initiatives for Biodiversity, Research and Development, Pokhara, Nepal, and Bioversity International, Rome, Italy, pp16–40

Subedi, A., Sthapit, B., Rijal, D., Gauchan, D., Upadhyay, M. P. and Shrestha, P. (2012) 'Community biodiversity register: consolidating community roles in management of agricultural biodiversity,' in B. Sthapit, P. Shrestha and M. Upadhyay (eds) *On-farm Management of Agricultural Biodiversity in Nepal: Good Practices* (revised ed), Local Initiatives for Biodiversity, Research and Development, Pokhara, Nepal, pp37–40, www.bioversityinternational.org/uploads/tx_news/On_farm_management_of_agricultural_biodivesity_in_Nepal_Good_Practices_revised_edition_2012_1222_.pdf, accessed 24 July 2014

6   Support and networking

*Ronnie Vernooy, Bhuwon Sthapit
and Pitambar Shrestha*

Community seed banks mobilize a range of actors in conservation, plant breeding and rural development to find new ways of collaborating with farmers and strengthening the multi-functionality of farmers' seed systems. Community seed banks tend to be small-scale organizations that store seed on a short-term basis and serve individual communities or several communities in surrounding villages. Such local efforts can have a multiplier effect if the community seed banks cultivate partnerships and engage in networking and sharing of information and seeds with other informal and formal seed system actors.

Some community seed banks have excelled in building relationships, but, overall, the networks that our case studies describe differ considerably. Some are stable, but remain limited in scope with few connections. Others span a large geographic area, include many social actors from various fields and have a large number of connections. The latter are part of, or becoming part of, a more-or-less formal group, network, association or federation of community seed banks along with other rural development organizations, such as non-governmental organizations (NGOs), cooperatives, farmers' enterprises and farmers' unions. Such connections increase the chances of accessing new materials and information. Currently, one such network operating at the state level in Brazil includes more than 240 community seed banks (Chapter 39). Likewise, the Spanish seed network, 'Resembrando e Intercambiando', is an informal federation that brings together 26 local seed networks that are distributed throughout the country (Chapter 36).

Some community seed banks interact regularly with researchers, mainly but not always on the initiative of the latter (e.g. Brazil, Costa Rica, Guatemala, Malaysia, Mali and Uganda cases) or extension agents (e.g. Bhutan, China and Zimbabwe cases), while others have little or no contact with these professionals or prefer not to interact with them (e.g. some examples from India). In India, some individual enthusiastic scientists and seed curators have established their own community seed banks by collecting local seeds from surrounding villages using their own resources (e.g. Debal Deo in Orissa, Laxman Shukla in Lucknow for mango; see Sthapit et al., 2013). Some community seed banks cooperate with national gene banks or national-level agencies in charge of plant genetic resources (e.g. Bhutan, Ethiopia, Mexico and Zimbabwe), while some have started to explore working together (e.g. India and Nepal) or envision doing so (e.g. South Africa). National guidelines for such cooperation that spell out roles, rights and duties are still lacking everywhere.

In some countries, community seed banks are part of a dynamic network alongside the formal research system, jointly conducting participatory plant breeding and participatory variety selection and exchanging knowledge and experiences. Some community seed banks have evolved into more than just seed-oriented organizations and serve as platforms for social learning, mobilization and community development more broadly (e.g. Nepal cases).

The most common relations found among our case studies are between community seed banks and international or national NGOs (e.g. the Community Technology Development Trust, the Norwegian Development Fund, LI-BIRD (Local Initiatives for Biodiversity, Research and Development), USC Canada and Welthungerhilfe, all described in this book, as well as ActionAid and OXFAM-NOVIB). In some cases, national and international research organizations (notably Bioversity International) provide technical and financial support. Through these support organizations, some community seed banks have started to interact with the national government agencies that set policies on plant genetic resources (e.g. Honduras). However, even when long-term relations exist, they are seldom stable because of their often highly personal nature, and they will most likely never be stable, given the financial uncertainty that affects these organizations.

Sometimes, community seed bank leaders take the lead in establishing and maintaining a network; sometimes, there is much greater participation by members. In some cases, women farmers play a strong role in almost all operations of community seed banks; in other cases, women and men share roles and activities. Networking in developed countries (e.g. Australia, Canada, European countries and the United States) appears to function well with strongly committed members, focussed objectives and sound self-financing mechanisms. In developing countries, most networking is facilitated, at least initially, by donors or national or international NGOs, and local buy-in takes time and is sometimes hindered by distrust.

Many factors influence these dynamics, e.g. geography, roads and communications infrastructure, local culture, the role of local leaders, municipal or district politics, the occurrence of natural disasters, civil unrest or war, national policy development, international development priorities and the international financial situation. How does the nature of the web of relations have an influence on the operations and performance of community seed banks? In what ways does promoting networking make sense? How easy is it for a locally focussed organization to build a wider web of useful relationships? What can community seed banks do to create such links: organize annual seed diversity fairs and participatory exchanges?

Unfortunately, the case studies do not allow for an in-depth sociological assessment of how the nature of networks affects their performance and sustainability, which would require longer-term field research; however, they offer some insights, nonetheless. We offer these insights in the following sections, grouping the case studies into two categories: light and dense webs, i.e. those with few linkages and those with multiple linkages, respectively. It remains a challenge to apply network analysis more deeply as part of a coherent conceptual framework to assess community seed banks and their value as dynamic and viable core participants of seed and information exchange networks. Before presenting the two types, we briefly review the kinds of support community seed banks receive and its significance.

Support

The case studies provide ample evidence that a combination of material, technical, financial, social, political and moral support is important for the establishment and continuous operations of community seed banks. Many seed banks received financial and material support to start up, build a seed-storage facility and acquire basic equipment and materials. In Oaxaca, Mexico, the Sistema Nacional de Recursos Fitogenéticos para la Alimentación y la Agricultura provided support for the construction of ten community seed banks (Chapter 23). In Nicaragua, several international NGOs financed the creation of a network made up of a central bank and a series of family-based community seed banks (Chapter 26). In Bangladesh and Sri Lanka, national and international NGOs shared the costs of the establishment of a number of community seed banks (Chapters 9 and 28). Although farmers are sometimes able to generate enough local resources to establish a community seed bank and build a basic facility, there is no doubt that external support is of great help.

However, establishing a community seed bank requires not only material resources, but also human capacity. The case studies of organizations supporting community seed banks in Part II are all good illustrations of this principle. The approach developed by LI-BIRD in Nepal emphasizes the need – from the very beginning – to empower community seed bank members through training and capacity building in technical and institutional aspects of seed conservation and community seed bank management, governance and networking (Chapter 34).

National extension, conservation and research agencies, national and international NGOs and international research organizations all provide technical training to members of community seed banks in a wide range of subjects: soil health, participatory crop diversity assessment, participatory variety selection and plant breeding, technical seed management, data registration, seed production and marketing, organizational development and enterprise development. The case of Bhutan is characterized by a few, but very strong, support connections between the community seed bank and government agencies, with the district agriculture officer and staff coordinating activities at the dzongkhag level; the National Biodiversity Centre (NBC) offering technical and financial support (and initial coordination); and the United Nations Development Programme's Global Environment Fund project, 'Integrated Livestock and Crop Conservation Project', providing financial support through the NBC (Chapter 10). In Trinidad, the community seed bank obtained new technology (seed threshers, driers and a greenhouse) through the main national plant genetic resources agency (Chapter 29).

In the United States and Canada, community seed banking efforts rely heavily on volunteers who assist with many aspects of on-farm growing, seed cleaning and packaging. In the United States, volunteers also help with the retail store run by the community seed bank. Several case studies mention the importance of moral support, which is a form of legitimization of the establishment and operations.

These various forms of support, when properly appropriated by members of community seed banks, can strengthen operations and performance. However, a high degree of dependence on a single or a few support providers can have a negative effect. As community seed banks mature, the nature and level of support they benefit from will change. More demand-driven forms of support can be expected to replace supply-driven forms. The organizations committed to providing long-term support to community seed banks included in this book seem to have accepted this dynamic evolution and adjusted their support accordingly. USC Canada, for example, reflects that as community seed banks mature, its support is redirected to the national level, through targeted training, collaboration with other institutions and policy efforts. In terms of focus, USC Canada mentions that it is now paying more attention to market development and income generation opportunities, gender equality and youth engagement (Chapter 37).

Sometimes, despite strong support from national and international agencies and attention paid to human capacity development, community seed banks do not evolve beyond initial steps. As the case study from Malaysia makes clear (Chapter 20), this can be due to several factors, including cultural values that do not encourage seed sharing, lack of strong community support to maintain operations and labour shortages.

Light webs

In a number of countries, community seed banks have not yet become part of dense webs although this does not mean that they are not solid in terms of operations, governance and performance. In Nicaragua, the only important external support has been that of the national Programa Campesino a Campesino (PCaC; farmer-to-farmer programme) of the Unión Nacional de Agricultores y Ganaderos (UNAG; the national union of farmers and livestock ranchers), which channels resources received from European NGOs and provides technical support (Chapter 26). The PCaC–UNAG network is in turn part of an alliance of organizations called Seeds of Identity supported by SWISSAID. The PCaC is known for its close and long-term cooperation with farmers, but its financial dependence on outside sources has caused some problems.

In Rwanda, the community seed bank, newly set up with the involvement of Bioversity International, is being connected with other agencies, such as a local youth cooperative, the Rwanda Agricultural Board, a government agency housing the national gene bank and the international NGO Caritas (Chapter 27). However, these connections are incipient and not very clearly defined. In Uganda, the newly established community seed bank works most closely with the national gene bank in Entebbe under the Plant Genetic Resources Centre of the National Agricultural Research Organization (NARO). The community seed bank receives technical guidance, and the gene bank stores duplicate accessions of its varieties (Chapter 30). NARO facilitated the link with support from Bioversity International.

In China, the first community seed bank in Xiding, Yunnan province, relies heavily on research support from provincial-level agencies and technical support from the local extension service bureau. It has not yet made other connections with formal-sector agencies, which, in the Chinese context, would require paying careful attention to formal cooperation procedures. Exchanges with other incipient community seed banks in southwest China are envisioned and could be useful in terms of sharing experience and seeds, as well as ideas for building more community seed banks in the country (Chapter 15).

In Bolivia, an early attempt to link community seed banks with formal rural development and seed-sector agencies did not last long, because of changes in the national political situation. Currently, a second attempt is benefitting from technical and financial support from an international donor agency project implemented by Bioversity International in cooperation with the Fundación para la Promoción e Investigación de Productos Andinos and four other national agencies. Partners are seeking how best to build a supportive network and policy and legal environment to guarantee sustainability (Chapter 11).

Dense webs

In a number of countries, community seed banks have become immersed in much denser webs characterized by a large number of and/or frequent connections with multiple and diverse social actors in both the formal and informal sectors. The case studies suggest that such dense webs can have a positive impact on the performance of community seed banks and offer opportunities to develop strategies in support of sustainability.

However, a caveat is necessary, as the experience in Mali suggests (Chapter 22). In Mali, a number of community seed banks, established with technical and financial support from USC Canada, now cooperate with other similar local and regional initiatives through networks and in partnership with a number of subregional organizations. When USC Canada support was withdrawn from one of the community seed banks, it continued to operate independently; in contrast, another community seed bank closed after funding ended. Although operating under similar, well-resourced network conditions, these banks differed in terms of level of empowerment of their members: leadership, motivation, sense of ownership and organizational skills.

A similar experience can be found in the Dalchowki case study, Nepal (Chapter 24). Although the community seed bank there collaborated with like-minded NGOs and government agencies (including the national gene bank) to receive technical and material support and seemed well connected, it suffered ups and downs in its development trajectory, mainly because of internal factors.

The Bhutan government is developing a national strategy to establish and support community seed banks. This represents an institutional model that could guide solid operations, good performance and sustainability (see Chapter 8). In Zimbabwe, community seed banks have benefitted from similar kinds of connections, although not backed up by a formal policy or national strategy (Chapter 38). The Zimbabwean community seed banks have developed close working relations with the national gene bank, which provides training and storage of seed samples collected by the community banks and participates in seed fairs. The national extension service has provided technical support from the beginning. The Community Technology Development Trust, the NGO supporting the community seed banks, has signed a memorandum of understanding with the Zimbabwe farmers' union to facilitate scaling up of the seed banks and networking among farmers at the national level.

Case studies from Brazil (Chapters 12 and 13) indicate that many hands working together can move a lot of soil. In the state of Paraiba, community seed banks are part of a network of farmers' and community associations, small cooperatives, unions, parishes and local NGOs that, together, have contributed to stronger farming systems and the realization of greater social equity and local sustainable development. In the state of Alagoas, community seed banks have joined forces with a cooperative of small-scale farmers and a large network of civil society organizations. These constellations of organizations have resulted in important policy and legal changes in support of community seed banks (Chapter 39). In Nepal, an ad hoc committee of the national network of community seed banks, formed in 2012, is promoting the exchange of knowledge and seeds and developing a catalogue of local varieties conserved in community seed banks across Nepal with support from LI-BIRD (Chapter 34). The committee is trying to bring all community seed banks in Nepal into the network. It is planning to meet with the national gene bank in late 2014 to discuss developing linkages.

Another way to build a dense web is through the execution of projects. Community seed banks alone are unlikely to be able to do this, but projects can be carried out through the agencies that support the banks. For example, the Native Seeds/SEARCH's project activities and impact in the southwest of the United States have created a dense web of connections through which knowledge and resources flow in multiple directions. These efforts also included the recent establishment of the first 'seed library' or small community seed bank with free exchange of seeds in Arizona and support to set up a sophisticated network among eight public libraries in Tucson (Chapter 31). This case might be atypical, but it points to the potential that well-functioning community seed banks can have in facilitating other initiatives.

Reference

Sthapit, B., Lamers, H. and Rao, R. (eds) (2013) *Custodian farmers of agricultural biodiversity: selected profiles from South and South East Asia*. *Proceedings of the Workshop on Custodian Farmers of Agricultural Biodiversity, 11–12 February 2013, New Delhi, India*. Bioversity International, New Delhi, India, www.bioversityinternational.org/e-library/publications/detail/custodian-farmers-of-agricultural-biodiversity-selected-profiles-from-south-and-south-east-asia/, accessed 26 January 2015

7 Policy and legal environment

*Ronnie Vernooy, Pitambar Shrestha
and Bhuwon Sthapit*

Across the world, community seed banks operate in countries with diverse political regimes and policy and legal contexts. Our review of the literature indicated that, surprisingly, very little attention has been paid to analyzing the policy and legal environment in which community seed banks operate. This chapter aims to fill that gap. Our analysis is guided by a number of questions: Which policies and laws concerning conservation and management of crop diversity on farm and in situ affect the operations of community seed banks? How are they affected? What public policy interventions have supported the operation of community seed banks? Are community seed banks recognized and rewarded as an expression of farmers' rights? If so, are they legally protected? What kinds of policy instruments *could* be put in place, if none exist, to create incentives for community seed banks to maintain crop diversity and contribute to other ecosystem services derived from biodiversity in agricultural landscapes?

From the previous chapters, a number of key objectives for policies and laws that could support community seed banks have been suggested:

- Encourage the conservation and recovery of local plant species and varieties maintained by smallholder farmers and their communities.
- Value and reward farmers' collective efforts to safeguard agricultural biodiversity and associated cultural values and knowledge.
- Value and protect these local genetic resources and related knowledge.
- Maintain fair access to and availability of these resources (through proper access and benefit-sharing arrangements).
- Facilitate links between local and national and international efforts.
- Support farmers technically and financially to organize themselves, and strengthen their organizational capacity.
- Disseminate and promote the results realized by communtiy seed banks.

The case studies offer a wide array of ways in which current policies and laws affect community seed banks, both positively and negatively. The various scenarios are summarized below. On the positive side, in recent years promising changes have been taking place in a number of countries, some of which have been mentioned in previous chapters. We believe that this positive trend will likely continue and expand, given the potential of community seed banks as well as increasing awareness of this potential among key decision-makers and their interest in integrating community seed banks into the broader framework of policies, strategies and programmes.

On the positive side: from sympathy to support

In Mexico (Chapter 42), community seed banks are receiving financial and technical support from the federal government; this support seems unique in terms of its size and scope. Nevertheless, the authors of the case study from Oaxaca (one of the pioneering states in which the support programme operates) argue that more could be done. Although community seed banks are now part of the national conservation system, they argue that public policy should support the in-situ conservation of genetic diversity in community seed banks by producers. This strategy would meet the challenges posed by climate change and transgenic materials. Legislation is also needed to protect farmers' biocultural resources. Community seed banks in Oaxaca should be part of a national strategy of in-situ conservation of the country's plant genetic resources. Creation of other community seed banks should be encouraged in Mexican states that are strategically located near indigenous and mestizo groups who are dealing with high levels of genetic diversity or threatened or endangered species.

In Nepal (Chapter 41), the national policy environment has become more favourable for community seed banks. The department of agriculture has mainstreamed community seed banks in its plans and programmes as a strategy to increase access to quality improved seeds and to conserve local crops. The recently amended national seed regulation has relaxed its requirements for registering local crop varieties making it possible for individual and organized farmers to register their locally bred strains.

With input from nongovernmental organizations (NGOs), Nepal's government pioneered a Community Seed Bank Guideline (2009), a comprehensive document developed to guide planning, implementation and regular monitoring of community seed bank activities. The guideline focusses on marginalized, subsistence, indigenous peoples and war-affected households, who often have poor access to seeds. It shares a clear vision and outlines strategies to coordinate and collaborate with various governmental and nongovernmental institutions; the complementary roles community needs to play; and a capacity-building and community empowerment plan. The guideline has been used by some government agencies to establish and support a number of community seed banks, but it has not been widely disseminated. Only the District Agriculture Development Office has the mandate to establish community seed banks and only 17 districts can establish them. So far, seven seed banks have been set up in seven districts. The strategy of the National Agricultural Genetic Resources Centre includes building a network of community seed banks as a key part of a complementary conservation strategy.

In 2014, Bhutan's National Biodiversity Centre followed Nepal's example by drafting a guide for community seed banks. The guide has six chapters that include definitions, objectives, functions, organizers and collaborators, scope and establishment and management guidelines. Wider dissemination of such guides might be of help to other governments interested in promoting seed banks.

The country with the most supportive policies and laws is Brazil (Chapter 39). Over the last few years, three Brazilian states (Paraíba, Alagoas and Minas Gerais) have approved laws aimed at providing a legal framework for existing community seed banks created and maintained by small-scale farmers' associations with the support of NGOs and sometimes local governments. In four other states (Bahia, Pernambuco, Santa Catarina and São Paulo), similar bills are being discussed in their legislative assemblies. A special community seed bank programme allows Paraiba's state government to buy seeds of local varieties for distribution among farmers and community seed banks. Previously, only certified seeds of improved varieties had been used for this purpose. This law has also allowed farmers to use seeds of local varieties to produce food and sell it to public schools and hospitals (through contracts with state government agencies). The state of Minas Gerais approved its community seed bank law in 2009. It established, for the first time, a legal definition of a community seed bank and offered some protection to farmers in terms of access and availability: 'a germplasm collection of local, traditional and creole plant varieties and, landraces, administered locally by family farmers, who are responsible for the multiplication of seeds or seedlings for distribution, exchange, or trade among themselves.'

Promising developments

In a number of countries, there are signs that more supportive policies and laws are on the way. The case studies describing such promising signs include those in Mesoamerica (despite the negative conditions in Nicaragua; see below) and South Africa. In South Africa, the Department of Agriculture, Forestry and Fisheries (DAFF) considers community seed banks to be a means to strengthen informal seed systems, support conservation of traditional farmer varieties and maintain seed security at the district and community levels. The Departmental Strategy on Conservation and Sustainable Use of Genetic Resources for Food and Agriculture proposes, among other focus areas, both ex-situ and in-situ conservation of plant genetic resources for food and agriculture. DAFF is collaborating with Bioversity International to set up a small number of community seed banks in the country in selected regions of mainly smallholder farms (Chapter 43).

In Central America (Chapter 40), the recently developed Strategic Action Plan for Strengthening the Role of Mesoamerican Plant Genetic Resources for Food and Agriculture in Adapting Agricultural Systems to Climate Change makes community seed banks central. The plan was formulated in 2012–2013 with funding from the Benefit-Sharing Fund of the International Treaty on

Plant Genetic Resources for Food and Agriculture. Its development involved stakeholders from six countries in the region under the scientific guidance of Bioversity International's Regional Office for the Americas. The resulting plan, supported by the Central American Council of Ministers, is structured in thematic sections focussed on in-situ/on-farm and ex-situ conservation, sustainable use, policies and institutions. Each section outlines actions to be carried out over the next ten years (Chapter 40).

In Zimbabwe, there have been discussions on the need for a comprehensive farmers' rights legislative framework. The proposed framework will provide for the establishment of community seed banks interacting closely with the national gene bank and the South African Development Community Regional Gene Bank. Such cooperation has great potential in terms of strengthening conservation and sustainable use efforts at the national level (Chapter 38).

In Uganda, the community seed bank of Kiziba (Chapter 30) is registered at the district level as a seed-producing group and operates under various policies, principally under the draft national agricultural seed policy (2011) currently under review. The community seed bank also operates under the Seed and Plant Act (2006) which is the legal framework concerning the promotion, regulation and control of plant breeding and variety release, seed multiplication and marketing, seed import and export and quality assurance of seeds and planting materials. The Seed and Plant Regulations (2009) provide guidelines for enforcement of the act.

Contradicting policies

Although only mentioned explicitly by the authors of the Rwanda case study (Chapter 27), but most likely also relevant in quite a number of countries, policies and laws sometimes contradict each other. In Rwanda, for example, the government has started to support the establishment of community seed banks in selected areas. However, the policy of land consolidation and growing a single priority crop has a negative impact on community seed bank activities because the local varieties of different crops cannot be grown freely by farmers. This is also hindered by the government's distribution of improved varieties of seeds and fertilizers to farmers under the crop intensification programme.

On the negative side: unsympathetic, no support, difficult to obtain support

A number of countries make it difficult to establish and operate community seed banks. Some governments consider them 'competitors' of the government-controlled conservation system. Others are worried about community-based organizations at large.

For example, in China, current agricultural and biodiversity-related policies do not favour conservation by farmers and their communities, although in recent years some opportunities for local initiatives have been created (Song and Vernooy, 2010). The negative environment is likely one of the reasons why, despite the enormous size of the country and its farming population, few attempts have been made to set up a community seed bank. In fact, the one described in Chapter 15 might be the first. Policies and laws at the provincial level have an effect as well. The Yunnan Provincial Protection Regulations for new varieties of registered horticultural plants and the Yunnan Agricultural Environmental Protection Ordinance mentioned by the case study authors have had a positive impact on conservation and agricultural biodiversity activities. However, awareness of the need to protect agricultural biodiversity on farm is weak in the country.

In Spain, the situation is not much different. The 'Cultivate diversity. Sow your rights' campaign in which the Spanish seed network participates (Chapter 36) demands a change in public policies related to the conservation and use of local varieties and local seed production. However, so far this long-term effort has not led to any concrete policy or legal changes.

Some countries, such as India and Ethiopia, do have farmers' rights acts or provisions, which, in principle, are favourable towards community seed banks, but actual implementation may not be evident. In India, the community seed banks established by the National Board of Plant Genetic Resources are under its strong control and operate as mini-gene banks (Malik et al., 2013). One of the problems is that smallholder farmers are not allowed to produce and market seeds. In some cases, there are restrictive laws, such as a seed certification law, based on criteria related to distinctiveness, uniformity and stability that were developed for the formal seed system. In Nicaragua (Chapter 26), the lack of supportive conservation policies on native genetic resources combined with the promotion of a few varieties of staple grains by research and extension agencies has resulted in the loss of local varieties in recent decades. The case study from Bangladesh (Chapter 9) also reports this.

Community seed banks and recognition of farmers' rights

Andersen and Winge (2011) have pointed out that community seed banks contribute to the realization of farmers' rights as defined by the International Treaty on Plant Genetic Resources for Food and Agriculture (ITPGRFA). They ensure a diversified supply of seeds adapted to local conditions; protect knowledge related to local varieties; reduce dependence on seed sources outside the community; promote the multiplication of seeds, sharing with other farmers and crop improvement activities; provide benefits through NGO sponsorship; and ensure access to seed reserves in times of stress.

As the case studies illustrate, all community seed banks fulfill at least one of these functions, but only a few do so by making explicit reference to farmers' rights. For example, the authors of the Zimbabwe case study refer to the ITPGRFA and mention that support of community seed banks is a way 'to experiment with the domestication of the ITPGRFA' (Chapter 38). Zimbabwe is one of the few countries where there have been discussions on the need for a comprehensive farmers' rights legislative framework.

Concerning legal protection, which supposedly comes with the protection of farmers' rights, the case studies offer a very mixed panorama from operating without any clear protection to formal forms of recognition, most notably acquired by functioning as cooperatives. This remains an area where more technical support would be welcome.

In its advocacy of community seed banks, Norway's Development Fund has argued that governments should establish or support community seed banks as part of their obligations to implement farmers' rights and other provisions of the ITPGRFA, such as sustainable use and conservation of crop genetic diversity. The Development Fund has also requested that parties to the ITPGRFA support the upscaling of community seed banks to reach as many farmers as possible, especially in marginalized areas (Chapter 35). These seem valid demands, but to date they have not received much attention or support from national governments, although the governments of some countries have begun to consider community seed banks more seriously (see, for example, the case studies of Mesoamerica and South Africa, Chapters 40 and 43).

Policy measures to support community seed banks

National seed policies and related laws normally address seed production (multiplication), standardization, certification and commercialization; variety improvement, registration and release procedures; protection of intellectual property (often mostly concerning breeders' rights); technical support to the seed sector (research and extension services); and farmer organization. As such, they have an immediate impact on the operations of many community seed banks, particularly those that focus on providing access to and availability of seeds. Specific measures spelled out in policies and laws can offer concrete support to community seed banks, but, to date, more often than not, they have the opposite effect. In Zimbabwe, farmers are not allowed to sell farm-saved seed. In Mexico, legislation to protect farmers' genetic resources is still lacking, although community seed banks do receive technical and financial support from the government. In Nicaragua, various civil society organizations are campaigning for enactment of a legal framework to promote and protect seeds of local varieties.

Apart from those related to seeds, other policies and laws may be relevant. In Nepal, for example, the Agrobiodiversity Policy, first developed in 2007 and revised in 2011 and again in 2014, gives implicit credit to community seed banks through its focus on conserving, promoting and sustainably using agro-biodiversity; securing and promoting farming communities' welfare and rights to their indigenous knowledge, skills and techniques; and developing appropriate options for a fair and equitable sharing of benefits arising from the access and use of agricultural genetic resources and materials. Community seed banks have the potential to support the Nagoya Protocol by helping to ensure benefit-sharing at the community level. However, a serious policy gap remains: support is needed for appropriate incentives based, for example, on a quality assurance system for community seed banks.

Policies and laws concerning cooperative development or farmer organization, more generally, can be a strong support for community seed banks. They could provide legal recognition and protection, technical and financial support, opportunities for the commercialization of seeds and other incentives, both monetary and non-monetary (e.g. prizes and awards), as well as opportunities to make farmers' voices heard at the national level. In a number of countries (e.g. Burundi, Mali and Mexico), community seed banks have acquired formal cooperative status giving them the chance to solidify and expand their operations.

Specific policies and laws concerning community seed banks are still rare. The most inspiring case is found in Brazil (as mentioned above), where three states have approved specific laws aimed at providing a legal framework for existing community seed banks and four other states are discussing similar bills. We can only hope that more countries will follow this example.

References

Andersen, R. and Winge, T. (2011) 'Linking community seedbanks and farmers' rights,' in *Banking for the Future: Savings, Security and Seeds*, Development Fund, Oslo, Norway, pp5–6

Malik, S. K., Singh, P. B., Singh, A., Verma, A., Ameta, N. and Bisht, I. S. (2013) *Community Seedbanks: Operations and Scientific Management*, National Board for Plant Genetic Resources, New Delhi, India

Song, Y. and Vernooy, R. (eds) (2010) *Seeds and Synergies: Innovating Rural Development in China*, Practical Action, Bourton on Dunsmore, UK, and International Development Research Centre, Ottawa, Canada

8 Sustainability

*Pitambar Shrestha, Bhuwon Sthapit
and Ronnie Vernooy*

In previous chapters, we discussed key aspects of the operations and performance of community seed banks. All of those factors influence what we could call organizational viability. However, sustainability, or long-term organizational viability, is the greatest challenge facing community seed banks. As the case studies in this book indicate, there is considerable variability in the performance of community seed banks in terms of technical and operational capacities, such as adherence to phytosanitary standards, quality seed production, technical rigour in monitoring germination and ensuring viability of stored seed, management of information about stored varieties and growing conditions, governance and operational management. Technical and operational challenges are compounded by lack of legal recognition (although, in some countries, improvements are underway in this regard) and scarce financial resources. Past experience has shown that community seed bank initiatives are usually quite effective during their initial years, but with the withdrawal of external support, many cut back on activities or stop altogether. As in other organizational efforts, when community seed banks are established without proper foundations, long-term survival is difficult.

The variation among our case studies, along with the recent growth in the number of community seed banks, raises the question: What capacities must community seed banks have to be and remain effective in the long run? Our case studies suggest that a number of conditions must be met: legal recognition and protection, options for financial viability, members with adequate technical knowledge and effective operational mechanisms. Careful and systematic planning right from the start is another important factor. In this chapter, we elaborate on some aspects of sustainability of community seed banks, namely, human and social capital, economic empowerment, policy and legal environment and operational modality.

Building human and social capital

Community seed banks function on the principles of participation, collective decision-making and shared responsibility for resources, risks and benefits. The process of farmers working together and participating in activities strengthens their capacity for collective action and builds human and social capital. The technical aspects of community seed bank management are a crucial part of this process. The effective operation and survival of seed banks depend on providing access to quality seeds, and this can only be realized with committed, trained and capable human resources.

Community seed banks usually follow traditional knowledge-based practices that are relatively simple and low cost, but some use modern equipment and the latest technologies. In addition to the physical facilities of the banks, the technical knowledge acquired and used by members plays a significant role in maintaining the quality of seeds. When members are fully equipped with the technical knowledge they need to conserve and produce genetically and physically pure seed (as discussed in detail in Chapter 5), chances of long-term functioning of the seed bank are good.

Another important aspect of building human capital – and ensuring sustainability – is the transfer of leadership roles, knowledge and expertise of senior members to second-generation leadership and young members. This is partly determined by the governance mechanism (Chapter 4). Networking of community seed banks in a country or state creates a platform for learning and sharing of experiences, but it can also contribute to developing human and social capital. In Brazil, Mali, Mexico and Nepal, various types of networks have been set up, both as a result of strengthened capacities and as vehicles for further strengthening of community seed banks. In other cases, community seed banks are networking with national gene banks (e.g. China, Zimbabwe and planned in Nepal). Such collaboration is another way to strengthen the capacity of community seed bank members, particularly in the technical aspects of seed handling, including disease and pest management and, to a lesser degree, operational aspects.

The community seed banks in the case study countries are functioning at various levels of technical capacity. Some are highly professional, while others are beginners; some are receiving technical support from public research or extension agencies and nongovernmental organizations (NGOs), while others are functioning on their own after receiving support from external agencies for a number of years. Community seed banks in Bhutan, Bolivia, China, Costa Rica, Mexico and Trinidad receive technical support from public research institutions. In Zimbabwe, both the government extension agency and the Community Technology Development Trust provide guidance in technical and management aspects of community seed banks.

Economic empowerment

Community seed bank members commonly volunteer their time and labour to carry out the work of the facility. They attend meetings and discussions; search for and collect seeds; maintain records; clean, dry and store seeds; distribute seeds for production and regeneration; monitor and supervise; build and maintain physical assets – all at no cost to the seed bank. Many of them also contribute small amounts of seeds and planting material to be stored and distributed through the seed bank free of charge.

But how long will members be able to continue this work? For how many generations? How many members? What economic incentives are there for being part of a community seed bank? Answers to these questions are not easily found in the case studies. Depending on the types of seeds and volume of annual transactions, proper seed management requires regular involvement of one or more people throughout the year to ensure that day-to-day functions are carried out smoothly. To be financially viable and not completely dependent on voluntary labour, a community seed bank should be designed in such a way that it generates economic incentives at two levels: for its members (in particular those playing key roles) and for the organization as a whole. One important reason why community seed banks become less functional when external support is withdrawn is the lack of economic incentives to support the livelihoods of member families.

Overall, the case studies are characterized by lack of attention to economic empowerment and financial sustainability, except for production and marketing of farmer-preferred varieties of local and improved seeds. In cases where this strategy is successful, it has generated economic benefits at both levels: seed producer members and the seed bank. It has also gone hand in hand with making seeds available to needy members and others, usually at a lower price than other sources. Community seed banks in Costa Rica, Nepal and Zimbabwe are producing and selling seeds in large volumes and doing well financially. Some are in the process of developing community seed banks as seed enterprises, e.g. Uganda (Chapter 30).

A unique approach, developed in Nepal and now disseminated elsewhere, is the establishment of a community biodiversity management fund (Shrestha et al., 2013; Chapter 34). These funds (approximately US$5,000–10,000 per community seed bank) were created using donor funds (through projects) and contributions from the community (ranging from 10 per cent to 25 per cent). They are set up as revolving funds available to seed bank members to finance income-generating activities. They provide easy access to small amounts of credit (without collateral or complex procedures) to the members as well as generating some income for the community seed bank in the form of interest (12 per cent a year). The interest is used to cover staff salaries, the regeneration of rare local varieties and other operational expenses. Exploring opportunities for further dissemination of this mechanism and similar ones could provide immense support to many community seed banks around the world. However, successful implementation of a community biodiversity management fund will require social and human capital building from the outset.

Policy and legal provisions

Despite the growing number of community seed banks over the last three decades, to date very few countries have developed relevant policies, laws, acts or guidelines for implementing or supporting them. Without legal recognition, community seed banks are less likely to be sustainable in the long run. Most community seed banks have been established with support from NGOs through project funds, usually of short duration. For seed banks to find their own funding, they require legal recognition and registration in most countries; many funding agencies also often hesitate to provide support to an organization that is not a legal entity. On the positive side, obtaining legal recognition contributes to building confidence among community seed bank members by requiring them to speak on equal terms with public, private and civil society organizations.

Among the case studies in this book, Brazil seems far ahead in terms of bringing community seed banks into the legal framework, as three states have already approved community seed bank laws and four are discussing such laws (Chapter 39). These laws have allowed state governments to buy and distribute seeds of local varieties produced by community seed banks; previously, only certified, formal-sector seeds could be used. Mexico has integrated community seed banks into its National System of Plant Genetic Resources for Food and Agriculture (SINAREFI) coordinated by the National Seed Inspection and Certification Services, a public institution. This represents strong institutional recognition, and community seed banks receive financial and technical support from SINAREFI projects.

Because of the absence of a policy and legal framework in most of the countries covered in this book, some community seed banks have been registered as cooperatives or local NGOs or societies, while many others are still functioning as informal community-based, self-help institutions based on mutual trust and cooperation. Registering a community seed bank as a co-operative or a local NGO requires some legal procedures, which can be a burden for members. However, it also creates opportunities to obtain funding and programme support and, thus, allows the bank to continue its activities when other resources are unavailable.

Another strategy is for community seed banks to become part of a network connected to the national level gene bank. The Nepalese national gene bank has proposed such a plan to promote collecting and regenerating locally adapted materials in their natural habitats and to create ex-situ–in-situ links. However, there is yet no adequate policy or legal framework to carry this plan forward.

Operational modality

The methods adopted by community seed banks for participation and decision-making by members relate to the key tasks to be carried out. The case studies indicate that rules and regulations are usually established by the members themselves and efforts are usually made to respect them. In most cases, both women and men farmers are active participants.

The operational dimension is important in terms of sustainability, because it is through the practices related to seed circulation among members and non-members that a community seed bank comes to life and remains active. Clear roles and responsibilities of the management team are features of well-governed community seed banks. As the cases demonstrate, there is room for further strengthening of the contributions of women and custodian farmers.

The modus operandi of a community seed bank may vary – and we consider this a strength – depending on farmers' own organizational processes, who participates in which activities and decision-making (e.g. not every member has to invest the same amount of time and effort in all the tasks at hand), levels of knowledge and skills that members gain through interactions and the amount of training available. Usually, an executive committee of elected or selected farmers is responsible for overall management, both technical and financial, but some community seed banks form separate committees for the various tasks.

In Bangladesh, for example, the community seed bank has two committees. The Natural Resource Audit Committee with seven members is responsible for regenerating seeds and recording and maintaining data. The Specialized Women Seed Network with 11 members carries out the tasks of seed handling, safe storage, distribution and exchange (Chapter 9). The Kiziba community gene bank in Uganda has divided major tasks among a general manager, a records manager, a distribution manager, a quality control manager and mobilizers (Chapter 30). In Costa Rica, a technical committee looks after seed delivery, quality analysis and seed storage (Chapter 16).

A unique operational modality is used by the Toronto Seed Library in Canada and is being adopted in many other parts of North America and Europe. Its name alone shows that the library is not functioning as a community seed bank, but as a free-to-all public space for the exchange and use of seeds rather than collection and conservation. The public, retail stores and seed companies are all invited to donate seeds, which are then distributed through the library's branches to gardeners and seed savers (Chapter 14). Such an approach functions well in areas where the public has a strong interest in and commitment to environmental issues.

The case studies in this book illustrate how difficult it is to combine these four dimensions of sustainability. Some community seed banks have made progress on the policy and legal sides, some have developed promising options for financial viability, some are working hard to improve technical knowledge and skills and many are paying attention to developing more effective operational mechanisms. Our assessment is that much remains to be done. Learning from each other could be one mechanism, and we hope this book will facilitate such learning.

Reference

Shrestha, P., Sthapit, S., Subedi, A. and Sthapit, B. (2013) 'Community biodiversity management fund: promoting conservation through livelihood development in Nepal,' in W. S. de Boef, A. Subedi, N. Peroni, M. H. Thijssen and E. O'Keeffe (eds) *Community Biodiversity Management: Promoting Resilience and the Conservation of Plant Genetic Resources*, Earthscan from Routledge, London, UK, pp118–122

Part II

Case studies from around the world

9 Bangladesh

The Mamudpur Nayakrishi Seed Hut

M. A. Sobhan, Jahangir Alam Jony,
Rabiul Islam Chunnu and Fahima Khatun Liza

Purpose and evolution of the seed hut

The Mamudpur Nayakrishi Seed Hut (NSH) was established in 2001, when Rina Begum, along with other farmers, became interested in collecting local seeds to improve their livelihoods (Plate 1). The farmers had participated in a training session in biodiversity-based farming held by Unnayan Bikalper Nitinirdharoni Gobeshona (UBINIG), a policy research organization working with the farming community. After joining the Nayakrishi Seed Network, whose aim is to collect and maintain seeds of local crop varieties, they decided to establish a 'seed hut' in the village of Mamudpur on land donated by Rina Begum. In a seed hut, a group of farming households takes joint responsibility for looking after seeds and genetic resources that they collect and propagate on behalf of the community.

The Mamudpur NSH is associated with the Community Seed Wealth Centre and is supported by the UBINIG Tangail Centre. UBINIG has been warning of the harmful effects of conventional agriculture and promoting and conducting training sessions on biodiversity-based farming at the community level. Rina and her husband, Mainuddin, were among 25,600 poorer farmers in Tangail district who were concerned over modern chemical-based agriculture as well as the loss of crop diversity and aquatic and animal genetic resources. Nayakrishi Andolon, a farmers' initiative to undertake biodiversity-based farming, soon became popular in more than 300,000 farming households in over 19 districts of the country.

More than 20 farmers practising nayakrishi (community-based farming) in Mamudpur joined the seed hut cooperative led by Rina Begum, Tara Banu and Tafizuddin. Currently, a committee of seven women and four men is responsible for its operation. Since 2009, UBINIG, in collaboration with the Community-based Biodiversity Management South Asia Programme, has been providing support for construction, repair and maintenance of the seed hut, training of farmers, seed production and the distribution of seeds to farmers (Plate 2). The farmers provide physical labour for construction, management and maintenance and take care of running the day-to-day activities, such as production, regeneration and enhancement of plant genetic resources at the community level. The cost of establishing the seed hut amounted to 60,000

Bangladeshi taka (BDT) or US$800. Annual maintenance, management and improvement costs come to about BDT 40,000. UBINIG provided 50 per cent of the total original cost and 50 per cent was contributed by farmers.

For the farmers in Mamudpur, the focus was not only on stopping the use of chemicals, but also on conserving their own seed. They were already familiar with the Community Seed Wealth Centre, where they had been exchanging seeds. Although the NSH is not a formal organization, it is well known in the community and has informal links with various government departments, such as the Department of Agricultural Extension, the Bangladesh Rural Development Board, academic institutions, nongovernmental organizations (NGOs) and local government. The seed hut acts as a meeting place for the nayakrishi farmers to discuss their crops, seeds and other related issues. It provides training sessions, workshops and seminars and the participants take part in fairs and exhibitions.

Currently, 1,350 farmers from four villages (Mamudpur, Ghunikishore, Baraiatia and Kuchiamari) are directly involved in NSH activities. In Mamudpur, 75 per cent of farming households practise nayakrishi farming. Women there are experienced in seed conservation techniques and maintain a variety of crops grown in the homestead area. Mamudpur NSH has a Specialized Women's Seed Network formed by UBINIG in consultation with the community, and its members are key actors in conservation and maintenance of plant genetic resources. UBINIG has been organizing training, information-sharing sessions and exchange visits for its members, which have helped them gain more experience. The network also documents pertinent information on seed collection, conservation and distribution.

Functions and activities

The NSH preserves seeds of local varieties suited to the community. Currently, it holds 1,507kg of seed; the main species are rice (17 species), wheat (one), barley (one), pulses (five), oilseeds (six), vegetables (40), spices (11) and fibre crops (two). Small and marginalized farmers are particularly interested in the cultivation of indigenous varieties of crops following nayakrishi principles. They prefer local seeds, because of their resistance to common pests and pathogens, over commercial varieties and hybrid seeds, which are costly and require the application of chemical fertilizers, pesticides and irrigation. Between 2010 and 2012, 974 farmers (349 in 2010, 217 in 2011 and 308 in 2012) used seeds from Mamudpur NSH. Women farmers have been especially interested in cultivating vegetables and fruits. Local seeds of these crops are adapted to the mixed culture practised on homesteads and in the adjoining highlands.

Seeds are distributed among the nayakrishi farmers on demand and with their commitment to deposit seed in the NSH after the harvest. For example, Aynal Houque, a farmer from Adazan village, Basail, received 50g of safflower seed, which he cultivated as a mixed crop. Now he has 300g of seed that he will share with five other farmers after returning 50g to the NSH. In 2012,

11 varieties of rice seeds (Lalchamara, Hizaldigha, Sadadepa, Laldepa, Patjag, Latashail, Notashail, Kalijira, Salla, Bawailadihga and Lakhidigha) were distributed among 56 farmers for planting during the May–August season; these varieties are popular because of their suitability in the flood-plain ecosystem. For the same season, 41 farmers received vegetable seed, and for the January–April crop period (a drier season), 192 farmers received vegetable and spice seeds. All recipient farmers were able to return seeds to the NSH after harvest. The status of stored seeds is checked regularly for viability and arrangements are made for seed multiplication.

Neglected and underused seeds are collected, regenerated and maintained with special care because they are grown by only a few farmers. During 2010–2012, lesser-used crops identified and regenerated by the NSH included safflower, satpotal (a rare variety of ridged gourd), elephant foot yam, bean, local red radish, aniseed, tosa jute, finger millet and a number of local rice varieties including Begun Bichi, Chitkashaita, Hiali Baron, Sadabaronlakkhidigha, Shamubanga, Karchamuri and Ashaira. Eight farmers are involved in identifying endangered and threatened species and varieties for collection, multiplication and maintenance. The NSH has been playing a vital role in taking stock of these resources and developing an appropriate strategy for their multiplication and maintenance. Farmers are actively conserving barley, fox-tail millet, sesame and chili – examples of species that were neglected or underused in the past but are now important in terms of adaptability to changing environmental conditions and yield potential. The Mamudpur NSH has paid special attention to conservation of such varieties through collection and exchange with other NSHs in the area. Five farmers are experienced in handling rice seeds, and nine specialize in vegetables, pulses and spices. The assigned seed-producing farmers are given 16 varieties, including rice (eight), vegetables (four), pulses (two) and oil seed (two). Surplus seeds are available at the nayakrishi sales outlet.

The NSH is participating in a programme to improve aus varieties by combining drought tolerance with high yield. (Aus is a pre-monsoon, rain-dependent, fast-growing rice grown during the January–April season.) There are 277 aus varieties now under cultivation in Bangladesh. Six selected varieties are in the third year of participatory varietal selection trials. Two varieties of aman rice, Kalakut and Lalcheyshail, have also been selected by nayakrishi farmers using a participatory approach. The seeds are maintained at the seed hut and distributed to farmers for crop production.

The Mamudpur NSH also supports local research. For example, the Department of Agricultural Extension (DAE) at Upazila and at the district level has regular communication with the seed hut and uses seeds from it. Government policies have been based on conventional agriculture, and its promotion of mainly introduced crops has eroded local varieties. However, recently the government has become interested in incorporating local varieties of aus rice into its cropping system, and the DAE and UBINIG have an agreement to promote these varieties at the community level. In 2012, DAE collected 17 accessions of local rice seed from Mamudpur NSH.

Nayakrishi farmer researchers also regularly use seed from Mamudpur NSH. Among them, five farmers from Mamudpur are conducting research on productivity, land pattern suitability and selection of new varieties. Their findings help other farmers increase their yields and grain quality.

Two DAE staff stationed at Mamudpur carried out research on the productivity of five varieties of local rice seed from the NSH. Their yields were high, and they are now practising nayakrishi on their own farms. Local varieties of rice, vegetables, pulses, oil seeds and jute seeds are also frequently used in research.

Traditional knowledge plays a key role in the practice of nayakrishi. For example, only unblemished fruits free from infection and pest infestation are selected for seed harvesting. Rice panicles of a certain length with a large number of grains are harvested separately for seed collection, threshed and dried separately in the sun. Quality control consists of a bite check. When the grain is completely dry, it is cooled and stored in containers, often earthen pots, sealed with a mixture of fresh cow dung and mud. Seeds with a thick coat are stored in transparent bottles; those with a thin coat are stored in coloured bottles. Pulse and wheat seeds are stored in tin containers. Neem leaves are placed around seed containers to prevent disease and insect infestations.

Governance, management and networking

Two committees are responsible for the management and coordination of the NSH: the Natural Resource Auditing Committee, with seven members, and the Specialized Women's Seed Network, with 11 members. The Specialized Women's Seed Network is engaged in cleaning the NSH, collecting seeds from harvested plants, drying seeds and containers and ensuring that stored seeds are kept dry. It meets weekly to approve the cropping plan for the season, seed distribution and seed exchanges.

Nayakrishi farmers and members of the Specialized Women's Seed Network participate in regular meetings of the NSH. Every nayakrishi farmer can exchange seed and genetic resources with this NSH. The Mamudpur NSH communicates regularly with the Atia Union Parishod (local government institution), the DAE in the Delduar subdistrict and the Bangladesh Rural Development Board at Delduar. People from educational institutions in Delduar have visited the Mamudpur NSH, and it is well recognized by local government, the DAE, the Bangladesh Rural Development Board and academic institutions. During the untimely flood and drought in 2011, when farmers in Mamudpur and neighbouring villages lost their field crops, Mamudpur NSH distributed vegetable and oil seeds to 73 farmers as back-up support.

In collaboration with the Community Seed Wealth Centre, the NSH has been regularly participating in agricultural and plant fairs organized by the Upazila DAE and has won five first-place prizes. The NSH has also been participating in various events organized by NGOs and other civil organizations. The NSH is a component of the Nayakrishi Seed Network, which in turn maintains a link with the National Agricultural Research System's gene bank. Through the Nayakrishi Seed Network, the NSH has collected 900 accessions of rice seed from the Bangladesh Rice Research Institute and has regenerated these varieties through the Community Seed Wealth Centre. Seven of these varieties are maintained by Mamudpur NSH through regular cultivation by the farmers. During 2012, 117 women farmers linked with Mamudpur NSH exchanged seeds with three other NSHs and Community Seed Wealth Centres.

Technical issues

Eight specialized farmers are involved in high-quality seed production and practise integrated crop management. The members of the Specialized Women's Seed Network select mature, robust, disease-free fruit for collection of seeds. The network members are knowledgeable and experienced in seed maintenance and management, and their expertise is useful to all farmers as they ensure the availability of high-quality seeds.

All crops maintained at the seed hut are regenerated every year in the appropriate season under the close observation and monitoring of the seven members of the Natural Resource Auditing Committee. Pertinent data are recorded over the season from sowing to postharvest handling. Morpho-agronomic data are also recorded, mainly by the Natural Resource Auditing Committee with the collaboration of NSH members. Weekly meetings are held at the NSH, and information is exchanged among seed users in group discussions, group meetings and exchange visits. Farmers' knowledge and skills are strengthened at monthly meetings of the Specialized Women's Seed Network, exchange visits and various training sessions.

Achievements and prospects

The use of local varieties of crops has increased in Mamudpur, as has the use of on-farm resources such as crop diversification, mixed cropping and cow dung and compost. The application of chemical fertilizers has decreased and no pesticides are now used. More and more farmers are growing local varieties. Women farmers, especially, are playing an important role in the efficient management of the NSH. Seventeen local varieties of aman rice have been reintroduced. In 2001, 11 major crop varieties were grown in the Mamudpur area; now, 89 local crop varieties are available from the NSH and these are well suited to local flood-plain agro-ecological conditions.

The farmers feel confident and believe that the work of the NSH is their strength. Recently, rainfall patterns and soil moisture conditions have become variable, with drought sometimes followed by heavy rain and flooding. Based on their observations and practical experience, the farmers are now selecting crop varieties that can withstand changing climate conditions. The aus paddy varieties Kala manik, Karchamuri, Vaturi and Lohachure; aman paddy varieties Maynagiri, Kaika, Patishaile, Jhuldhan, Sada depa and Lal depa; sesame; jute;

and foxtail millet are suitable in dry and drought conditions. The aman paddy varieties Hizaldigha, Chamaradigha and Bawailadigha are suitable in flood conditions. Radishes, sweet potatoes and grass peas are suitable in heavy fog conditions.

Most households have become self-sufficient, earning about BDT 8,000–12,000 (about US$100–155) a month and are now able to buy cows or repair their house. Total productivity has increased through the use of mixed cropping and crop rotation. For example, one popular practice is to broadcast a mix of aman and aus rice in April–May. In 70–90 days, the farmers harvest the aus rice and leave aman rice as a standing crop. Then in October–November, 15–20 days before the aman rice is ready to harvest, the farmers sow black grams and grass pea. After harvesting aman rice, the pulse crops remain until January–February when the mature crop is harvested. This system has not only increased productivity but has also increased soil fertility.

By growing varieties of vegetables and pulses in their fields and homesteads, farmers have ensured a supply of balanced and nutritious food free from contamination by chemical fertilizers and pesticides. Their cash income comes mainly from aus and aman rice; mustard, sesame and lin seeds; lentils and black gram; barley; millet; and many varieties of vegetables.

The NSH has been able to cooperate with the community to improve livelihoods and food security with very little outside support. The community holds meetings on its own initiative and finances the NSH with its own contributions. The NSH stores and multiplies seeds; the seeds are used by its members and the surplus harvest is sold; and the money earned is used for running the NSH. The farmers are happy and content.

10 Bhutan

The Bumthang community seed bank

Asta Tamang and Gaylong Dukpa

History and purpose of the community seed bank

Bhutanese farmers save their seeds in traditional ways and share them in and between communities. In Bumthang (one of 20 administrative districts, or dzongkhag, in Bhutan), farmers grow crops that are adapted to high altitudes, such as buckwheat, a traditional staple crop that is strongly associated with the Bumthang culture. However, despite the importance of bitter buckwheat, sweet buckwheat and barley in terms of food security and culture, in the late 1970s these crops were declining, largely due to the promotion of potato production by the Food Corporation of Bhutan. Nowadays, rice has completely replaced buckwheat as a staple crop.

In an effort to maintain agro-biodiversity and resilience in the farming system, the National Biodiversity Centre (NBC) organized workshops for farmers in the province in 2009. NBC staff observed that knowledge of diversity in the communities was limited. The idea of conservation was new to Bumthang farmers; they knew nothing about community seed banks in Bhutan or in the region. In 2009, after a study visit to Nepal by an assistant dzongkhag agricultural officer to observe on-farm conservation initiatives, the idea of a community seed bank, based on strong cooperation among farmers and support from the NBC, was born.

To avoid future conflict regarding ownership of land, precautions were taken to establish the seed bank on government property with the approval of the governor of the dzongkhag. An existing storehouse was renovated and converted into a 'treasure house': the Bumthang community seed bank in the town of Chamkhar in the district of Choekhor. Once the structure was sound, agricultural extension officials collected germplasm of cereals and vegetables from all areas of Bumthang. The seed samples collected from the field were processed to reduce the moisture level and then put into earthenware pots for short- to medium-term storage (Plate 3). The community seed bank was formally inaugurated by the minister of agriculture and forests on 17 December 2011, the National Day of Bhutan.

The community seed bank was established in recognition of the importance of agricultural biodiversity for national food security, agricultural resilience and sustainable development in the face of such emerging challenges as global warming and climate change. The seed bank houses the seeds of traditional varieties collected from the fields of farmers who are still cultivating them. Its main purposes are to:

- maintain the existing genetic diversity of Bumthang;
- restore the lost genetic diversity of Choekhor buckwheat;
- increase/enhance genetic diversity in the field so as to build resilience to climate change;
- improve the accessibility and availability of diverse genetic resources in Bumthang;
- enhance and promote the use of local varieties through improved cultivation to add value and make them commercially attractive;
- preserve traditional food culture and practices related to local varieties.

Management, operations and support

The key supporters of the community seed bank include the community; the district agricultural officer and his staff, who coordinate activities at the dzongkhag level; the Bumthang dzongkhag administration; the NBC, which offers technical and financial support (and initial coordination); and the Integrated Livestock and Crop Conservation Project (of the United Nations Development Programme's Global Environment Facility), which provided financial support through the NBC. Currently, the Dzongkhag Agricultural Sector manages the community seed bank, which is still in the initial stages of building up its collections, assisted by the Bumthang Buckwheat Group. The Bumthang Buckwheat Group is registered with the Department of Agriculture, Marketing and Cooperatives under the Ministry of Agriculture and Forests. Currently, this group has nine active members, eight of whom are women. The dzongkhag and NBC are in the process of developing guidelines and a framework for the management and operations of the community seed bank, which may also be useful to other community seed banks in the country.

Initially, in 2011, information associated with germplasm was scant. Now, seed samples that were collected in 2011 are being replaced with fresh seeds from the same locations. As the seeds are replaced, associated information provided by farmers is being documented. Farmers are able to describe how the variety performs under drought conditions, whether it is resistant to disease and the length of time it takes to mature. This valuable information will be useful to other farmers as well as to breeders in their search for useful traits. A start has been made with germplasm samples of cereals and vegetables. The size of the seed samples is 1–5kg for cereals and 0.2–0.5kg for vegetable crops.

The community seed bank carries out the following activities:

- maintains the existing crop diversity of Bumthang;
- restores the threatened crop diversity of Choekhor (particularly buckwheat);

Plate 1 Chapter 9/Bangladesh: Rina Begum, a champion seed custodian
Credit: UBINIG

Plate 2 Chapter 9/Bangladesh: Exchanging seeds among members of the seed hut
Credit: UBINIG

Plate 3 Chapter 10/Bhutan: Part of the collection of the Bumthang community seed bank
Credit: Ronnie Vernooy/Bioversity International

Plate 4 Chapter 11/Bolivia: The garden of local potato varieties of the community of Cachilaya (province of Los Andes, La Paz)
Credit: Fundación PROINPA

Plate 5 Chapter 13/Brazil (Minas Gerais): Re-use of plastic bottles to store seed
Credit: Carlos Alberto Dayrell

Plate 6 Chapter 14/Canada: Poster for the 1st independent Toronto seed exchange
Credit: Toronto Seed Library (poster illustrator: Caitlin Taguibao)

Plate 7 Chapter 15/China: Delivery of maize seeds to the Xiding gene bank
Credit: Dong Chao/YAAS

Plate 8 Chapter 17/Guatemala: Dedicated and trained staff members manage the community seed banks
Credit: Gea Galluzzi/Bioversity International

Plate 9 Chapter 18/India (Kolli Hills): Adding value to millets
Credit: E. D. Israel Oliver King/ MSSRF

Plate 10 Chapter 20/Malaysia: Expert farmer plant breeder from Nepal teaches Malaysian farmers about participatory variety selection
Credit: Paul Bordoni/PAR

Plate 11 Chapter 21/Mali: The use of traditional seed containers
Credit: USC Canada

Plate 12 Chapter 22/Mali: Part of the collection of the Badiari community seed bank
Credit: USC Canada

Plate 13 Chapter 23/Mexico (Oaxaca): Seed containers handed over to members of the community seed banks
Credit: Flavio Aragón-Cuevas

Plate 14 Chapter 24/Nepal (Dalchowki): Monitoring the production seed lot of Guzmuzze broad-leafed mustard
Credit: Bharat Bhandari/USC Canada Asia

Plate 15 Chapter 25/Nepal (Tamaphok): The president of the community seed bank explains the use of the specially designed stamp for administration purposes
Credit: Ronnie Vernooy/Bioversity International

Plate 16 Chapter 26/Nicaragua: A collection of 'creole' or traditional maize varieties, La Labranza no. 2 community seed bank
Credit: Jorge Iran Vásquez Zeledón/PCaC

Plate 17 Chapter 26/Nicaragua: Members of the La Labranza no. 2 community seed bank
Credit: Jorge Iran Vásquez Zeledón/PCaC

Plate 18 Chapter 27/Rwanda: Rwanda Agricultural Board researchers meet with members of the Rubaya community seed bank
Credit: RAB

Plate 19 Chapter 28/Sri Lanka: The community seed bank of Haritha Udana
Credit: Lal Wakkumbere

Plate 20 Chapter 30/Uganda: Recognition of exceptional efforts to maintain local bean diversity
Credit: Joyce Adokorach

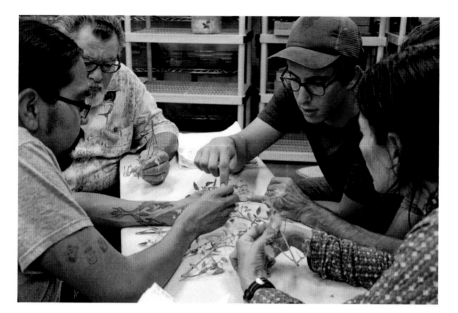

Plate 21 Chapter 31/USA: Learning about seeds at the Seed School
Credit: Native Seeds/SEARCH

Plate 22 Chapter 32/Burundi: One of the seed storage facilities built with Welthungerhilfe support
Credit: Welthungerhilfe

Plate 23 Chapter 33/Honduras: The interior of the community seed bank of the CIAL
in Ojo de Agua, Jesús de Otoro
Credit: Gea Galluzzi/Bioversity International

Plate 24 Chapter 34/Nepal (LI-BIRD): The community seed bank in Bara
Credit: Pitambar Shrestha/LI-BIRD

Plate 25 Chapter 35/Norway, the Development Fund: Field day in Ejere, Ethopia, to evaluate durum wheat varieties in diversity block
Credit: EOSA

Plate 26 Chapter 36/Spain: Diversity fair organized by the Spanish seed network members
Credit: The Spanish Seed Network

Plate 27 Chapter 38/Zimbabwe: Cereal grains are an important part of the collection of the Chibika community seed bank, UMP
Credit: Hilton Mbozi/CTDT

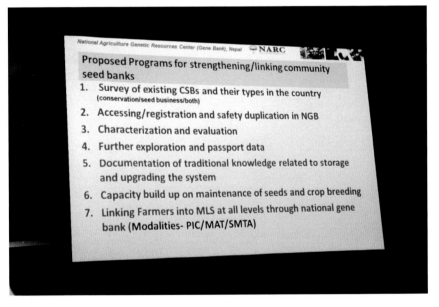

Plate 28 Chapter 41/Nepal: Action plan proposed by the national gene bank to connect the national gene bank to the more than 100 community seed banks in the country
Credit: Ronnie Vernooy/Bioversity International

Plate 29 Chapter 42/Mexico: Storing seeds in the community seed bank of Santa
Maria Peñoles
Credit: Ana María Sánchez

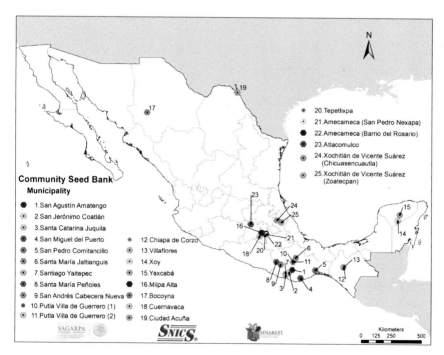

Plate 30 Chapter 42/Mexico: Distribution of community seed banks in Mexico: 1–11
Oaxaca, 12 and 13 Chiapas, 14 and 15 Yucatán, 16 Distrito Federal, 17 Chihuahua, 18
Morelos, 19 Coahuila, 20–23 Estado de México, 24 and 25 Puebla
Credit: Map prepared by the authors

Plate 31 Chapter 42/Mexico: Seed storage in one of the community seed banks
Credit: Flavio Aragón-Cuevas

Plate 32 Chapter 43/South Africa: The first ever organized seed fair in Mutale, Limpopo
province
Credit: Ronnie Vernooy/Bioversity International

- increases and enhances genetic diversity in farmers' fields to build resilience and adapt to climate change;
- improves the accessibility and availability of diverse seeds to needy farmers in Bumthang;
- enhances and promotes the use of local varieties through improved cultivation to increase the value and marketability of crops;
- preserves the traditional food culture and practices associated with local crops;
- showcases the seed diversity of Bumthang.

The major costs involved in setting up the community seed bank included renovation of the building, purchase of containers to hold germplasm, an entrance gate and fencing. This material and work was supported by NBC through the Integrated Livestock and Crop Conservation Project. Setting up of the seed bank also required the collection of germplasm and associated information and labeling and proper documentation by agriculture extension officials coordinated by the Dzongkhag Agricultural Office. Labour was provided freely by buckwheat farmers.

Seed flows

Extension officers are involved in collecting seed samples from various districts within the county. The seeds are collected using a standard protocol provided by the NBC. Once the seeds are collected, they are cleaned and processed to scientific standards. Finally, they are stored in earthenware pots. Information about the seeds is entered into spreadsheets using a format provided by NBC. Seeds collected earlier are also being replaced and NBC is helping to fill the gaps in the collection. In the future, seed germination tests will be carried out by giving seeds to some farmers.

Dzongkhag agricultural officers and extension officials visit farmers' fields to assess the suitability of the seed for multiplication and renewal. Multiplication of the seed samples is carried out by growing each sample every alternate year so that the seed retains its viability. The routine growing of the seed samples exposes crop varieties to prevailing weather and climate conditions and helps them adjust and adapt to changes. The seed material that is returned to the bank after every growing season is expected to be more adapted to the environment, pests and disease as well as the weather. Seeds are provided on a returnable basis to interested farmers who are allowed to grow crops for themselves and return the amount of seed they borrowed. About 1,000kg of seeds of two buckwheat varieties, i.e. bitter buckwheat and sweet buckwheat, have been distributed – to eight households in 2011, 17 in 2012 and nine in 2013. The farmers most interested in this process are women.

All Bhutanese are eligible to use seeds from the community seed bank. We are not aware of any sex discrimination in the availability of its resources. However, the transfer of material and associated traditional knowledge out of the country will be guided by the draft national Access and Benefit-sharing policy, which states that:

> The access to duly registered *ex situ* collections of genetic resources for food and agriculture that fall under Annex-1 of the International Treaty for Plant Genetic Resources for Food and Agriculture (ITPGRFA) and are under the management and control of the government as well as in the public domain shall be in ac*cordance* with the terms and conditions of the Multilateral System of Access and Benefit-sharing, including the conclusion of a Standard Material Transfer Agreement (SMTA) while the access to other genetic resources in *ex situ* collections in the Actualization Phase shall be based on an ABS Agreement between the user of such resources and the National Focal Point.
>
> Ministry of Agriculture and Forests,
> Royal Government of Bhutan, 2014, p10

Connections

As the community seed bank is still in the early stages of establishment, it does not have any links with other groups, other than the NBC, which is providing technical guidance and is seen as the backbone of the seed bank. However, the Buckwheat Group is involved in product development and marketing and, thus, is registered with the Department of Agriculture and Marketing Cooperatives.

Connections with the national seed system is an area that will be explored once a proper management system for the seed bank is in place. In 2009, the national gene bank conducted a first round of germplasm collection from Bumthang. There is a need to assess the gaps in the 2009 collection and obtain missing seeds for the community seed bank before depositing them in the national gene bank. In the future, two-way flow of germplasm is expected to make the community seed bank more dynamic.

Achievements and challenges

With the formation of the Buckwheat Group and community seed bank, cultivation of buckwheat has been revived in Bumthang. The value of this crop has also increased dramatically, from 35 Bhutanese ngultrum (BTN) per kilogram of buckwheat flour back in 2009 to 80 BTN/kg in November 2013 (about US$1.34/kg). The group has managed to increase both the area under production and the yield of buckwheat and barley in Bumthang.

The community seed bank has grown rapidly in popularity. Along with the 'Buckwheat House' (a buckwheat product-processing and market outlet), it is now the most visited site and a must-see attraction for visitors to Bumthang, including farmers, students, tourists, government officials and dignitaries. Farmers visiting the community seed bank from other parts of the country have started requesting seeds. The Bumthang seed bank will serve as a case study in the government's 11th five-year plan (July 2013 to June 2018), which includes the establishment of three more community seed banks in the country. Although the seed bank has enjoyed some success, it faces some challenges as well. For example, buckwheat is a low-yielding crop with a poor response to chemical fertilizers. Bumthang has adopted organic farming practices, but the availability of farmyard manure is limited. It has also been difficult to change the traditional cultivation practices of farmers. Further, the dzongkhag staff are engaged in numerous tasks and do not have enough time to devote to community seed bank matters.

Efforts are being expanded to barley cultivation, and there is a plan to include Bumthap chili, as chili is an important ingredient in Bhutanese food. Later, work will be extended to include amaranth as well. With an expected increase in demand in the future, farmers will focus on seed production and distribution of locally adapted landraces.

Reference

Ministry of Agriculture and Forests, Royal Government of Bhutan (2014) *Access and Benefit Sharing Policy of Bhutan, 2014.* Thimphu, Ministry of Agriculture and Forests, Royal Government of Bhutan

11 Bolivia

Community seed banks in the Lake Titicaca area

*Milton Pinto, Juana Flores Ticona
and Wilfredo Rojas*

Establishment of quinoa and cañihua ex-situ collections

In Bolivia, the first efforts to establish a germplasm collection of quinoa and other Andean crops date back to the 1960s. The first quinoa germplasm bank was originally managed by the Patacamaya Experimental Station and later by the national quinoa programme of the Instituto Boliviano de Tecnología Agropecuaria, which operated until 1998. With the closure of the institute, the Patacamaya Experimental Station began to report to the prefecture of La Paz. During this process, the germplasm collection received no economic support and, as there was no clear policy on quinoa management and conservation, this work was discontinued (Rojas et al., 2010). Finally, the authorities decided that the Fundación para la Promoción e Investigación de Productos Andinos (PROINPA; foundation for promotion of and research into Andean products), established in 1998, should manage the conservation of quinoa and cañihua in the germplasm bank (Rojas et al., 2010).

Consolidation of the National Andean Grains Bank was achieved over 12 years (1998–2010), during which PROINPA managed the collection of these two crops. Conservation standards were improved, documentation was modernized and primary information was generated and used in various fields, from plant breeding to agro-industry. These achievements have been possible through collaborative projects that established links between the bank and various users: professors, scientists, technicians and rural communities doing in-situ conservation (Rojas et al., 2010). Management protocols were developed and adapted for each ex-situ conservation stage (Jaramillo and Baena, 2000). During the utilization phase, interaction with communities increased to promote the direct use of germplasm. Thus, in-situ conservation efforts were progressively included until both ex-situ and in-situ components were integrated in recognition of how the advantages of one component make up for disadvantages of the other.

In-situ conservation: from quinoa and cañihua to agro-biodiversity

In the area around Lake Titicaca, in-situ conservation of quinoa and cañihua started in 2001. Studies of the number of varieties of both crops being grown under traditional management systems (Rojas et al., 2003, 2004) showed a decrease in diversity compared with the range of varieties conserved in the germplasm bank. Case studies illustrated what internal and external factors were influencing farmer families to continue or discontinue planting and conserving quinoa and cañihua varieties (Alanoca et al., 2004; Flores et al., 2004).

At this point, farmers expressed an interest in getting to know and recovering the diversity of varieties and traditional knowledge that existed in their communities. Thus, in the 2004–2005 growing season, work was initiated to study annual patterns and characteristics of a range of crops and varieties and document associated traditional knowledge.

Linking ex-situ and in-situ conservation

The process included annual participatory evaluation of local quinoa and cañihua varieties, as well as material from the germplasm bank. Sharing of knowledge related to agro-biodiversity was promoted among families in six communities bordering on Lake Titicaca. At fairs held between 2002 and 2004, the various uses of quinoa and cañihua were exhibited; later, between 2005 and 2010, exhibits were related to the diversity of seeds, their uses and handicrafts (Pinto et al., 2010). Farmers were encouraged to visit the National Andean Grains Bank, and, in turn, its staff attended several rural and urban fairs.

These activities created opportunities to inform the community about the role of the National Andean Grains Bank, and the importance of conserving seed and diverse varieties and crops was explained to farmers. The farmers not only agreed to have their varieties included in the bank's collection, but they also proposed that families migrating out of the region leave their genetic material with the bank, so that it would be available if they returned. Community seed banks were then established in an effort to connect ex-situ and in-situ conservation.

Establishing community seed banks

The process had two stages: 'quinoa and cañihua community banks' and 'agro-biodiversity community banks'. The first was supported by the Sistema Nacional de Recursos Genéticos para la Alimentación y la Agricultura (SINARGEAA, national system of genetic resources for food and agriculture), and work was carried out from 2005 to 2008 (Pinto et al., 2006, 2007).

Quinoa and cañihua demonstration plots were established in 13 communities located in the Bolivian altiplano and in the inter-Andean valleys, using accessions identified and selected during the earlier characterization and evaluation process. The purpose was to promote the direct use of germplasm and, thus, involve farmers and use their criteria in participatory selection processes. Native community authorities participated in and endorsed the process. Quinoa seed banks were established at Antarani (Pacajes) and Patarani (Ingavi) and cañihua banks were set up in Coromata Media (Omasuyos) and Rosapata (Ingavi).

During the first year, farmers carried out participatory variety selection; in the second and third years, an expert was assigned to take care of all cropping activities: planting, harvesting and storing local and selected varieties.

The quinoa and cañihua community seed banks were in operation as long as SINARGEAA existed, but were not officially registered, as these efforts, which took place during structural and political changes in the country, were viewed as pilot projects. Community seed banks were turned into seed multiplication facilities for teaching and places where both farmers and experts could exchange knowledge on management and use of different varieties.

However, this three-year process was never supported, adopted or recognized by local authorities who changed from year to year – a critical factor affecting operation of the seed banks. Activities were carried out on the initiative of families and specific functions and tasks were not defined. However, the families in charge started distributing seed to farmers interested in a specific quinoa or cañihua variety.

Agro-biodiversity community banks

The second attempt to establish community seed banks has been supported since 2011 under the Project on Neglected and Underutilized Species, which is funded by the International Fund for Agricultural Development (IFAD). This project is now in the process of implementing a network of 'custodian farmers' and, at the same time, institutionalizing the community seed banks as part of a strategy to monitor agro-biodiversity and traditional knowledge. The focus is on agro-biodiversity and getting to know and address interspecific and intraspecific diversity of crops useful to people for food, medicine and other functions. This project is being developed in eight communities near Lake Titicaca and receives support from four partner institutions. The experience is also being shared with the communities of Cachilaya and Coromata Media under the coordination of PROINPA.

After holding meetings with local authorities, farmers and two farmers' associations in Cachilaya and Coromata Media, custodian farmers were identified (four in Cachilaya and six in Coromata Media) and given the responsibility of conserving and using a number of crop varieties. Criteria for selecting these farmers included experience in crop management and commitment to crop diversity, in addition to being well known and respected by the community for their knowledge of ancient traditions. Potatoes were chosen as the focus because they constitute the main crop in the altiplano, followed, in order, by quinoa, cañihua and barley, which is used for feeding livestock. Seed and land were provided by the custodian farmers in each community (Plate 4).

The Instituto Nacional de Innovación Agropecuaria y Forestal (INIAF, national agricultural and forestry innovation institute), created in 2008, was invited to be part of this initiative. INIAF reports directly to the national government and is currently in charge of the national germplasm banks where collections of Andean root crops (potato, yam, ulluco and mashua) and grains (quinoa, cañihua and amaranthus) are conserved. One of INIAF's main tasks is establishing a national genetic resources system, under which community seed banks could be registered and acknowledged. (To date, the potato seed banks in Cachilaya and Coromata Media have not been officially registered.)

At the beginning of the Neglected and Underutilized Species project (2011–2012) work focussed on ensuring that custodian farmers became familiar with the diversity of crops they managed. The potato community seed banks were established later (2012–2013) with participation by other farmers in both communities. The custodian farmers are responsible for managing the banks.

The farmers asked that issues such as seed health, soil fertility, yield and commercialization of products be included in the project. Hands-on and theoretical training was provided during 2012 and 2013 to address this request and topics included such concerns as damage caused by the Andean weevil and the potato tuberworm moth and organic fertilization. Community seed banks also serve as a place for seed multiplication and for learning and teaching, as farmers can share and practise what they have learned in training courses.

To date, no fixed rules have been established for borrowing or depositing seed in the community seed banks. Seed exchange among farmers is informal. For example, a farmer who is interested in a variety will ask for it in person from the custodian farmer. No record is made of the transaction or receipt issued.

The bank in Coromata Media holds 45 native potato varieties, while the one in Cachilaya holds 54. Over 90 per cent of these varieties are considered to be underutilized. Both men and women have access to this material. In some cases, researchers also request potato seed, especially of the varieties that exhibit favourable characteristics, such as early maturation or resistance to or tolerance of adverse biotic and abiotic factors. Researchers are looking for characteristics that allow them to breed varieties that are adapted to different climates and to climate change.

In the communities, there are marked differences between men and women in terms of knowledge of potato varieties and their uses. Men consider varieties from the productive angle, looking for those that can be sold in local markets. Women, on the other hand, think about culinary attributes, identifying varieties by their names and differentiating those that are for fresh and direct consumption from those that can be used for stored products, such as chuño or tunta (freeze-dried potatoes). However, the roles played by men and women are complementary in terms of managing agro-biodiversity, recording and documenting traditional knowledge and, especially, the activities of the community seed banks. Although no benefits have yet been derived from the establishment of the potato seed banks, both men and women farmers now know much more about the management of the main potato pests and diseases. The farmers who participated in crop-cycle activities (plant-ing, ploughing, phytosanitary control, harvest, seed cleaning and storage) had a chance to observe the encouraging results of the management practices and the low incidence of pest attack in the varieties kept in the community seed banks.

In addition to support from IFAD's Neglected and Underutilized Species project, community seed banks are technically and financially supported by the farmers' associations in Cachilaya and Coromata Media and by PROINPA. However, the most important factor is the moral support they receive from local authorities in both communities. Bolivia does not have a national agency to liaise with and strengthen community seed banks, nor are there local, municipal or departmental policies designed to provide support to this type of initiative. In light of this situation, meetings have been held within the framework of the IFAD project to bring together custodian farmers, experts from public institutions such as INIAF and the municipality to initiate joint actions and consolidate the seed banks. Funding from the IFAD project currently covers the maintenance costs of the potato seed banks; however, efforts are being made with farmers and municipal governments to provide for the future of these seed banks.

Achievements and challenges

Finding out about the diversity of locally available native potato varieties and recording the associated knowledge aroused great interest among farmers in the Cachilaya and Coromata Media communities. Effective practices were put in place to control the main potato pests, and more seed is now available for exchange and distribution. The amount of seed borrowed by farmers has increased, as well as the availability of seed in the community seed bank.

One of the main challenges that lies ahead is the fact that community seed banks have not been recognized as local institutions benefitting farmers, and little is known about their functions and reach. In meeting this challenge, we must work with the farmers in a participatory manner. Who should be in charge of managing the community seed banks? Should it be the custodian farmers? Should this be a rotating post among community farmers? What are the direct benefits to farmers? These questions are being discussed, and we must find answers if the seed banks are to contribute effectively to conservation and use of the important genetic resources they hold.

Acknowledgements

We would like to express our sincere thanks to the farmers of Cachilaya (Los Andes) and Coromata Media (Omasuyos) in the Titicaca Lake region of Bolivia, who, without seeking personal gain, contribute to the conservation and management of agricultural biodiversity through their community seed banks.

References

Alanoca, C., Flores, J., Soto, J. L., Pinto, M. and Rojas, W. (2004) 'Estudios de caso de la variabilidad genética de quinua en el área circundante al Lago Titicaca,' Annual report 2003/2004, McKnight project on sustainable production of quinoa, Fundación para la Promoción e Investigación de Productos Andinos, El Paso, Bolivia

Flores, J., Alanoca, C., Soto, J. L., Pinto, M. and Rojas, W. (2004) 'Estudios de caso de la variabilidad genética de cañahua en el área circundante al Lago Titicaca,' Annual report 2003/2004, Sistema Nacional de Recursos Genéticos para la Alimentación y la Agricultura project on Management, conservation and sustainable use of high Andean grain genetic resources in the framework of SINARGEAA, Fundación para la Promoción e Investigación de Productos Andinos, El Paso, Bolivia, pp102–108

Jaramillo, S. and Baena, M. (2000) 'Material de apoyo a la capacitación en conservación ex situ de recursos fitogenéticos,' International Plant Genetic Resources Institute, Cali, Colombia

Pinto, M., Flores, J., Alanoca, C. and Rojas, W. (2006) 'Implementación de bancos de germoplasma comunales,' Annual report 2005/2006, Sistema Nacional de Recursos Genéticos para la Alimentación y la Agricultura project on Management, conservation and sustainable use of high Andean grain genetic resources in the framework of SINARGEAA, Fundación para la Promoción e Investigación de Productos Andinos, El Paso, Bolivia, pp280–288

Pinto, M., Flores, J., Alanoca, C., Mamani, E. and Rojas, W. (2007) 'Bancos de germoplasma comunales contribuyen a la conservación de quinua y cañahua,' Annual report 2006/2007, Sistema Nacional de Recursos Genéticos para la Alimentación y la Agricultura project on Management, conservation and sustainable use of high Andean grain genetic resources in the framework of SINARGEAA, Fundación para la Promoción e Investigación de Productos Andinos, El Paso, Bolivia, pp200–205

Pinto, M., Marin, W., Alarcón, V. and Rojas, W. (2010) 'Estrategias para la conservación y promoción de los granos andinos: ferias y concursos,' in W. Rojas, M. Pinto, J. L. Soto, M. Jagger and S. Padulosi (eds) *Granos Andinos: Avances, logros y experiencias desarrolladas en quinua, cañahua y amaranto en Bolivia*, Bioversity International, Rome, Italy, pp73–93

Rojas, W., Pinto, M. and Soto, J. L. (2003) 'Estudio de la variabilidad genética de quinua en el área circundante al Lago Titicaca,' Annual report 2002/2003, McKnight Project, Fundación para la Promoción e Investigación de Productos Andinos, El Paso, Bolivia

_____ (2004) 'Genetic erosion of cañahua,' *LEISA Magazine on Low External Input and Sustainable Agriculture*, vol 20, no 1, p15

Rojas, W., Pinto, M., Bonifacio, A. and Gandarillas, A. (2010) 'Banco de Germoplasma de Granos Andinos,' in W. Rojas, M. Pinto, J. L. Soto, M. Jagger and S. Padulosi (eds) *Granos Andinos: Avances, logros y experiencias desarrolladas en quinua, cañahua y amaranto en Bolivia*, Bioversity International, Rome, Italy, pp24–38

12 Brazil

Gene banks, seed banks and local seed guardians

*Terezinha Aparecia Borges Dias,
Irajá Ferreira Antunes, Ubiratan Piovezan,
Fabio de Oliveira Freitas, Marcia Maciel,
Gilberto A. P. Bevilaqua, Nadi Rabelo dos
Santos and Cristiane Tavares Feijó*

There is tremendous potential for on-farm conservation in Brazil, given the 215 indigenous communities (that occupy about 12 per cent of the land) and the large number of non-indigenous farmers, most of whom practice subsistence agriculture. Beginning in the 1970s, an extensive network of gene banks was set up led by the Brazilian agricultural research corporation (Empresa Brasileira de Pesquisa Agropecuária or EMBRAPA). In the last decade, EMBRAPA has been restructuring its research programme in favour of on-farm conservation and the interface with ex-situ conservation. This move was not only in response to an internal desire to start working on on-farm conservation, but also the result of the demands of numerous traditional farmers, true seed guardians, to restore varieties that had disappeared from their fields.

In Brazil, public policies geared towards traditional indigenous agriculture, especially in terms of strengthening on-farm conservation and the promotion of local seed banks, are still incipient (for a more detailed discussion of policies that affect community seed banks in Brazil, see Chapter 39). Not considered priorities, such initiatives suffer from lack of support from the public sector and delays in the release of the few funds raised for this purpose. However, references to seed guardians and community seed banks can be found in national plans, such as the Política Nacional de Gestão Territorial e Ambiental de Povos e Terras Indígenas (national territorial and environmental management policy of indigenous peoples and lands), the Política Nacional de Segurança Alimentar e Nutricional (the national policy for food and nutrition security; PNSAN, 2010), the Política de Desenvolvimento do Brasil Rural (development policy of rural Brazil) and the more recent Política Nacional de Agroecologia e Produção Orgânica (national policy for agro-ecology and organic production; PNAPO, 2012). The latter, especially, along with its implementation plan, emphasizes the need for the Brazilian state to support farmers' local conservation initiatives and indicates the need to develop guidelines for access to germplasm banks by farmers, through their organizations.

More recently, as a result of awareness rising about the importance of conservation of so-called Creole varieties (i.e. locally adapted), the agricultural research community has increased even further the adoption of on-farm conservation strategies. Nowadays, organized farmers and seed guardians are taking the initiative to conserve Creole varieties through community seed banks, including several based on partnerships with governmental institutions (see Chapter 13 for another case study from Brazil).

Krahô people

The Krahô indigenous people live in 28 villages in a territory of 302,000ha in northeast Tocantins state, in the municipalities of Itacajá and Goiatins. In the last 50 years or so, the Krahô have lost agricultural genetic resources, and their food security system was disturbed when the government tried to change their family-based agricultural culture into a collective system with new agricultural practices and a predominance of rice monoculture (Schiavini, 2000). In the early 1990s, supported by Fernando Schiavini of the national Indian foundation (Fundação Nacional do Índio; Funai), members of the union of Krahô villages began to discuss their situation and plan for counteraction. In 1995, a group of Krahô leaders approached EMBRAPA to rescue their traditional seeds, most notably several maize varieties. Interactions between the Krahô and EMBRAPA later led to the signing of the first contract (through Funai) regarding access to genetic resources and associated traditional knowledge in Brazil. This precedent enabled the introduction, at the national level, of the principle of prior informed consent at the genetic heritage management council (Conselho Gestor do Património Genético) as a major step towards implementing the Convention on Biological Diversity.

Since 2000, several local seed banks have been established following extensive surveys of on-farm agro-biodiversity (Dias et al., 2008b) and the identification of guardians of agro-biodiversity (Silva, 2009). In addition, fairs have been held to exchange traditional seeds and confer diversity awards (Dias et al., 2008a). These fairs have been organized by the union of Krahô villages, with support from Funai and EMBRAPA and a wide network of other supporters including Brazilian government agencies, the rural extension agency of Ruraltins state, the University of Brasilia and local prefectures.

The Krahô local seed bank conducts on-farm conservation through a network of farmers and guardians who maintain varieties by practising their traditional agriculture. Species maintained by the local seed bank include: rice (20 varieties), faba bean (15), yam (15), sweet potato (13), cassava (13), bitter cassava (macaxeira; ten), maize (ten), common bean (six), pigeon pea (five), pumpkin (11) and squash (three).

As a result of these activities, the Krahô people are now self-sufficient in terms of their agricultural practices, and they have no need to obtain seeds from any outside entity, public or private.

Paresi people

The Paresi are inhabitants of the plateaus in Mato Grosso state. The population of approximately 2,005 lives in about 60 villages on ten indigenous territories, an area close to 1.3 million ha.

In 2010, a study of Paresi agriculture revealed impoverishment of genetic diversity (Maciel, 2010). With the support of the community, Maciel raised awareness of the issue and organized discussions and study tours culminating in a fair to reintroduce and exchange traditional roots and seeds. Since then, villages have continued holding fairs annually and these exchanges have contributed to improving the quality of the household diet and increasing the diversity of species grown locally. Plants such as arrowroot, yam, winged yam varieties and especially indigenous maize or soft maize (milho fofo), considered extinct in the area for 50 years, are again under cultivation.

To increase crop diversity, farmers are using diversity kits with several types of cassava, pineapple and soft maize. The multiplication of the varieties in the kits takes place in the village and on the Botucatu campus of the Universidade Estadual Paulista under the direction of the faculty of agricultural sciences. Varieties of purple and white winged yam, various sweet potatoes, peanuts and pigeon peas originating from the producers' fair in Tangará da Serra, Mato Grosso, are also part of the kit. The Paresi seed fairs have contributed to the establishment of a larger seed conservation network in the region.

Guarani Mbyá people

In Paraná state, EMBRAPA's Centre for Temperate Climate Agricultural Research (CPACT) has recently started promoting the use of Creole seeds. CPACT is working with the Guarani Mbyá people to address genetic erosion of their crops, including varieties of beans, maize, groundnut, squash and cassava. Of the 35 varieties of the Creole cultivars held by CPACT, villagers selected seven: Rim de Porco, Unha de Princesa, Preto Comprido, Vermelho Anchieta, Amendoim Unaic, Fogo na Serra and Mourinho. Of these, only the Mourinho bean was representative of a variety considered truly Guarani. The other varieties were selected because they were similar to those cultivated by the Guarani in the past (Feijó et al., 2014). The varieties were multiplied and distributed to the indigenous farmers who reintroduced Mourinho beans into their fields.

Community associations in the Canguçu region

The União das Associações Comunitárias do Interior de Canguçu e Região (UNAIC), in the municipality of Canguçu, Rio Grande do Sul, is an association of family farmer groups. It was founded in March 1988 and its principal objectives are the protection of the rights of family farmers and the promotion of sustainable rural development based on agro-ecological practices.

The production of Creole seeds was initiated in September 1994, stimulated by partner institutions, such as the Pastoral Rural da Igreja Católica and the Support Centre for Small-Scale Farmers. At the same time, with support from EMBRAPA, seed exchange between the state and farmers was initiated. In 1997, a community seed bank was established to promote the exchange of cultivars among farmers and the multiplication and preservation of these varieties. In 1999, the production of Creole varieties of maize and beans became a UNAIC programme. A register was set up at the former plant production department of the Rio Grande do Sul state government. As a result, new markets were opened with emphasis on the commercialization of seeds via an exchange programme set up by the government, allowing access to these seeds by traditional communities as well as settlers under agrarian reform.

In 2002, UNAIC inaugurated a seed-processing unit, donated by the Rio Grande do Sul government, the first grain-processing unit in Latin America and also the first exclusively administered by family farmers. The unit opened at the time of the first state fair for Creole seeds and popular technologies, whose main objectives were to publicize the seed preservation work done in Canguçu and to exchange information on the production of Creole seeds in the state. This event, which had its sixth anniversary in 2013, contributed to raising awareness in the local community about the importance of biodiversity conservation.

Since its formation, UNAIC has rescued and multiplied 19 cultivars of Creole maize, seven of beans, two of wheat and four of species intended for green manure. UNAIC's work has directly benefitted 40 farming families and indirectly helped a significant number of other farming families, settlers under agrarian reform, quilombolas and other traditional communities that have acquired the Creole seeds produced and commercialized by UNAIC.

References

Dias,T.A. B., Madeira, N. and Niemeyer, F. (2008a) 'Estratégias de conservação on farm: premiação agrobiodiversidade na Feira de Sementes Tradicionais Krahô,' abstract, Proceedings of the II Simpósio Brasileiro de Recursos Genéticos, 25–28 November, Brasília, Fundação de Apoio à Pesquisa Cientifica e Tecnológica and EMBRAPA Recursos Genéticos e Biotecnologia, p350

Dias,T.A. B., Piovezan, U., Borges, J. and Krahô, F. (2008b) 'Calendário sazonal agrícola do povo indígena Krahô: estratégia de conservação "on farm,"' abstract, Proceedings of the II Simpósio Brasileiro de Recursos Genéticos, 25–28 November, Brasília, Fundação de Apoio à Pesquisa Cientifica e Tecnológica and EMBRAPA Recursos Genéticos e Biotecnologia, p315

Feijó, C.T., Antunes, I. F., Eichholz, C.,Villela, A. T., Bevilaqua, G. P. and Grehs, R. C. (2014) 'A common germplasm bank as source for recovery of cultural richness,' in *Annual Report of the Bean Improvement Cooperative*, vol 57, Prosser,Washington, USA, pp261–262, www.alice.cnptia.embrapa.br/bitstream/doc/987751/1/digitalizar0038 .pdf, accessed 22 July 2014

Maciel, M. R. A. (2010) 'Raiz, planta e cultura: as roças indígenas nos hábitos alimentares do povo Paresi, Tangará da Serra, Mato Grosso, Brasil,' PhD thesis, Universidade Estadual Paulista 'Júlio de Mesquita Filho,' Botucatu, Brazil

PNAPO (Política nacional de agroecologia e produção orgánica) (2012) 'Decreto n° 7.794 de 20 de Agosto de 2012,' Presidência de República, Casa Civil, Brasília, Brazil, www.planalto.gov.br/ccivil_03/_ato2011-2014/2012/decreto/d7794.htm, accessed 22 July 2014

PNSAN (Política nacional de segurança alimentar e nutricional) (2010) 'Decreto 7.272 de 25 de Agosto de 2010,' Presidência de República, Casa Civil, Brasília, Brazil, www.planalto.gov.br/ccivil_03/_ato2007-2010/2010/decreto/d7272.htm, accessed 22 July 2014

Schiavini, F. (2000) 'Estudos etnobiologicos com o povo Krahò,' in T. B. Cavalcanti (ed.) *Tópicos atuais em botánica*, EMBRAPA Recursos Genéticos e Biotecnologia: Sociedade Botânica do Brasil, Brasília, Brazil, pp278–284

Silva, S. M. O. (2009) 'Guardiões da agrobiodiversidade do povo indígena Krahô: uma abordagem sobre a preservação da biodiversidade agrícola,' thesis, Instituto Cientifico de Ensino Superior e Pesquisa, Brasília, Brazil

13 Brazil

The Minas Gerais seed houses for conservation in times of climate crisis

Anna Crystina Alvarenga
and Carlos Alberto Dayrell

This cane here is from the time of the great grandfathers; it has been handed over from generation to generation. When someone loses her variety, there is a neighbour who has it. Look, my canes have finished, I am going to ask, then give it later back to her, the planting material comes back. So it goes, life never ends.
— Maria Cecília talking with her husband, Imir de Jesus, Community Quilombola Vargem do Inhaí, Diamantina, Minas Gerais [recorded by the authors in December 2013 while preparing a video about the roles of farmer guardians of traditional seeds and climate change]

Background and regional context

The northern area of the state of Minas Gerais is situated in the southern part of Brazil's semiarid region. It is a region of great sociocultural and agrarian diversity. The Cerrado (tropical savannah), Mata Atlântica (Atlantic forest) and Caatinga (desert) harbour a wealth of transitional plant ecosystems from highlands to savannah, enclaves of wet forest and temporary flooded areas. In this region, communal use of environmental resources is based on custom. Its peoples and traditional communities still manage and conserve a wide range of species and plant varieties for food, fibres, medicines and energy, both for home consumption and to sell. These people are the real guardians of agro-biodiversity; however, they are on the fringe of policies that recognize their territories and traditional strategies to coexist with the environment.

In 2013, a survey was conducted by a team of guardians of agro-biodiversity among 41 families in a region of the Minas Gerais outback. In cleared areas alone, 22 food species were identified, including 328 varieties; among them were 46 varieties of cassava and 49 of maize. When other units of the production system are considered (in addition to kitchen gardens), a single family interacts with hundreds of plant species, thus becoming a living germplasm bank with an enormous wealth of knowledge of the phenologic, adaptive, dietary and culinary qualities of these plants.

A few decades ago, this diversity was being maintained, but it is now in jeopardy. Large development companies, greedy for land, are expropriating traditional territory, promoting the standardization of the food culture and distributing hybrid and transgenic seeds. More recently, climate change is causing continuous losses, and traditional agro-biodiversity conservation strategies are seriously compromised.

Emergence of seed houses

To support the struggle of local communities to defend their rights, a commission on agro-biodiversity (Comissão de Agrobiodiversidade do Norte de Minas) was created and later became a network (Rede de Agrobiodiversidade do Semiárido Mineiro). The commission was led by several popular organizations, including unions and local networks. Among the strategies they developed was the conservation of Creole seeds managed by the guardians through the creation of regional 'seed houses' (Plate 5). One of these seed houses, known as Generation House, is located in an agro-ecological experimentation and training area of the Centro de Agricultura Alternativa do Norte de Minas, a rural area of Montes Claros, in the northern region of Minas Gerais. It has been operating since June 2010, and its main objective is to guarantee the medium-term conservation of genetic material managed and maintained for generations by farmers and guardian farmers, using ex-situ, in-situ and on-farm methods.

The regional seed houses represent a conservation approach that complements other strategies and actions of a network of men and women peasant farmers, organizations and social movements in the field of agro-ecology as well as federal teaching and research institutions. This socio-technical network aims to strengthen strategies based on relations between individuals and institutional stakeholders with common goals at the regional and local levels. Together with the guardians, the network carries out such activities as agro-biodiversity surveys. The objective is to strengthen agro-biodiversity as managed by the communities, identifying the diversity, species density and varieties resistant to climate change; broadening the local diet; ensuring local and regional food security and sovereignty; and conserving traditional native seeds as well as the biodiversity of the region's agricultural systems.

Seed production and conservation

To guarantee this cultural and genetic heritage and secure access to quality seeds in quantities sufficient to meet farmers' demands, some communities, families and groups have established local seed production fields for commercial purposes. This process is usually associated with participatory crop improvement. The seed production fields are also used as complementary conservation tools and a buffer against cultivars developed under artificial conditions and genetically modified varieties.

Another strategy used to conserve and maintain traditional seeds is the community seed house (Casas de Sementes Comunitárias) and family seed stocks. These are collections of the germplasm of local cultivars, maintained and managed by farmers. In addition to contributing to the conservation of agro-biodiversity, these collections guarantee good-quality seeds in sufficient quantities, at the appropriate time, thus ensuring farmer autonomy. They also help prevent genetic erosion and the consequent substitution of so-called 'improved' varieties for traditional seeds.

With a view to using different approaches to conservation – ex-situ, in-situ and on-farm methods – the network negotiated with the Brazilian agricultural research corporation (Empresa Brasileira de Pesquisa Agropecuária or EMBRAPA) the use of the concept of 'trustee' for the shared management of its collected accessions. The agreement includes the people and communities of northern Minas Gerais. The accessions will be conserved in the main collection at EMBRAPA's genetic resources and biotechnology centre (Recursos Genéticos e Biotecnologia). EMBRAPA will ensure the seeds' long-term conservation, minimizing contamination of the local materials by transgenic seeds.

An important forum for strengthening the network and its activities is local and regional agro-biodiversity fairs. These fairs provide an opportunity for people and communities to share their experience and knowledge, exchange seeds and other materials and discuss conservation of natural resources and public policies.

Management and functioning of Generation House

Regulations to guide operations at Generation House were agreed to by the technical staff of peasants' organizations and researchers from research and teaching institutions. The first step was the election of a management commission, composed exclusively of guardians; these three men and one woman are responsible for ensuring that the rules for collecting, monitoring and regenerating seeds are followed. The second step was to define the mandate of the regional seed house as a place for the medium-term conservation of species' diversity and accession of traditional varieties – especially those that play an important role in the communities' agro-food strategies and those that are at risk of being lost.

Samples of seeds, on average 1.5–2kg, are collected or donated by the regional seed house guardians. They are documented in a management system, in which it is also possible to register morphologic, phenologic, geographic and utilization information, in addition to any other information deemed relevant by the guardians. Subsequently, they are given codes, which help with proper identification, and then stored in a room with controlled relative humidity (20 per cent) and temperature (20°C).

Monitoring the accessions involves annual physiological tests to ensure the seeds' viability and regenerating seeds as needed. When a critical situation is noted, such as viability below 80 per cent or seed quantity less than 400g (depending on the species), a report is issued. Technical staff and trainees from federal research and teaching institutions review the reports and submit recommendations to the management committee on the need for regeneration and multiplication processes. Currently, the regional seed house stores about 70 accessions of seven species and 62 varieties.

14 Canada

The Toronto Seed Library

Katie Berger, Jacob Kearey-Moreland and Brendan Behrmann

Purpose and evolution

The Toronto Seed Library was born when Jacob Kearey-Moreland heard a friend mention the idea of a tool library. Jacob brought the idea to his fellow coordinator of Occupy Gardens Toronto, Katie Berger, who decided to take on the creation of a seed library as her major research project for York University's master of environmental studies programme. With the moral support of the Toronto Seedy Saturday and Sunday steering committee and the national Seeds of Diversity network, work to set up the library started. Kearey-Moreland and Berger, along with Brendan Behrmann, a librarian recently graduated from the University of Toronto's iSchool, are the current coordinators. The Toronto Seed Library is registered with the Seed Library Social Network (www.seedlibraries.org/).

The initial organizational and operational set up was shaped with input from the public in early 2013. A 'learning by doing' approach was adopted, and collecting and lending seeds began right away. During the first season, thousands of seeds were collected, sorted and shared with hundreds of people; about 3,000 small packages of seeds were distributed. At the same time, a seed awareness and education campaign was carried out through seed sharing and saving events (Plate 6), workshops and social media. Bi-weekly events including volunteer information sessions, seed sorting and packaging parties, basic seed-saving workshops and branch launch events were organized. Coordinators also helped organize a large anti-genetically modified alfalfa demonstration (9 April 2013) and the March Against Monsanto (25 May 2013). On 7 May 2013, they made a presentation at the York–University of Toronto–Ryerson Library Staff Conference themed 'Why libraries matter'.

Between April and June 2013, five community branches across the city opened: Permaculture Project GTA Headquarters Branch (Scarborough); Toronto Tool Library Branch (Parkdale); Saint Stephen-in-the-Fields Church Branch (Kensington Market); Regenesis@York University Branch and High Park Nature Centre Branch, all of which welcome folks to borrow seeds during opening hours or by appointment.

International cooperation is taking place with other individuals and organizations related to the Fortnight of Seed Freedom called for by Dr. Vandana Shiva as part of the international movement for seed sovereignty.

Goals and operations

The Toronto Seed Library is governed by the idea that seeds should not and cannot be privately owned, but should be shared freely among all people at the local and community levels. Its coordinators believe that seeds should not be commodified in any way; thus, the seed library does not charge users for seeds. Borrowers are encouraged and enabled to participate to the degree they wish. Regular volunteer orientation sessions are held for those looking to find their role in the seed library.

Although seed libraries and community seed banks have many functions in common, traditionally 'banks' focus on conserving seeds for future use while a library's primary focus is dissemination of seeds to as many people as possible. The Toronto Seed Library avoids association with or the use of the term 'banks' as these institutions are the cornerstone of modern capitalism and are fundamentally antithetical to the ideology and values behind the Toronto Seed Library project. Just as traditional libraries help to facilitate literacy, the seed library helps to spread seed and food literacy.

The Toronto Seed Library provides a freely accessible alternative to the genetically modified seeds produced by large corporations, as well as print and other resources for new seed savers and gardeners and a platform for seed–food–environmental education. Through educational outreach and events, it promotes the introduction of seed saving and sharing into the mainstream, encourages people to 'connect' with seeds and take an active part in growing food and advocates increased biodiversity and awareness of its relation to cultural diversity.

Seeds are donated to the library by individuals, seed companies and retail stores. Currently, most donors are mid-sized to large businesses, with a smaller portion from individual seed savers and community groups. However, as people in the area become more informed about and skilled at seed saving, it is hoped that the vast majority of seeds will come from community members and groups. The library accepts all seeds regardless of condition. For example, seeds that have outlived their shelf life and no longer meet commercial standards and seeds with questionable origin are shared freely for the purpose of engaging new gardeners, growing experience, experimentation and food production. However, only organic seeds – either certified or believed to be organic – are loaned for the purpose of seed saving.

When seeds are donated, the only information required is the type of seeds and where and when they were grown (e.g. holy basil, Hart House garden, 2012). Sometimes people provide additional information, which is passed along to borrowers. More general traditional knowledge about seed farming and saving is communicated through seed-saving workshops run by elders in our community.

In addition to the five branches, a very active 'roaming branch' travels across the city and disperses seeds at a wide range of food, gardening and environmental events. Community members can check out seeds from any branch in the city. The only requirements for borrowing seeds are to sign up to receive electronic updates and seed-saving information and to make an informal commitment to try to save some seeds from the plants grown and bring them to the library.

Currently, the mailing list includes almost 1,000 people, the vast majority of whom borrowed seeds from the seed library during the 2013 growing season. Borrowers are an incredibly diverse group and vary depending on the branch or event location. Because of the coordinators' personal and professional connections with local universities, students have made up a large proportion of participants. All types of urban farmers use the library, from allotment tenders to balcony-container farmers. Numerous reports from library users provide evidence that they are now harvesting and enjoying much higher-quality produce than they previously had access to.

Within the seed collection, there is a very small stock of rare seeds that are reserved for experienced seed savers who can ensure their reproductive success. Seed supply has been greater than could be handled, and the plan is now to establish a more sophisticated growing programme linked with more established seed farmers and savers in the region outside the city where there is more room to grow.

The variety of seeds in the library is constantly increasing, particularly through connections with Toronto's various ethnic and cultural communities. Gardens across the city are growing a diversity of crops, which are locally adapted and passed on through families and cultural communities and are now being shared through the Toronto Seed Library.

In addition to the three coordinators, six semi-regular volunteers help with running events, outreach, graphic design, etc. In terms of other participants, thus far joining the seed library mailing list has been the informal equivalent to becoming a member.

Costs and support

The main monetary costs have been for packaging materials, specifically paper envelopes to hold the seeds. Another large portion of funds has been used to print posters and flyers for outreach. The seed library is in the process of establishing a web site, which will also require money to maintain. No money has been spent on seeds or labour, as these resources have been donated by businesses and the community.

The seed library receives technical support in terms of seed identification, cleaning and storing methods, etc. from experienced elders in the Toronto seed community. It receives financial support from individual donors, with countless contributions of CA$1–20 used primarily for outreach materials and costs related to holding events. Several large donations of seeds from two corporations were received and accepted with the understanding that no conditions were attached, as the seed library does not advertise or promote corporations indirectly or directly. Strong moral support comes from the established seed-saving community within the greater Toronto area, as well as established food and gardening organizations that recognize the potential benefits of a free city-wide community seed library. Moral support has also come from a variety of city councillors, academics, farmers and consumers.

Links and networking

The seed library fosters connections with other emerging seed libraries in the Toronto area, around Ontario and, to a lesser extent, across North America. This includes hosting meetings with neighbouring seed librarians and communications via telephone, social media and email with more distant partners. The Toronto Seed Library has been a source of inspiration for new seed libraries in the region, including those in rural communities, such as Orillia, Ontario. The seed library actively supports campaigns run by the National Farmers' Union and the Canadian Biotech Action Network. Links have not yet been formed with the formal gene bank network in Canada.

The library plans to develop closer ties with the Canadian Seed Library (CSL), a project of Seeds of Diversity, the pre-eminent national organization that has led the domestic resurgence in seed saving. The CSL is housed in a farm just outside Toronto; from it, seeds are mailed across the country to experienced member seed growers, primarily hobby seed savers and small-scale seed farmers. The Toronto Seed Library hopes to become integrated with the CSL to offer community-based seed libraries within public libraries, so that anyone can borrow and grow seeds and have free and easy access to the knowledge and resources they need to grow their own food and seed supply. Community-based seed libraries are the next phase in the evolution of seed banks, with their emphasis on sharing of seeds, knowledge and resources.

Policy and legal environment

Next to the United States, Canada has the most highly developed industrial food system in the world. Most Canadian farmers are integrated into the corporate food and seed regime, which is heavily regulated and subsidized by the highest levels of government. The Toronto Seed Library has no direct involvement in legislation or lobbying for farmers' rights, except in terms of raising awareness of issues affecting rural communities and farmers. The seed library is specifically interested in municipal food policy, which supports the integration of the Toronto Seed Library within the Toronto Public Library system and the Toronto District School Board. There are 97 public libraries and hundreds of public schools in Toronto. If even a small fraction of these institutions housed a branch of the seed library, this could contribute significantly to an increase in food and seed awareness and even in food and seed sovereignty and security in Toronto, as well as increasing support for an improved regional food system.

The Toronto Seed Library has been informally lobbying the municipal government and community partners to include the Toronto Seed Library project as part of the new GrowTO Action Plan for scaling up urban agriculture in Toronto. Formal partnerships with the Toronto Public Library and the Toronto District School Board would significantly increase the capacity of the seed library by harmonizing its efforts with those of existing institutions, infrastructure and government programmes. Federal and provincial seed regulations do not affect the daily operations of the seed library, as they largely apply to commercial and large-scale operators.

Challenges

Current challenges for the seed library include funding and the time and energy commitment needed from the coordinators and volunteers. Although the coordinators have been working full time on the project, the Toronto Seed Library has grown at an unexpected rate, and it has often been difficult to manage without paid staff.

There is also a risk that users may not be able to return seeds or will return seeds of lesser quality, as most participants are first-time growers; currently, the library has few safeguards to ensure the quality of returned seed. Quality-control standards are being developed to be implemented in the second season, spring 2014.

Space is a major challenge in Toronto, particularly for seed production, and labour and time constraints keep the library from putting many of its ideas into practice. Although the project is still in its infancy, it is confident of ongoing and future support from larger institutions, such as the Toronto Public Library and the Toronto District School Board, as well as colleges, universities and other food and farming organizations.

Sustainability and prospects

Sustainability can be achieved through collaborative partnerships with public libraries, schools and community groups. Using open-source philosophy and technology, the seed library can establish a platform that enables the mass participation and collaboration necessary to maintain a free, self-perpetuating public resource. The Toronto Seed Library could be part of a national or international network of seed libraries. Just as public libraries exchange books and other items within and between systems, so can the seed library exchange seeds with regional partners and others with similar climate conditions. Furthermore, the seed library hopes to collaborate through educational and promotional materials and collective action to secure further public support.

Acknowledgements

The Toronto Seed Library would like to thank the following people and organizations for their inspiration and support: Vandana Shiva and the

International Seed Freedom Movement, Maria Kasstan and Seeds of Diversity Canada, Ralph Adams, Li Keller and Occupy Gardens Toronto, Angela Elzinga Cheng and FoodShare Toronto, Toyin Croker and the Permaculture Project of the Greater Toronto Area, Jodi Koberinski and the Organic Council of Ontario, Krista Fry and Scadding Court Community Centre, Emily Martyn and the Regent Park Community Food Centre, Kate Raycraft and Dig In, the University of Toronto, Susan Berman and the Toronto Community Garden Network, Mariam Alkabeer, Vince McLaughlin, Maggie Helwig, Emily Rourke, Alexandra Cleaver, Caitlin Taguibao, Jako Raudsepp and our partners at the University of Toronto.

15 China
The Xiding gene bank in Yunnan

Yang Yayun, Zhang Enlai, Devra I. Jarvis,
Bai Keyu, Dong Chao, A. Xinxiang, Tang Cuifeng,
Zhang Feifei, Xu Furong and Dai Luyuan

Purpose and evolution

Since 2006, a team of Chinese researchers and Bioversity International colleagues has been engaged in the project, 'Conservation and use of crop genetic diversity to control pests and disease in support of sustainable agriculture' in Xiding township, Menghai county, Xishuangbanna prefecture of Yunnan province. Menghai is an area of rich agricultural biodiversity, especially in terms of rice and maize varieties. Farmers use specific selection criteria when saving and improving varieties to respond to the demands of the environment. In the mountainous regions of Yunnan, the diverse ecological niches, even within the same agricultural region, require specially adapted crop varieties. Socioeconomic, cultural and market forces also influence farmers' portfolios of crops and varieties. Although this has led to rich overall biodiversity in this part of China, intensification and modernization of agriculture have made it difficult to maintain. Only a few agricultural scientists are paying attention to the negative trend.

The research team has identified more than 300 rice and maize varieties known to local farmers from ancient times. With time, some of these varieties have disappeared for various reasons, such as low yield or lack of resistance to diseases and pests. Genetic resources, in the form of landraces, are precious to agriculture development, particularly for crop variety breeding as they could be a source of important adaptive traits. The maintenance of these traits on farm is essential for sustainable agriculture and for their capacity to adapt to climate change.

In 2010, with support from the Institute of Agricultural Science in Xishuangbanna Dai Autonomous Prefecture, the Menghai county agricultural bureau, the Xiding government, the Xiding agricultural sciences station and the village committee, we set up the Xiding gene bank in the committee building, Manwa village, Menghai county.

This gene bank is a farmer-owned facility that conserves the diversity of local crop seeds and provides a seed-exchange service to farmers. The specific objectives of the Xiding gene bank are to collect seeds from current and ancient local crop varieties, demonstrate them to local farmers and make them available through seed exchange. The efforts of the community gene bank are supported by participatory propagation.

To ensure efficient management of the bank according to established standards and procedures, we established the Xiding Crop Gene Bank Management Committee and the Expert Advisory Committee. The latter consists of 12 experts from scientific institutions in Yunnan who provide technical support for management of the community gene bank. As far as we know, this initiative represents the first of its kind in China. The above-mentioned 'Pest and disease' project provided some initial financing and technical support through funding from the United Nations Environment Programme and the Global Environment Facility. Currently, some funds are provided through the International Fund for Agricultural Development and in-kind support from the Chinese authorities.

Functions and activities

The main functions of the community gene bank are conservation, demonstration of Xiding's crop diversity and the organization of biodiversity fairs, which help connect the past with the future by ensuring the continuing availability of genetic resources for research, breeding and improved seed delivery. In 2010, the gene bank started with 20 local varieties of rice and ten of maize (Plate 7). By 2013, the collection had grown to nearly 70 varieties of rice and ten of maize, as well as seeds of other crops, such as sunflower, white gourd and peanut.

The different varieties have different characteristics. Most are drought tolerant and some are resistant to disease and pests. About 300g of seed of each accession is kept in the community gene bank. Seeds are replaced every year by the research team and some local farmers. Farmers dry their seeds directly after harvest on a bamboo screen, check for pests and diseases and remove affected seeds. The seeds are then treated with organic material, such as ashes or pepper, to protect them from disease. Women are often in charge of seed selection.

The rice genetic resources group at the Yunnan Academy of Agricultural Sciences (YAAS) covers the cost of reproducing seeds. The community provides the storage site and government institutions provide the technical support, e.g. the correct methods of collecting, storing and managing the seeds. Duplicate seeds are stored in the YAAS gene bank in modern facilities for mid-term conservation backed up by a complete documentation system. Both farmers and breeders have access to these seeds, on request by telephone or email.

The establishment, operations and management of the gene bank are guided by rules and regulations formulated by the agencies and farmers involved. For example, for germplasm entering the bank, the following guidelines have been agreed to:

* Farmers from the various villages bring their seeds (about 300g each) to the gene bank, encouraged by notices at crop seed diversity fairs and

locally displayed posters. At field days, farmers are exposed to different species of rice, corn, etc. from the gene bank, and gene bank personnel explain how seeds are stored and how farmers have access to them.

- The gene bank administrator collects passport data and registers the name of the variety, its origin, time of collection and its characteristics.
- The seeds are then stored in a bottle sealed with a paper label containing all the associated information.

Farmers who want to obtain seeds that are different from their own must deposit an equal quantity in the gene bank. To guarantee seed viability over the long term, some seeds must be propagated by the gene bank. Every year, about half a bottle of each variety is planted in the local breeding area in Gasa township, Jinghong city.

The aim is to make available to users as many accessions as possible along with associated data. Transactions are free. To obtain an accession from the gene bank, a farmer must fill in an application. The staff of the gene bank draw up a contract with the seed seeker based on compliance with China's Seed Law under the Crop Germplasm Resources Management Measures. The farmer is responsible for complying with the local or national requirement for seed importation, in particular the phytosanitary regulations to prevent the spread of pests or invasive species that could seriously affect local production.

Farmers may not apply for recognition of new varieties and other intellectual property protection for germplasm obtained from the gene bank. Those who access germplasm from the gene bank have to promptly report to the gene bank and later give feedback about the performance of the obtained germplasm. If this is not done on time, the gene bank is no longer obliged to provide germplasm. We usually provide 20g of seed for each request. When the quantity of a variety falls below 200g, we will use 100g to multiply the stock at the local breeding base in Gasa township.

Apart from the more common crops and varieties, the community gene bank also aims to collect local neglected and underused species. Farmers are interested in finding rare varieties, such as Abie, a kind of glutinous rice that has large grains and a very good taste, but is prone to disease and has a low yield. In some villages, such as Bada in Xiding township, farmers planted this variety up to a few years ago, but now can no longer find seeds. They are hoping that through the community gene bank they will be able to conserve and continue to use some of these neglected species.

About 100 villagers from ten villages and about ten technical staff from the agricultural extension service are currently involved in and benefitting from the gene bank's collection. Researchers, including staff of YAAS, Institute of Agricultural Sciences of Xishuangbanna (XIAS), use the collection mostly for crop evaluation, genetic improvement and scanning for useful genes. Women farmers are involved in decision-making, especially about seed storage, seed distribution and the daily management of the gene bank.

Policy and legal environment

The community gene bank has not yet been officially registered. If it can attain legal status, it will become more influential, standardized and sustainable. There is a need to better inform government agencies at all levels about the relevance of community gene banks. Currently, they do not understand the need for relevant laws and regulations, ensuring the normal operation of gene banks, standardized seed identification, registration and preservation, reproduction and use and distribution.

A series of laws and provincial and local regulations, promulgated in Yunnan, have had an impact on the conservation and sustainable use of agricultural biodiversity; examples are the provincial protection regulations for new varieties of registered horticultural plants and the agricultural environmental protection ordinance. However, in general, the institutional environment is not very supportive and awareness of the need to protect agricultural biodiversity is poor. One major problem is that farmers can easily be bypassed when it comes to registering intellectual property rights over biological resources. A more general problem is that laws are not enforced strictly and people tend not to obey them.

The research team has identified some effective ways to create an enabling policy and legal environment. These include the development of special regional laws and regulations that consider Yunnan's unique natural conditions and that offer strengthened special protection of its natural resources. A second alternative is to develop national agricultural biodiversity laws and a regulation system. A third mechanism is to increase government accountability for biodiversity conservation. Finally, there is a need to increase public awareness, education and training related to agricultural biodiversity. The research team has also proposed the establishment of a traditional variety protection system based on farmers' rights that encourages farmers to participate in regional and national germplasm conservation projects, strengthens community capacity development, promotes technology transfer and increases public financial support.

Sustainability and prospects

To make the community gene bank more effective, its staff must be trained in areas such as documentation, seed procurement, handling and overall management. There is also a need to increase awareness of the community gene bank through television and local government communication channels, connect it with crop conservation activities at the regional level and attract more support from farmers' organizations in the province. We plan to strengthen ties with the YAAS gene bank, which has more experience in conservation, and also to learn from the national gene bank system. Achieving financial sustainability will require more support from local government and other local organizations.

All in all, there is still a long way to go to make the bank part of a national or international network of community gene banks. First, we must obtain financial support from the local government and, at the same time, apply for national or international funding. Second, there is a need to continue creating awareness through diversity fairs; for further training in field crop cultivation and management and in pest and disease control; and for actively participating in conserving germplasm at the gene bank and through other crop genetic diversity activities.

16 Costa Rica

Unión de Semilleros del Sur

Flor Ivette Elizondo Porras, Rodolfo Araya Villalobos, Juan Carlos Hernández Fonseca and Karolina Martínez Umaña

Rescue, conservation and production of quality bean and maize seed

In the early 1990s, small farmer associations began to form in the Brunca Region in southern Costa Rica in response to the need to improve marketing opportunities by eliminating or reducing intermediaries and to organize seed-storage facilities that would allow the farmers to sell large volumes to packagers and industries. During this same period, research evolved from the traditional approach, where plant breeding is done by researchers and varieties are delivered to farmers, to a participatory scheme, where farmers are involved in the breeding process (Hocdé et al., 2000).

The need for bean producers in the Brunca Region to have access to high-quality seed of local varieties and, later, of varieties released through the participatory process led to the creation of local seed production units in Costa Rica. Previously, the only source of certified seed was the national production council (Consejo Nacional de Producción, CNP), regulated by the Seed Law (ONS, 1981, 2005), which did not allow the inclusion of local varieties. In addition, the main objective of the CNP is to supply seed of nationally grown varieties, not the local varieties developed through participatory plant breeding.

Local seed production started in 1995 with the widely disseminated variety Sacapobres (free from poverty), which matures early (Araya and Hernández, 2006) and produces high yields (Morales, 1994; Mora, 1995). The regional programme for agronomic research on basic grains (Programa Regional de Reforzamiento a la Investigación Agronómica sobre Granos en Centroamérica) supported this initiative (Silva and Hernández, 1996). In 2000, the participatory plant breeding effort, which integrated farmers' criteria and knowledge with that of breeders and other stakeholders, strengthened bean research in Costa Rica (Hocdé et al., 1999).

At the time, there was no organization responsible for seed production and no guidelines to regulate the process (Araya et al., 2010). In 2004, the Costa Rican bean research and technology transfer programme (Programa de Investigación y Transferencia de Tecnología Agropecuaria en Frijol, PITTA Frijol) was established with the collaboration of the Ministry of Agriculture and Livestock, the National Institute of Agricultural Technology Innovation and Transfer, the University of Costa Rica, the CNP, the National Seed Office and the National University. PITTA Frijol introduced a quality control protocol for local bean seed production (Araya and Hernández, 2007), and set up technical committees for participatory plant breeding and seed production (Elizondo et al., 2013). A protocol for postharvest seed handling was developed later (Araya et al., 2013c).

The Unión de Semilleros del Sur (union of southern seed producers) was formed in 2010 when regulations were established for its operation (Araya et al., 2013a). Research committees of four producer organizations, including 754 members, make up the union. In 2011, the name of these committees was changed from research to technical committees because their activities included local seed production in addition to participatory research.

Technical committees and operations

Members of the technical committees are appointed by the board of directors of each member organization; the boards also establish an administrative, logistic and economic strategy to support the committees. In addition to the PITTA Frijol support team, the technical committees include a coordinator and a secretary; a treasurer is named when the organization does not have an administrator; and sometimes a promoter or extension agent is needed, depending on the purpose of the committee (Araya et al., 2013b). These committees plan seed production for a minimum period of two years, based on demand and logistic and financial capacity. They also arrange for planting areas, set dates, select plots and designate farmers responsible for seed production. Seed producers receive training and are assigned varieties to propagate based on soil fertility and humidity on their land. The committees help out with the procedures required to register seed producers and their seed production lots, for both internal control and to obtain an official record. In terms of research, they also define the bean ideotype and evaluate and select materials to be released and registered as varieties.

In each seed production cycle, one of the main activities is recording information provided by each producer in a database that includes an entry number, inputs provided, audit records, records of seed received, quality analysis results and production costs. Supervision of plots is based on local production protocols defined by members in a participatory way (Araya and Hernández, 2007). Each seed producer harvests and delivers clean and dried (13 per cent maximum moisture content) seed to the local association. The technical committee audits the three stages: seed delivery, quality analysis (moisture content, inert matter, varietal mixture, discoloured seed, seed damaged by fungi or insects, mechanical injuries, wrinkles, pre-germination and contaminating seed of other crops or weeds) and seed conditioning. A form is filled out for each stage.

The Unión de Semilleros del Sur has two storage chambers with a total capacity of 32t for storing bean seed and germplasm of the main commercial varieties, plus 1kg of each of the varieties that form the community's reserve. A log book is kept for recording incoming and outgoing commercial seed and germplasm. Each local variety has passport data. Seed cleaning of local varieties to be stored in the chambers is done at the University of Costa Rica's experimental station (Estación Experimental Fabio Baudrit Moreno, EEFBM) during at least three multiplication cycles. After that, seed committees are responsible for seed propagation. All varieties in the seed chambers have backup seed samples in EEFBM's germplasm bank. Each organized farmer group administers its own resources in the seed bank and storage costs are included per hundredweight of stored seed.

Seed of commercial varieties is available for direct sale to members who have access to credit provided by the farmers' associations. PITTA Frijol and the Panamerican agricultural school (Escuela Agrícola Panamericana El Zamorano) are currently using some of the local varieties in breeding efforts. The technical committee of the Guagaral farmers' association is planning to hold biodiversity fairs to share information on the genetic and organoleptic characteristics of the seed they produce.

The participation of women in the seed production process has been important. Women record all committee activities, record and update trial and seed propagation information, ensure that agreements are met and convene meetings. They also participate actively in supervising and managing seed lots. Women influence the choice of local varieties for commercial bean production for household consumption based on organoleptic characteristics.

Over the years, the technical committees have taken on the tasks of rescuing, increasing and conserving native varieties. The first initiative originated in 2010 in collaboration with the Food and Agriculture Organization's (FAO's) Seeds for Development project. Common beans (*Phaseolus vulgaris*), lima beans (*Phaseolus lunatus*) and maize were included in these collections. Collected seed was cleaned of pathogens and propagated at the Fabio Baudrit experimental station in time to make quality seed available in 2013 and start local multiplication. In parallel with the increased seed availability in Guagaral, local knowledge about seeds is increasing. In areas where a farmers' association is close to a school, children have received training in biodiversity issues, the importance of rescuing local varieties and the use of passport data for collecting seed of varieties grown in their communities.

Solidarity networks

Solidarity networks were set up by the farmers' associations that make up the Unión de Semilleros del Sur to provide credit to members, obtain bank loans to invest in seed production, facilitate community access to seeds of improved and local varieties, reduce the cost of these varieties and provide storage and conditioning facilities for the grains produced. Approximately 750 families have benefitted. Information on seed production is disseminated in reports prepared by the technical committees and presented during the annual meeting of the association. Information is also shared locally at churches, on posters, in workshops and meetings and with those who visit the association's facilities. In addition, producers organize information-sharing activities, such as field days and demonstrations. All members of the technical committees and the board of directors, as well as producers and local, regional, national and international extension agents usually participate in these activities.

PITTA Frijol provides technical support to the Unión de Semilleros del Sur by holding workshops and periodic meetings with the technical committees and by supervising seed production plots. The committees have also received training in organizational and entrepreneurial skills, local seed production and breeding of new bean varieties. Biodiversity fairs are being planned for the near future. Support to establish a fund as seed capital is being provided by the government and regional organizations, such as the Collaborative Program on Participatory Plant Breeding in Mesoamerica and FAO's Seeds for Development project.

One of the main achievements of the union is the availability of locally produced seed, which has been graded as 'authorized seed' by the National Seed Office. Evidence has shown that quality seeds result in better seedling establishment, even under drought or flood conditions and in low-fertility, clayey soils.

The main challenge faced by the Unión de Semilleros del Sur is sustainability of the seed production process and long-term conservation of germplasm – a problem because of the high relative humidity and temperatures in the areas where seed-storage chambers are located. Another challenge is improving and enlarging storage areas and finding resources to increase the seed capital.

References

Araya, R. and Hernández, J. C. (2006) 'Mejora genética participativa de la variedad criolla de frijol Sacapobres,' *Agronomía Mesoamericana*, vol 17, p347

_____ (2007) 'Protocolo para la producción local de semilla de frijol,' Estación Experimental Fabio Baudrit Moreno, Alajuela, Costa Rica

Araya, R., Elizondo, F., Hernández, J. C. and Martínez, K. (2013a) 'Reglamento de la Unión de Semilleros del Sur,' Food and Agriculture Organization, San Jose, Costa Rica. Project GCP/RLA182/SPA

_____ (2013b) 'Guía para el funcionamiento del comité técnico: mejora genética participativa y el control de calidad de la semilla en la agricultura familiar,' Food and Agriculture Organization, San José, Costa Rica. Project GCP/RLA/182/SPA

Araya, R., Martínez, K., López, A. and Murillo, A. (2013c) 'Protocolo para el manejo pos cosecha de la semilla de frijol,' Food and Agriculture Organization, San José, Costa Rica. Project GCP/RLA/182/SPA

Araya, R., Quirós, W., Carrillo, O., Gutiérrez, M. V. and Murillo, A. (2010) 'Semillas de buena calidad,' Food and Agriculture Organization, Costa Rica. Project GCP/RLA182/SPA. Brochure

Elizondo, F., Araya, R., Hernández, J. C., Chaves, N. and Martínez, K. (2013) 'Guía para el establecimiento de comités técnicos: el fitomejoramiento participativo y la producción de semilla de calidad,' Food and Agriculture Organization, San José, Costa Rica. Project GCP/RLA/182/SPA

Hocdé, H., Hernández, J. C., Araya, R. and Bermúdez, A. (1999) 'Proceso de fitomejoramiento participativo con frijol en Costa Rica: la historia de "acapobres",' Fitomejoramiento Participativo en América Latina y el Caribe. Proceedings of an International Symposium, Quito, Ecuador, August 31–September 3, 1999

Hocdé, H., Meneses D. and Miranda B. (2000) 'Farmer experimentation: a challenge to all!' *LEISA Magazine*, vol 16, no 2, www.agriculturesnetwork.org/magazines/global/grassroots-innovation/farmer-experimentation-a-challenge-to-all, accessed 13 January 2014

Mora, B. (1995) 'Validación de cultivares mejorados de frijol común en diferentes localidades de Pejibaye en el inverniz de 1995,' work report, Ministerio de Agricultura y Ganadería, San José, Costa Rica

Morales, A. (1994) 'Ensayos de verificación de cultivares promisorios de frijol,' work report, Ministerio de Agricultura y Ganadería, San José, Costa Rica

ONS (Oficina Nacional de Semillas) (1981) 'Reglamento a la Ley de semillas número 6289,' ONS, San José, Costa Rica

_____ (2005) 'Reglamento para la importación, exportación y comercialización de semillas,' ONS, San José, Costa Rica

Silva, A. G. and Hernández, M. (eds) (1996) *Producción local de semilla de calidad: la experiencia Centroamericana*, Programa Regional de Reforzamiento a la Investigación Agronómica sobre Granos en Centroamérica, San José, Costa Rica

17 Guatemala

Community seed reserves restore maize diversity

Gea Galluzzi and Isabel Lapeña

The Huehuetenango region of the Cuchumatanes highlands in western Guatemala is an important centre of maize diversity. Although farmers there have developed a wealth of open-pollinated local varieties, changing environmental and socioeconomic conditions are beginning to have a negative impact on their ability to maintain local genetic resources on farm. Over the last ten years, climate variation and a series of natural disasters have considerably affected maize-based production systems. Increasing fragmentation of land holdings has weakened traditional forms of seed exchange and knowledge sharing. Declining productivity has started to affect families' food security; current production levels are only able to meet home consumption needs for half the year. This has led to a tendency among farmers to devalue and abandon their local varieties and to buy seeds of commercial varieties and hybrids on the market. However, these seeds are expensive. They often do not perform well in the low-input, harsh growing conditions of the area and may not suit the cultural preferences of traditional communities.

Convinced that the maintenance and continued evolution of locally adapted genetic resources through collective, community-based innovation are key elements in achieving resilience of local communities and agro-ecosystems, Asocuch, a Guatemalan association of agricultural cooperatives, took action to halt the loss of agricultural biodiversity. Asocuch joined forces with government agencies, Fundación para la Innovación Tecnológica, Agropecuaria y Forestal and the Instituto de Ciencia y Tecnología Agrícola, to implement a Guatemalan component of the Collaborative Programme on Participatory Plant Breeding in Mesoamerica.

Starting in the Quilinco community, maize landraces conserved by farmers were collected and characterized to form a base collection representative of the on-farm diversity available in the area. This initial collection was used to develop a participatory breeding process in which farmers were trained in selection techniques that gradually improved the performance of local varieties based on farmers' preferences. In parallel, community efforts focused on conserving the initial collection in a rudimentary 'seed reserve'. Over the years, the collection has grown with the inclusion of the gradually improved materials from the breeding programme. The Quilinco seed reserve now holds

657 maize accessions and another seven community seed reserves have been established in other communities in the area. Up to 1,000 farmers have been trained in mass selection and seed conservation, and significant increases in local landrace yields have been achieved (a detailed report about two of the seed reserves, Sololá and Quilinco, is available in Spanish, Fuentes López, 2013) (Plate 8).

These efforts have not only contributed to strengthening the seed and food security of more than 5,000 people in the region, but they have also enabled the conservation of locally adapted maize varieties. Recently, community members have begun selecting best-performing adapted landraces and started larger-scale multiplication efforts to produce packets of seed for sale. They plan to expand their operations and find markets farther away.

However, challenges remain in terms of dissemination and wider adoption of these seeds. Currently, no policy mechanisms allow registration or certification of improved landrace varieties produced by farmers and agricultural cooperatives; thus, their achievements are limited to the informal sector and wider commercial distribution is not possible. Benefit-sharing and intellectual property issues surrounding this type of community-based innovation in terms of access and availability are not clear either.

Asocuch is currently participating in technical and policy discussions around the drafting of a national seed law and advocating the inclusion of a seed category and related regulations appropriate for registering, sharing and commercializing the improved landraces produced by the farmers of the Cuchumatanes.

Reference

Fuentes López, M. R. (2013) 'Tema 4: vincular los agricultores al TIRFAA/SML: el potencial y los desafíos de fortalecer el acceso a los RFAA a través de bancos de genes/semillas basados en la comunidad. SUB TEMA: Estudios de caso de reservas comunitarias de semillas en Guatemala,' Bioversity International, Rome, Italy

18 India

Community seed banks and empowering tribal communities in the Kolli Hills

E. D. Israel Oliver King, N. Kumar and Stefano Padulosi

Agrarian tribal communities engage in many practices related to the production, selection, storage and exchange of seeds in their subsistence farming. These practices have been evolving since time immemorial and are the backbone of the traditional farming systems of small and marginal farmers in the hill regions even today. They have helped farm families cope with the vagaries of monsoon and weather changes. Local seed systems that are self-sufficient enable community members to find seeds even in times of crisis. Their contribution to the maintenance of crop diversity on farm and diversified livelihood options is invaluable. However, these best practices have begun to decline over the last three decades because of farmers' increasing use of commercial crops.

The Kolli Hills in Tamil Nadu, South India (78° 17′ 05′ to 78° 27′ 45′ E and 11° 55′ 05′ to 11° 21′ 10′ N) are low-ranging hills spread over an area of 441.41km². The area is inhabited by a homogenous group of tribal people known as the Malayali Gounders, who have maintained inter- and intra-specific minor millet diversity on farm through a set of practices based on the local environmental and social conditions. Currently, 21 landraces of finger millet (seven), little millet (seven), Italian millet (five), common millet (one) and kodo millet (one) are being cultivated by these communities under various agro-ecological conditions.

The introduction of high-yielding varieties and commercial crops has affected the availability of seeds of traditional cultivars of millets. Adoption of cash crops and associated agricultural practices has, in fact, weakened dependence on community-based seed systems. This has led, in turn, to a decrease in the portfolio of diversity-based on-farm options with repercussions for the food and nutritional security of people.

In this context, strengthening access to and availability of traditional varieties is a key intervention in support of local communities. To that end, the community-based seed bank networks, which have been facilitated by the M. S. Swaminathan Research Foundation (MSSRF) in Kolli Hills represent an effective contribution that helped halt the erosion of indigenous crop diversity and strengthen the livelihoods and resilience of the local community.

Motivation and objectives

In 1997, the MSSRF initiated a programme to conserve small millets in Kolli Hills (MSSRF, 2002). At that time, conventional seed sharing was weak and took place at the individual level. As a first step, MSSRF began to identify the 'knowledge holders' and 'seed keepers' of the millet landraces to establish contact and share knowledge about millets and millet farming practices. A core group of 35 traditional millet farmers, both men and women, were motivated to establish community seed banks to ensure the sustainable supply of required seeds of local landraces; serve as a community-based ex-situ conservation facility and as a backup source of seed; enhance availability, use and enhancement of locally adapted seeds; and emerge as a seed and knowledge exchange network managed by a group of tribal people by institutionalizing the community seed bank as a common resource.

First steps

Participatory research appraisal conducted with farmers in various parts of the Kolli Hills revealed that intra-specific landraces were grown in different zones. Also, there was an extreme shortage of the seeds of some varieties and most had been mixed with others under the traditional method of farming.

A core group of millet farmers was trained by the MSSRF in the production of quality seed and its safe storage. The strategies for conservation of millets involved seed collection, multiplication, seed distribution and farmer-to-farmer exchanges mediated by the seed banks. The seed banks were built on traditional practices. MSSRF motivated the revival of traditional seed-storage practices, such as the use of thombai, a traditional grain storage structure that varies in size from a small compartment within a house to a separate hut-like structure nearby. These structures are 5–8cm above the ground to prevent damage by rats. Generally, they consist of two compartments with a small opening at the top. Women usually manage these structures and use dried leaves as a pest repellent. In addition, MSSRF facilitated the construction of new structures using local manual labour (King et al., 2009).

Governance and management

These revitalized and newly constructed seed banks are managed by the local communities. Over the last decade, MSSRF facilitated the establishment of community seed banks in 15 villages that now have their own safe seed storage and an institutional system for regular seed production, distribution and exchange.

New institutions, such as self-help groups consisting of 10–15 women and men farmers, have been organized to manage the seed banks. These groups are primarily credit-based institutions that are recognized by the formal banking system. Two women or men chosen from the group serve as seed bank managers. Based on local preferences, the required quantity of preferred varieties of seed is mobilized. Transactions are guided by local ethics and norms, such as:

• The borrower has to return one and a half or two times the quantity of seed borrowed.
• Transactions consist of the exchange of seeds, never cash.
• Seed has to be returned; otherwise, borrowers will not be able to use the seed bank again.
• If the seed is not returned after harvest in the same year, the interest rate doubles.
• The lender ensures good seed quality and trusts 'neighbourhood certification'.
• If the quality of the seed is poor, e.g. it contains inert dust particles and chaff, the lender cleans it before the transaction.

Technical issues

MSSRF provides training and capacity building periodically for both men and women; the training focusses mainly on seed quality, monitoring, storage and management. Community seed bank operations are largely dependent on an optimal level of literacy and require valuable time for monitoring; thus, seed exchange is difficult at times (King et al., 2009). This problem was resolved through training, especially in maintenance of records, receipts, interest on seed loans, etc.

The seed bank managers ensure the germination and physical purity of the seed material loaned and returned. They also constantly monitor the seed stock for pests. The availability of the seed stock in the bank and the balance sheet are discussed at monthly group meetings. The self-help group members share information on available varieties and quantities informally with neighbouring farmers. To allow greater outreach, seed bank managers participate in annual temple festivals, seed bank fairs and state-sponsored exhibitions.

Evolution to village millet resource centres

For over a decade now, the MSSRF has been promoting an integrated approach to reviving, conserving and enhancing the sustainable use of crop genetic resources, especially indigenous ones (King et al., 2009). It has supported community seed banks and managing institutions in implementing a 'four Cs framework': conservation, cultivation, consumption and commercialization. In 15 locations, community seed banks have evolved into village millet resource centres (VMRCs), where the local managing groups provide information support. Practices involved in the four Cs framework for sustaining seed banks are described below.

Participatory quality seed production and selection of better varieties

Community seed bank facilitators have been trained in the importance of weeding and thinning plants, identifying seeds, dealing with pest and disease infestation and postharvest processing, such as drying and safe storage. To promote millet production and broaden local genetic diversity, MSSRF accessed a few hundred accessions of three millet species from the germplasm bank of the International Crops Research Institute for the Semi-arid Tropics in Hyderabad and improved cultivars developed under a national programme from the All India Small Millet Coordinated Research Programme, Bangalore. At some seed banks, these were grown repeatedly and varieties that were better than the local landraces were selected by farmers (King et al., 2013a). In these experiments, farmers identified three varieties from among improved varieties as well as local landraces with yields 20–30 per cent higher than those under cultivation.

Increasing yield by improving cultivation practices

The availability of quality seed substantially contributed to the promotion of millet cultivation. However, compared with alternative crops, such as tapioca and pineapple, millet yield and the income from its production were poor. Thus, increased productivity was essential to maintain millet as a viable crop option. Together with the self-help groups, the MSSRF initiated agronomic measures such as row planting, reduced seeding rates, application of farmyard manure and intercropping millet with tapioca. These practices were able to increase the yield, and thus the economic return, of finger millet by 39 per cent, of little millet by 37 per cent and of foxtail millet by 30 per cent (King et al., 2013b). This result convinced farmers who are associated with the community seed banks to increase cultivation of millets using the improved practices.

Introducing drudgery-free grain processing technology

One of the important reasons for decreasing interest in millet cultivation and use was the hard work associated with its processing. All millets except finger millet have a hard seed coat requiring strong abrasive forces to extract the grain. Decortication had been accomplished using a mortar and pestle – a tedious and physically taxing process almost exclusively done by women. No suitable machinery was available to reduce this drudgery. The introduction by MSSRF of small mechanical milling facilities in the VMRCs signaled a major change for the women and contributed substantially to revival of interest in millet cultivation and consumption. Currently, pulverizers and dehulling mills are managed by VMRCs in nine settlements. A collaborative project with the University of Agricultural Sciences, Dharwad, and McGill University, Canada, which was supported by the Canadian International Food Security Research Fund and the International Development Research Centre, has resulted in new prototype machinery for processing little millets with a recovery efficiency of 90–95 per cent (Dolli et al., 2013). Further research is ongoing to customize this machinery for other small millets. Another important spinoff from the mechanization of millet processing was local interest, particularly among women, in building a value chain for millets.

Developing and promoting new marketable millet products

Building a value chain for millets required specialized training in product development, maintaining product quality and consistency, packaging, labelling and marketing. Selected members of VMRCs were trained in these areas at the Rural Home Science Colleges under Avinashilingam University, Coimbatore, and also at the agricultural universities at Bangalore and Dharwad (Vijayalakshmi et al., 2010; Yenagi et al., 2010; Bergamini et al., 2013). This training, which was planned and supported by the MSSRF, has empowered village women in terms of the production of all value-added items such as malt, rava and ready-made mixes of millets. Products with good commercial potential were identified through market studies and put into production through the collective work of the self-help groups. Different groups were encouraged to specialize in the production of different products (Plate 9). During the early stages of production and marketing, MSSRF assistance was extended in the form of further training in product quality, packaging, labelling, marketing and account keeping.

Establishing a market for value-added millet products

Although farmers had experience in selling their primary produce, they lacked the ability to market value-added products. Thus, MSSRF was required to provide assistance to the self-help groups in marketing the products in urban areas. This was done through a combination of approaches, including promotion campaigns, awareness raising and lobbying for policy changes. Slowly, members of the self-help groups with marketing skills were identified and promoted to undertake product marketing with local retail outlets. With help, they also established a retail outlet for all products in Kolli Hills under the banner Kolli Hills Agro Biodiversity Conservers' Federation (KHABCoFED) (Assis et al., 2010; King, 2012). Millet products branded 'Kolli Hills Natural Products' are available in natural food stores in 25 towns in Tamil Nadu. The most popular and best-selling millet products are ready-made mixes, milled rice of little millet and Italian millet and finger millet malt. Since 2001, the KHABCoFED has sold 9t of whole grain, 23.3t of little millet, rava and flour, 7.4t of value-added products for a total value of 15.2 lakh rupees (about US$2,500).

Establishing community institutions for the promotion of millets

MSSRF organized local farm women and men, who were interested in the cultivation of millets, into self-help groups and farmers' clubs. The self-help groups were encouraged to build collective savings from their income and lend money within the group; they are often linked with local banking services.

They were also trained and supported in collective activities, such as promotion of millet cultivation. MSSRF has facilitated training for 43 self-help groups and 29 farmers' clubs in the Kolli Hills, which include over 943 members (of which 420 are women). Among these, 47 groups (365 men and 247 women) are involved in the institutionalization of various operations to conserve, cultivate and market millets. Specific self-help groups or individual members are delegated to undertake specific activities according to their interest, such as improved production, variety selection, management of millet processing units, grain procurement and transportation to processing centres, building the value chain, etc. These self-help groups have been confederated under the KHABCoFED.

Costs and sustainability of VMRCs

A decade of participatory research and development efforts has enabled farm families to access and manage diverse local genetic materials all year through community seed banks and seed exchange networks. Communities have also been enabled to make their own choices of varieties based on local weather conditions. Millet production and yield have been increased through the selection of adapted varieties, use of high-quality seed and improved agronomic practices. Interventions to increase production and improve agronomic techniques have helped to increase yields and income and enlarge the food diversity basket. Millet processing machinery has reduced the drudgery associated with processing millet and improved food quality. Millet processing technologies, the development of new millet uses and linking products to markets through awareness and promotion campaigns have increased the use of millets. The value-chain interventions revolving around VMRCs have generated employment and income for millet producers and other actors in the chain. Community institutions built around these actions (self-help groups and farmers' clubs) have been able to promote their value-added products as they have improved access to suitable markets for millets. Enhanced local use and marketing opportunities have increased consumption of millets.

Furthermore, innovative practices developed in the process of networking community seed banks and recognition of custodian farmers and their enhanced role in the cultivation, processing, marketing of the underused and neglected millets have sustained community seed banks and have potential for larger replication in similar agro-ecologies.

Acknowledgements

We are grateful to Professor M. S. Swaminathan for his constant encouragement. We also acknowledge the support of international agencies – the Swiss Agency for Development and Cooperation, the International Fund for Agricultural Development, Bioversity International, the International Development Research Centre, the Food and Agricultural Organization – and the contribution of local communities in sharing their valuable knowledge.

References

Assis, A. L., Sofia, Z., Temesgen, D. and Uttam, K., with King, E. D. I. O., Swain, S. and Ramesh, V. (2010) *Global Study on CBM and Empowerment – India Exchange Report*, Wageningen University and Research Centre/Centre for Development Innovation, Wageningen, The Netherlands

Bergamini, N., Padulosi, S., Bala Ravi, S. and Yenagi, N. (2013) 'Minor millets in India: a neglected crop goes mainstream,' in J. Fanzo, D. Hunter, T. Borelli and F. Mattei (eds) *Diversifying Food and Diets using Agricultural Biodiversity to Improve Nutrition and Health*, Issues in Agricultural Biodiversity Series, Earthscan from Routledge, London, pp313–325

Dolli, S. S., Yenagi, N., King, E. D. I. O., Kumar, R., Sumalatha, B., Negi, K., Kumar, N. and Mishra, C. S. (2013) 'Drudgery reducing interventions in millet cultivation and their impact,' International Workshop on Promoting Small millets for Improved Rural Economy and Food Security, 8–9 February 2013, University of Agricultural Sciences, Dharwad, India

King, E. D. I. O. (2012) 'Resilience, the empowerment of tribal peoples' and access to markets, in the context of community biodiversity management in Kolli Hills, India,' 4th International Ecosummit, Ecological Sustainability Restoring the Planets Ecosystem Services, symposium 19. Community resilience: strategies for empowerment in agro biodiversity management and adaptation, EcoSummit 2012, Columbus, Ohio, USA

King, E. D. I. O., Bala Ravi, S. and Padulosi, S. (2013a) 'Creating economic stake for conserving the diversity of small millets in Kolli Hills, India,' in W. S. de Boef, A. Subedi, N. Peroni, M. Thijssen and E. O'Keeffe (eds) *Community Biodiversity Management: Promoting Resilience and the Conservation of Plant Genetic Resources*, Earthscan from Routledge, London, pp194–200

King, E. D. I. O., Kumar, B. N. A., Kumar, R., Kumar, N., Yenagi, N., Byadgi, S., Mishra, C. S. and Kalaiselvan, N. N. (2013b) 'Appropriate agronomic interventions for increasing productivity in nutritious and underutilized millets,' International Workshop on Promoting Small millets for Improved Rural Economy and Food Security, 8–9 February 2013, University of Agricultural Sciences, Dharwad, India

King, E. D. I. O., Nambi, V. A. and Nagarajan, L. (2009) 'Integrated approaches in small millet conservation. A case from Kolli Hills, India,' in H. Jaenike, J. Ganry, I. Hoeschle-Zeledon and R. Kahane (eds) *International Symposium on Underutilized Plant Species for Food, Nutrition, Income and Sustainable Development*, Acta Horticulturae 806, vol 1, International Society for Horticultural Science, Leuven, Belgium, pp79–84

MSSRF (M. S. Swaminathan Research Foundation) (2002) *Bio-conservation and Utilization of Small Millets*, MSSRF/MG/2002/14, MSSRF, Chennai, India

Vijayalakshmi, D., Geetha, K., Gowda, J., Bala Ravi, S., Padulosi, S. and Mal, B. (2010) 'Empowerment of women farmers through value addition on minor millets. Genetic resources: a case study in Karnataka,' *Indian Journal of Plant Genetic Resources*, vol 23, no 1, pp132–135

Yenagi, N. B., Handigol, J. A., Bala Ravi, S., Mal, B. and Padulosi, S. (2010) 'Nutritional and technological advancements in the promotion of ethnic and novel foods using the genetic diversity of minor millets in India,' *Indian Journal of Plant Genetic Resources*, vol 23, no 1, pp82–86

19 India

From community seed banks to community seed enterprises

G. V. Ramanjaneyulu, G. Rajshekar and K. Radha Rani

Origin and process

To restore farmers' habit of saving and using seeds from their own crops and to increase access to good-quality seeds, the Centre for Sustainable Agriculture has established community seed banks in 70 villages in the state of Andhra Pradesh and 20 villages in Maharashtra since 2004. Community seed banks are village-level institutions whose members are participating farmers. The community seed bank is managed by a committee of five volunteers (three women and two men) chosen by the villagers. In partnership with grassroots-level nongovernmental organizations (NGOs), the Centre for Sustainable Agriculture aims to:

- establish community managed seed banks at the village level;
- revive and conserve crop and genetic diversity with a special focus on food security;
- document the productivity of agro-diversity-based cropping systems;
- expand successful experiences over a larger area and into ongoing programmes;
- establish a state-level network of seed banks to share knowledge and resources.

As a first step, villages that wanted to initiate community-managed seed systems were selected with the help of a local NGO. Farmers met to discuss problems related to seeds, and they were briefed on alternative seed systems. Interested farmers were then chosen to participate in seed banks and assigned to groups to undertake planning, production and management. Some seed banks were registered as seed growers' associations (SGAs) under the civil societies act. Membership is open to all farmers, who meet periodically to discuss the plan of work. The process is illustrated in Figure 19.1.

The main functions of the community seed bank include:

- renewal of crop and genetic diversity in locations characterized by monoculture of commercial crops, exploitation of natural resources and extensive use of external inputs;

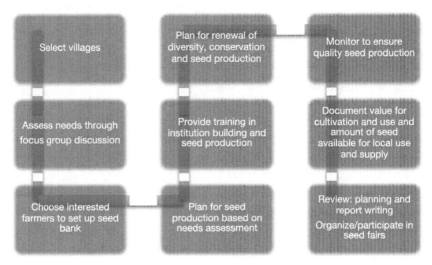

Figure 19.1 Steps in setting up and maintaining a community seed bank

- conservation of crop and genetic diversity in locations where diversity still exists but where farmers are facing the threat of chemicalization and monoculture;
- periodic mapping of diversity in the village and renewal of varieties that have lost their purity and vigour;
- participatory varietal selection and participatory plant breeding of specific crops, such as paddy cotton, groundnuts and vegetables, that are under threat due to erosion of diversity;
- selection of varieties suited to local conditions through participatory varietal selection; documentation of value for cultivation and use data for each variety and every agro-ecological situation;
- development, with innovative farmers and seed savers, of an inventory of available seed varieties along with information on their performance;
- organizing seed sharing and exchange, conservation of crop and genetic diversity and networking with similar bodies at the state and national levels;
- procuring breeder seeds from cooperatives and universities, mainly commercial crops, and multiplying and supplying them to farmers;
- assessment (by the seed bank committee) of village seed requirements and planning for seed production;
- encouraging farmers to produce/save/reuse seed carefully selected from their crops; helping farmers learn how to select and use farm-saved seed;
- holding enough stock to meet cropping requirements in case of crop failure or low rainfall, particularly in rainfed areas.

Currently, the community seed banks collectively hold 400 varieties of various crops. Their value for cultivation and use data are collected and published as a catalogue in Telugu and Marati for farmers to use as a reference.

The Centre for Sustainable Agriculture provides three types of support to the community seed banks:

- *Financial support*: For purchasing seed and storage structures, seed bank maintenance, etc. The amount is deposited in a bank account opened in the name of the seed committee.
- *Technical support*: The Centre for Sustainable Agriculture and NGOs train seed committee members to identify and map diversity, maintain diversity and produce seed according to standards specified for various crops. Farmers are also trained in seed selection and postharvest management.
- *Monitoring*: Seed banks are periodically monitored by a coordinator appointed to look after this programme.

Since 2007/08, the farmers have formed producer organizations to pool and market their crops. For some crops, such as paddy, soybeans, chickpeas, wheat and red grams, demand from farmers in neighbouring villages has been increasing and some of the community seed banks have entered into informal marketing arrangements. As the farmers were already marketing their grain, some formed SGAs at the village level to collectively plan and market their seeds.

Seed growers' associations

An SGA is made up of about 15 farmers, 50 per cent of whom are women. At the beginning of every crop season, the association prepares a plan and procures seed from various sources; multiplication is carried out by the members.

During the growing season, members organize visits to seed plots to monitor management quality. At the end of the season, based on requirements, seed is procured by the SGA and stored in seed banks or retained by farmers. Seed is documented and catalogued; then, at the beginning of the growing season, it is distributed to farmers. The SGAs in Chowdarpally and Enebavi have become famous for the paddy and other varieties they produce.

Evolving into a seed enterprise

Community seed enterprises are extensions of the SGAs. Representatives of the SGAs make up the general body and executive of such enterprises, which may be producer companies or cooperatives. While the SGAs are non-registered informal groups of farmers, producer companies are registered and have all the requisite licenses and permits to breed varieties, produce seeds and brand and sell them. The main functions of seed producer companies are:

- developing seed production plans based on the demand projections of community seed banks and SGAs;
- procuring and multiplying breeder seed in bulk and supplying it to community seed banks and SGAs;

- identifying farmer breeders and following participatory plant breeding processes to select crop varieties that are stable and can withstand climate variation;
- owning and operating a central seed bank and processing unit. The role of the seed processing unit is to facilitate postharvest management of the seeds: harvesting, threshing, cleaning, grading and checking for viability and germination rate. As the seeds will not be used until the next season, they must be carefully stored at the central processing unit to maintain viability.

In 2012, a federation of seed growers was established as a seed producer organization: Naisargik Sheti Beej Producer Company Ltd, Wardha, Maharashtra. It has 35 members and is involved in producing and marketing soybean, wheat, chickpea, red gram, green gram and black gram seeds. In 2012/13, it produced about 50t of these seeds, and for 2013/14 the production plan was for 150t. Similarly, the six farmers' cooperatives in Andhra Pradesh are also involved in seed production and marketing.

Harvest, storage and treatment methods adopted by seed banks

For effective storage of seeds, locally available containers made with local materials (bamboo, earthen pots, gunny bags and iron boxes) are used.

Groundnut: Healthy pods are selected at the winnowing stage and stored in gunny bags treated with neem solution. Some farmers hang the gunny bags from the roof. At sowing time, this seed is treated with cow urine and ash.

Pulses (red, green and black gram): For seeds saved on farm, pods of healthy plants are selected before harvest. They are winnowed and then either treated with 1 per cent neem oil or mixed with ash and neem leaves. The treated seeds are stored in earthen pots covered with cow dung. Stored this way, the seeds remain viable and free of pests for a year.

Millets: Healthy seed heads are selected at harvest time, threshed manually and stored in gunny bags. If they become infested with pests, the seeds are sun dried between 11 am and 3 pm.

Cereals (maize/paddy): Maize farmers first identify healthy plants with a cob at the fifth node. These cobs are harvested separately and stored by hanging them from the roof at the entrance to the house. Seed for sowing is selected from the mid-portion of the cob.

Vegetables: To prevent cross-fertilization, farmers cover the flower with a paper bag. At maturity, the self-fertilized vegetables are harvested separately, seeds are separated from fruits that have been dried in the sun, ash is added and the seeds are stored in cotton bags.

Building links and networking

Individual community seed banks are mainly confined to a geographic area, based on local food needs, cropping patterns and specific agro-climatic conditions including soil types and rainfall. Most seed production is planned to meet local requirements. For example, groundnut seed produced in Anatapur district is intended mainly to fulfill local needs. However, some seeds might be shared with other network partners. Local NGOs, community biodiversity organizations and self-help groups facilitate such initiatives. The Centre for Sustainable Agriculture organizes state- and national-level seed fairs where all stakeholders are invited to share seeds and information. In a few cases, the National Bureau of Plant Genetic Resources and the state biodiversity board have links with seed banks.

In the states of Telengana, Andhra Pradesh and Maharashtra, about 70 seed banks have formed two networks with the support of the Centre for Sustainable Agriculture. Twenty seed banks have joined to form seed cooperatives. Two cooperatives own a mobile seed processing unit and have a marketing license. A network of seed banks is equipped with cold storage for germplasm. Various institutions have direct or indirect links with community seed banks to exchange knowledge and seeds.

Impact of seed banks

- Seed banks have increased crop diversity and access to seed by small and marginal farmers.
- Most small and marginal farmers are using their own seed or procuring it from a community seed bank.
- All farmers are cultivating a variety of crops: food, fibres, vegetables and oils seeds. They sow high-yielding varieties of local and traditional seeds. Hybrids (e.g. cotton) are used to some extent.
- Twenty-two traditional varieties of paddy, millets, sesame and brinjal are in use. Most millets grown by farmers are local types.
- In rainfed areas, such as Anantpur, which experience regular crop failures because of erratic rains, farmers are highly dependent on the seed banks for contingency crops.
- Networking of community seed banks has helped farmers learn from each other and exchange seeds.
- Documentation of characteristics and performance of plant varieties has helped farmers make better and more informed choices.

Challenges

A one-time investment and short-term involvement of farmers in community seed banks is not sufficient to conserve traditional varieties in the long term. Collection, regeneration, multiplication and distribution of seeds must be carried out continuously. Varieties must be improved and attention must be paid to rare endemic and endangered crop varieties that are more vulnerable than the common, widely used ones. Sociocultural changes and access to electronic media, coupled with the excitement created by the formal seed sector with its false promises, has resulted in a shift from food crops to commercial crops. Crop failure resulting from abiotic factors is also a challenge.

Support is needed from the public sector on several fronts to strengthen the seed banks:

- restructure the subsidy fund for direct farmer payment to encourage farmers to use their own seed;
- assist in revival of some of the traditional varieties whose use has been eroded over time;
- create a seed policy to favour locally valuable farmers' varieties;
- evaluate traditional seed and its suitability for various areas by generating data on its value for cultivation and use;
- government agencies can provide informal assistance in many ways, such as allowing seed producers timely access to certified seed and guiding farmers in multiplication processes;
- help small-scale entrepreneurs by establishing a legal framework for marketing truthfully labeled seed and quality declared seed;
- establish forward and backward links with government;
- make registration of farmers' varieties simple and accessible so that farmers can claim rights and benefits under the Plant Variety Protection and Farmers' Rights Act;
- educate farmers on reuse instead of focussing on seed replacement.

Moving forward

In ten years of working with community seed banks, we have learned that such banks are successful in tribal areas where subsistence farming is predominant and traditional varieties of food crops are grown. Although exchange and sharing is easier within community seed banks, when it comes to exchanges between seed banks, the issue of quality arises. In areas where commercial crops and monoculture are common, the utility of community seed banks is minimal. The Centre for Sustainable Agriculture tried to scale up the lessons from community seed banks and SGAs to deal with the seed crisis faced by farmers. However, two critical issues were quality assurance and financial support, either from the government in the form of subsidies or from markets in the form of profit margins. Both issues require more formal systems for planning, production, processing and quality management.

To strengthen the system, a discussion on creating an open-source seed network has been initiated to establish a new set of institutions and a legal framework that protects farmers' interests and ensures free and open access to the germplasm needed for crop improvement. Such a network would have to include:

- people engaged in conservation and revival of traditional varieties and their characterization who are willing to share with others;

- farmers and organizations who can develop value for cultivation and use data for existing traditional and improved varieties in various agro-climatic and growing conditions using participatory varietal selection;
- farmers and breeders engaged in selection and development of newer varieties using participatory plant breeding principles;
- farmers' institutions involved in production and marketing of seed to other farmers.

To implement such a model, there must be an independent organization that can bring together all the players, build confidence in each other, coordinate activities and act as a nodal agency. This agency can also bring together breeders and farmers and guide farmers on aspects of conservation, data generation, participatory breeding, registration and licensing as open source. Farmers could contribute their seeds to a common pool and obtain samples from it. This common pool of germplasm could also be used to exchange materials with others under material transfer agreements that have open-source clauses.

20 Malaysia

Exploring the utility of a community seed bank in Sarawak

Paul Bordoni and Toby Hodgkin

Background

The vast majority of the world's small farms (those less than 2ha) are located in Asia, where rice grown on hillsides (padi bukit) is an important staple. In particular, the livelihoods of indigenous Iban and Bidayuh farmers in Sarawak, Malaysia, are centred on hill padi. These farmers practise shifting cultivation, where forest is cleared to grow rice and later left fallow for many years to regain fertility. In recent years, increased allocation of arable land to cash crops, such as oil palm and pepper, has led communities to grow hill padi on steeper slopes at higher altitudes, where the land is more fragile and the climate more unpredictable. Population pressure and limitations on land procurement have led to a reduction in the fallow period, which reduces soil fertility and crop yields. These trends, which may be exacerbated by the effects of climate change, threaten the preservation of traditional agricultural biodiversity in these communities and the cultural identity that it embodies. Although, in many cases, the rice harvest does not meet family subsistence requirements, Iban and Bidayuh farmers continue to cultivate hill padi because of their strong cultural and religious connection with rice.

Historically, government and outreach agency approaches, which have aimed at increasing rice yields and replacing the shifting cultivation practice with more productive methods, have met with limited success. However, from 2010 to 2012, the Sarawak Institute of Agriculture Scientists, the Sarawak Department of Agriculture and the Platform for Agrobiodiversity Research worked together with indigenous communities in Sarawak to support the maintenance of agro-biodiversity and the adaption of their traditional farming systems to climate change. The objective of the project was to increase local diversity of crops and access to genetic resources by increasing awareness of the value of diversity in adapting to climate change. It also aimed to explore how community gene banks could respond to farmers' needs by promoting dialogue between farmers and research scientists at the participating institutes. The community participants were the inhabitants of the Bidayuh village of Gahat Mawang (Serian District) located 125km south of Kuching and Iban people living in the longhouses of Mujan, Murat, Mejong and Nanga Tebat in Skrang

(Sri Aman Division), 250km southeast of Kuching. The project involved 204 households.

Raising awareness of agricultural biodiversity

To increase awareness among community members about climate change and the value of agricultural biodiversity, several participatory methods were used:

- *Four-cell analysis*: In April 2010, farmers from Gahat and Skrang carried out an experiment to assess how crop biodiversity is managed in each community by measuring the extent and distribution of rice varieties. In this technique, farmers place slips of paper representing different varieties in one of four quadrants indicating how many households grow them (many or few) and over how large an area (large or small). Some crops, e.g. those grown in large quantities by many households, are considered stable, while others, those grown by few households in small quantities or over small areas, can be considered at risk, because if one family stops growing them or one disease or bad year wipes out the strain, the variety could disappear.
- *Crop catalogue*: A booklet in the local language and English describing and picturing the plants cultivated in Skrang is in preparation. It is based on information gathered in surveys and community discussions with Iban farmers. This document is intended to illustrate the rich diversity of crops the communities manage and to serve as a public awareness instrument.
- *Community biodiversity register*: A record is kept by community members of the local genetic resources, including information on the custodians, passport data, agro-ecology, cultural and use values. Farmers were introduced to this practice in February 2012. The biodiversity register allows careful documentation of crops planted and their performance from year to year. It helps the farmers recognize trends in crop yield in relation to variety, weather patterns, pests and other factors.
- *Participatory varietal selection workshop*: In January 2012, a farmer/plant breeder from Nepal gave a workshop on participatory varietal selection in Sarawak communities. Through this method, farmers learned to identify valued characteristics of traditional varieties and were very enthusiastic about trying it out (Plate 10).
- *Community seed fair*: In July 2010, a seed fair was held during the state-level Farmers, Fishermen and Breeders Day celebration at Betong. The fair encouraged lively discussion and the exchange of germplasm in and between communities.

Promoting dialogue

To address the second objective of promoting dialogue among farmers and scientists, a workshop was held at the rice gene bank in the Agriculture

Research Centre in Semongok in August 2010. This gene bank is a small, simple facility set up by the research centre's rice section under the Sarawak State Government to keep traditional seeds from being lost because of crop failure or when farmers switch to modern varieties. Conservation work began in 1963, when 305 accessions were collected; it continued over six Department of Agriculture explorations from 1991 to 1999 and now includes over 2,000 accessions of rice.

During the four-cell analysis conducted as part of the Platform for Agrobiodiversity Research project in Sarawak, an additional 95 varieties were identified, with priority given to traditional varieties identified as grown by few families over a small area. During the workshop, farmers provided about 100g of seeds of each variety to the gene bank managers. These samples were processed, cleaned, placed in glass jars sealed with wax and stored at a temperature of 16°C.

The workshop gave community members an opportunity to learn about conservation efforts undertaken by the government and fostered discussion about the potential roles that gene banks can play in meeting community needs. Farmers toured the facility and were shown how their seeds had been processed and stored. The farmers were fascinated by the simple air-conditioned storage facilities. Some remarked that, although they may not have money in the bank in Kuching, it was a consolation to know that they now owned something even more precious than money in the Agriculture Research Centre's rice gene bank.

Exploring the utility of a community seed bank

As a result of seeing the seed-storage facilities, many workshop participants expressed a desire for larger seed-storage facilities at the farm level to counter problems with weather. The success of hill padi cultivation depends on timing of the burning step in relation to the onset of the rainy season, and the farmers had experienced failed germination when the rains were late. Currently, they stored their seeds in containers made of natural material covered with plastic to protect them from moisture and pests. Workshop participants asked the Department of Agriculture to expand the gene bank facility to accommodate larger quantities of their seeds with the possibility of retrieving them for future cultivation. Alternatively, they suggested that the project set up a seed-storage facility in their villages. They suggested that many people would deposit their seeds in the bank, as many have experienced irretrievable loss of their heirloom varieties (see Box 20.1).

In response to the farmers' interest in better seed storage, focus group discussions were held in Gahat and Skrang in August 2012 to explore the potential for establishing a community-managed seed bank. Twelve community members attended these meetings; in Gahat, most participants were men. Farmers in Skrang welcomed the idea of a community seed bank, although their interest depended on the quality of the facility and the provision of a salary for its management. As in other aspects of the project, community members in Gahat were hesitant to engage in this activity at a community scale. A third of these farmers felt that such a facility was not required, as each family had its own varieties and ensured that they remained viable. However, another third were receptive to the idea because it could ensure that their children would one day have a chance to see their traditional varieties. One of these farmers suggested putting all their seeds in the gene bank facility at Semongok so as not to increase the workload of the farmers. In general, labour is an issue in these communities, as young people are leaving and those who remain have an increased workload.

Unfortunately, the modest gene bank at Semongok lacks the space to accommodate the needs of the communities. The potential for expanding the

---

Box 20.1 Provision of seeds for adaption to climate change

During the gene bank workshop, farmers expressed a desire to have access to rice varieties (particularly traditional varieties) that have better tolerance to pests and diseases, which they saw as major problems associated with climate change. The characteristics of rice most valued by the farmers were organoleptic and agronomic qualities, followed by postharvest features. There was also a request for high-yielding rice varieties that are able to grow well with minimal pesticide and fertilizer inputs. Gene banks may be able to provide varieties that will satisfy farmer demands.

During an earlier gene bank workshop, farmers were provided with seeds capable of growing in marginal, drought- and flood-prone environments, according to available records; the varieties were Buntal B, Serasan Puteh and Serendah Kuning. Several farmers who had grown these varieties were interviewed during the community discussion in January 2010 regarding their performance and reported that they ripened early but all three varieties were too short. According to one farmer, one variety was good but its panicles were too long. There were several reports of birds and monkeys eating the seeds. None of the three varieties performed well according to the farmers and, as such, they did not intend to plant them again. During the discussion, it was noted that some farmers had mixed the seed and planted it together with other varieties. The farmers had also rebranded the seed as 'padi Kuching' or named it after their own family.

This qualitative evaluation suggests that the seeds did not meet the expectations of the farmers. The passport data associated with the rice seeds at the seed bank lacked information on the environmental tolerances of the plants. Including more details on the environmental preferences of accessions in the gene bank would make it easier to select varieties more adapted to climate change.

facility to store more farmers' seeds as a 'hotel service' might be explored further. The cultural taboos related to padi seeds place constraints on seed exchange and sales. Although, in a way, this is a form of protection of farmers' rights over local varieties, it does not create the conditions needed for an effective and dynamic community seed bank.

Acknowledgements

This article was adapted from the technical report of the project 'Strengthening the maintenance and use of agro-biodiversity by indigenous and traditional agricultural communities adapting to climate change'. Special thanks to Gennifer Meldrum, Paul Quek, Dorothy Chandrabalan (Bioversity International), Teo Gien Kheng (Sarawak Institute of Agriculture Scientists/ Sarawak Department of Agriculture) and the farmers with whom we worked and who so generously shared their knowledge in an effort to build a stronger alliance between farmers and scientists.

21 Mali

An overview of community seed and gene banks

*Amadou Sidibe, Raymond S. Vodouhe
and Sognigbe N'Danikou*

Goals and progress

The first seed and gene banks in Mali were established in 1991 with the support of USC Canada, a nongovernmental organization (NGO) (Chapter 22); they were in the cercles (administrative units) of Douentza and Mopti. Later, seed banks were extended to the cercles of San, Tominian and Ségou thanks to the efforts of the Unité des Ressources Génétiques at the Institut d'Economie Rurale and its partners, Bioversity International, the Food and Agricultural Organization (FAO) and NGOs, such as the Fondation pour le Développement au Sahel and Aide au Sahel et à l'Enfance au Mali and donor support from the International Fund for Agricultural Development and the Global Environment Facility.

The seed and gene banks aim to contribute to food security through the conservation and sustainable use of plant genetic resources. Their specific objectives are to:

- safeguard local material threatened with extinction by consolidating local knowledge and community-level mechanisms for seed conservation, multiplication and distribution;
- improve knowledge of plant material and the traditional methods developed by village communities to conserve this material through its use;
- enable farmers in the target areas and others in similar climate conditions to obtain sufficient quantities of quality seeds that are adapted to their needs;
- address frequent losses of family seed supplies;
- decentralize seed production to the farmer level while reinforcing farmers' capacities in this domain;
- make up for the shortcomings of the formal seed system and end the purchase and use of poor-quality and 'fake' seeds;
- document farmers' knowledge about available genetic resources (agricultural and forest).

Through field interventions, seed and gene banks also enable the development of a favourable framework for the coordination of various actors in the formal and informal seed sectors.

The community bank concept has evolved over time. Diverse forms exist in different regions: banks initiated and managed by local communities, such as Diagani and Fodokan in the cercles San and Ségou, and banks set up by development projects for local communities, such as Pétaka and Basiari in Mopti. Community banks are often started by a small group of participants headed by a patriarch who initiates the activity. As people become aware of the benefits such banks provide, particularly the possibility of obtaining seeds after catastrophes and acute crises (prolonged drought, flooding, locust invasion, etc.), the number of members increases. Community gene banks are known for their contributions during crises, but they are not registered nor are they officially recognized by public authorities.

Functions and activities

Most of the banks play the dual role of conserving varietal strains (genes) and providing seeds for production. The conserved seeds come from various sources (producers, farmers' organizations, diversity fields and NGOs). Table 21.1 shows the species stored in the community banks and their provenances. At the beginning of the crop season, participating farmers receive a given quantity of seeds; once the harvest is complete, they return double that quantity to the bank. Banks are open to all farmers, both men and women. Women are more interested in market gardening and peanut and cowpea seeds. In some cases, they develop small seed conservation units that are often guarded by the

Table 21.1 Number of cultivars by species stored in the banks

Bank and supporting organization	No. of cultivars							
	Millet	Maize	Sorghum	Fonio	Rice	Peanut	Cowpea	Groundnut
Pétaka (USC Canada, Bioversity)	7★	4★	10†	—	33	2†	4†	7
Badiari (USC Canada)	7★	—	40	1★	6	—	13	1
Fodokan (FDS, ASEM)	7‡		12†	—	—	—	38 12†	16
Diagani (FDS, ASEM, Bioversity)	3★		12†	—	—	—	9	18
Marka (FDS, ASEM, Bioversity)	7‡ 10		3★ 15				12† 21	

Note: ASEM = Aide au Sahel et à l'Enfance au Mali, FDS = Fondation pour le Développement au Sahel.
★Varieties from Douentza.
†Varieties from the diversity fields.
‡Improved varieties from the diversity fields.

eldest women in their group. Certain farmers specifically ask to deposit their seeds at the bank, and then withdraw them at the beginning of the cold season.

The seeds of neglected and underused species are generally conserved in the form of genes for a period of one to five years depending on demand for their use, for both production by farmers and research by the National Research Institute, the University of Katibougou, Bioversity International and the FAO. The number of species in this category has grown considerably with the activities of NGOs and Bioversity. Innovative farmers, who are interested in domestication, collection, varietal creation and introduction of new varieties, also bring their discoveries to the banks.

Supervision and management

The management of a bank is under the supervision of the president of the farmers' group, which may be a farmers' association, a group of diversity field member farmers or a field school. The position is honorary and unpaid. At the bank managed by a diversity field in Pétaka, all information regarding the cultivars conserved and the inflow and outflow of material is recorded in a registry. Women work in the banks to make and clean storage containers. The women manage all of the tasks related to the conservation of market garden seeds and the seeds of other neglected species that are preferred by women.

Technical questions

The selection of varieties is carried out by the farmers themselves, based on their own criteria: resistance to drought, diseases and insects; productivity; and cooking and organoleptic qualities. The seeds of ancient varieties that have disappeared from a village are brought to the banks if they are discovered in other villages or at banks managed by research institutes or NGOs.

Seeds brought to the banks for storage are dried, cleaned and placed in an appropriate container (Plate 11). The task of cleaning and packaging most often falls to members of the farmers' groups. Information on bank activities is disseminated during member meetings and at seed fairs. NGOs and those involved in farm-based seed diversity conservation projects periodically organize capacity-building sessions for group members. Information received by farmers who are project participants is diffused to others through visits and village-level meetings. Important challenges include financing of the system and building the capacity of various actors.

Support, links and network management

The banks receive support from national research bodies, such as the Unité des Ressources Génétiques at the Institut d'Economie Rurale, NGOs and international research and development institutions in the form of capacity-building support and small equipment. Beyond this, despite tacit recognition of their important role in the conservation of local varieties and in facilitating farmers' access to seeds for production, the banks do not benefit from any financial or material support.

The banks are connected to farmers' organizations, which are the main facilitators. Currently, the banks are not linked through formal ties, i.e. there is no community bank network. Nonetheless, thanks to the Unité des Ressources Génétiques, certain banks have established collaborative relations with researchers and other banks. This has allowed for the medium–term conservation of the seeds of certain local banks in Unité des Ressources Génétiques' freezers. As a result of visits organized by farmers from Sikasso/ Siramana to Douentza, a bank is to be started in this village and local varieties were exchanged.

All laws and policies encourage local initiatives to maintain and conserve the diversity of plant genetic resources. They particularly support these banks, which constitute the only means for rural populations to access seed supplies following poor crop years. The rights of farmers are tacitly recognized, which justifies the country's ratification of the International Treaty on Plant Genetic Resources for Food and Agriculture.

Costs

The main costs of setting up and maintaining the banks are related to the construction of the premises and the equipment. Each member contributes his or her labour to erect walls and locate construction materials. Materials that must be purchased are paid for with funds generated by the joint activities of members in community fields (diversity fields, school fields, etc.) or donations from the more affluent members of the group or village or from NGOs and projects.

With regard to equipment, the storage containers and items needed for conservation are mainly made by members using local materials. Those acquired on the market are paid for by members' resources or donations. The banks can function without outside assistance because of their very low management costs. However, the establishment of a minimum bank user fee would facilitate payment for maintenance tasks by removing the need to wait for donations or for members to become available to provide their labour.

Accomplishments

The community banks have been highly effective in:

- conserving varieties of neglected and underused species;
- increasing genetic diversity at the village level by conserving and providing farmers a wider range of varieties, including some that have disappeared or those newly introduced from other areas or through research;

Box 21.1 Examples of community knowledge and practices

Women's local knowledge

The women of Doutza make a solution using diseased peanut plants to protect their fields from future attacks. When diseased plants appear in a peanut field, the women randomly remove one of these plants, bring it back to the village and mix it with potash and water in a traditional terracotta pot. The mixture is brought to a boil and then cooled. It is then taken back to the field and poured on the ground as a remedy to stop the disease from invading the whole field.

Men's local knowledge

When grasshoppers attack, the men of Dansa do the following: The person in charge of the task gets up without speaking, eating or drinking to collect some grasshoppers in various fields which he then brings to the shaman (féticheur). The shaman boils the grasshoppers in a clay pot with some tree bark and his 'secret' ingredient. Once cooled, the mixture is poured on the ground. Following this treatment, birds fly in from elsewhere to eat the grasshoppers.

- conserving and valorizing local knowledge related to the production and conservation of seeds of various species;
- capacity building among various actors in seed production and conservation;
- reinforcing cohesion between group members seeking solutions to shared problems.

The community banks are organized and managed on the basis of indigenous knowledge. Some of these local knowledge-based practices prove to be highly effective and inexpensive for farmers. These practices work equally well on field crops and on conserved seeds. Certain practices are specific to women and others to men (see Box 21.1).

Policy and legal environment and sustainability

Policy, laws and formal and informal institutions do not have a direct influence on the banks. The banks operate following traditional standards and rules, however, without traditional authorities exercising any particular control over their mode of operation. The banks do not receive any support from these authorities.

The sustainability of community banks will depend on the recognition and support they receive from local and national decision-makers. This recognition and support could be translated into laws recognizing the production and sale of seeds of local cultivars that are favoured by farmers. The sustainability of banks also will depend on reinforcing the cohesion of their founding members with a view to ensuring a commitment to the smooth functioning of the banks that goes beyond the investment of their labour. This commitment could evolve towards cash payments for bank services. Progressive payment for the time that members spend on daily bank infrastructure maintenance should also be considered. The community banks could be part of national, regional and international networks if they can reach a joint agreement on how material should be exchanged at different levels.

22 Mali

The USC Canada-supported gene and seed banks of the Mopti region

Abdrahamane Goïta, Hamadoun Bore,
Mariam Sy Ouologueme and Ada Hamadoun Dicko

Background and evolution

Mopti is a Sahelian region where food insecurity is a chronic problem for many reasons: the failure to value small farmers' knowledge, the impact of climate change, the degradation of farm lands and insufficient and irregular rainfall. Although these challenges are faced throughout Mali, the situation is more acute in regions such as Mopti, and small farmers there are under intense pressure to ensure that their seed – and, consequently, food – is secure. Agricultural production is under threat, primarily from drought, soil degradation and insect invasions. In Douentza, one of the eight cercles (administrative units) in Mali, agriculture and livestock breeding constitute the main economic activities of the local population of approximately 248,000 people.

USC Canada's Seeds of Survival (SoS) programme (Chapter 37) has been working with farming communities in the region since 1993 to reinforce the resilience of small farmers, both male and female, in their fight against food insecurity and to improve their livelihoods. SoS emphasizes the protection and renewal of local seeds and the value of farmers' knowledge through farmer-to-farmer exchanges. It is working with farmers in two cercles in the Mopti region – Douenza and Mopti – to set up community gene and seed banks, in addition to other activities to restore soils, mitigate climate change effects and improve incomes (Plate 12).

Eight community gene and seed banks have been established: six in Douentza cercle and two in Mopti cercle (Table 22.1). The SoS programme works with farming communities to carry out these community-based genetic resource conservation initiatives, with the technical and financial support of USC Canada, which is funded by the Canadian International Development Agency and other donors. To enable this approach, based on small farmer knowledge, to develop and respond to the needs of the local people, the first step was to establish each bank as a cooperative society, so that they could be legally recognized by the government of Mali and benefit from the various advantages attached to such recognition.

Table 22.1 Community gene and seed banks in Mopti region established through USC Canada's Seeds of Survival programme

Bank location	Cercle	Year established
Badiari	Douentza	1995/96
Doumbara	Douentza	2002/03
Pétaka	Douentza	2002/03
Gono	Douentza	2007/08
Koubewel	Douentza	2007/08
Dianwely	Douentza	2008/09
Ouomion	Mopti	2002/03
Pathia	Mopti	2012/13

Functions

The community gene and seed banks were organized out of a growing awareness among farming communities of the need to preserve their genetic heritage, which was threatened with extinction by climate change effects and insufficient and irregular rainfall. The first banks were established to respond to the risk of diminishing diversity of local agricultural seeds, the source of all seed production. The banks that have been established more recently, 2007–2013, were a response to threats related to genetically modified and hybrid seeds.

All of the banks play the same roles. Each is composed of both a gene bank and a seed bank, which together fulfill the six functions listed below.

Functions of the gene banks

• Conserve the diversity of agricultural seeds produced by small farmers, both men and women.
• Conserve traditional tools and products for the sustainable conservation of agricultural seeds.
• Transmit farmers' knowledge regarding the sustainable conservation of agricultural seeds through continuous learning.

Functions of the seed banks

• Conserve the seeds of farmers who do not have appropriate storage facilities.
• Supply seeds to farmers who face seed shortages during the sowing period (in the form of loans or sales at a reasonable price).
• Improve members' living conditions through loans in the form of credit.

Operations and management

The community gene and seed bank of Doumbara, the second oldest bank in the area, was launched as a cooperative society on 15 December 2003 under the name Faso Yiriwa, which means community development. It began with 40 founding members from 15 villages of the commune of Dangol-Boré, but because of the distance of some villages from the bank (over 30km), some of the initial members withdrew. However, the number of actively involved participants has increased, reaching 64 by 31 July 2013. The bank conserves 13 varieties of four species: three of millet, three of rice, four of cowpea and three of sorghum. In addition to biological material, each bank also keeps equipment, such as a scale, a spring balance and a 50m measuring tape, and management tools, such as a stock register, a sales ledger, a loan recovery accounts book, a payments ledger, a members' list, meeting minutes and a community biodiversity register.

Faso Yiriwa is currently supplied by 18 seed producers (men) and two women's groups, composed of ten and 36 women, from seven participating villages. They multiply the seeds in their villages and then deposit a certain quantity in the bank to be sold. To become financially self-sufficient, the bank retains 20 per cent of the total revenue earned from the sale of seeds.

The operating rules of cooperative societies must be made public: each member pays annual dues of 1,200 Central African Francs (CFA; or US$2.46) and a membership fee of CFA 2,000 (about US$4). A general assembly is convened at least once a year. During the annual meeting, the sale prices of seeds are decided in the presence of the seed multipliers. The seeds are brought to the bank after harvest, and each producer covers the cost of that transfer. Revenues from the sale of seeds, dues and membership fees are loaned to members of the cooperative society at an annual interest rate of 10 per cent. As of 31 December 2012, the net income of individual banks was between CFA 25,000 and CFA 252,970 (about US$50–518). The various banks' supply procedures vary from one location to another according to the customs and economic means of their members. For certain banks, such as the one in Doumbara, the members multiply the seeds in their villages and deposit a portion in the bank to be sold. The bank retains 20 per cent of the revenues generated from the sale of seeds. Other banks sell or lend a certain amount of seed to farmers who, after the harvest, return double the amount initially received to the bank. This is one means of facilitating access to seeds by the most vulnerable people.

Although many issues remain to be resolved, both women and men use material from the banks. No farmer, male or female, is excluded; however, priority is given to bank members. The use of the material by women and men is shaped by local customs. Women are interested in minor and market garden crops, such as sesame, cowpea, chili, shallots, tomatoes, etc., whereas men grow major crops, such as millet, sorghum, rice, manioc, etc. Women often grow species that are used as ingredients in sauces and other products, which allows them to maintain a small business and earn income to cover family expenses.

Management of each bank is based on the internal regulations of the cooperative society, which are applied by a general assembly, a board of directors and an oversight committee. The general assembly is the decision-making body and meets at least once a year with additional meetings on special occasions. The board of directors is in charge of implementing the decisions made by the general assembly, while the oversight committee ensures that the decisions are carried out correctly.

The knowledge and skills of the members are reinforced through field schools (where seeds are multiplied for the banks), exchange meetings, seed fairs, exchange visits and various training sessions on valuing and sustainably managing agricultural biodiversity. The banks work in cooperation with other similar local and regional initiatives through gene and seed bank networks, as well as with USC Canada's SoS programme. This programme works in partnership with other organizations from the subregion such as Biodiversité Échanges et Diffusion d'Expériences, Coordination Nationale des Organisations Paysannes du Mali, Coalition pour la Protection du Patrimoine Génétique Africain and the climate change network of Mali.

In Douentza cercle, village management, monitoring and activity assessment committees exist in all of the villages covered by the SoS programme and are in charge of coordinating all programme activities. With regard to the banks, the committees mobilize villages to manage seed multiplication fields destined to supply community gene and seed banks. They also are responsible for informing and raising the awareness of the population with regard to the evolution of the banks, on one hand, and, on the other, monitoring and applying decisions made by villages regarding the maintenance and development of seed conservation and supply infrastructure. They also serve as the interface between the communities and partners.

Network members, who are also members of the village management, monitoring and activity assessment committees, are specifically charged with addressing all issues concerning the community gene and seed banks: their functioning, difficulties encountered, corrective measures and contacts with different banks at the local, regional and subregional levels. This work is facilitated by the SoS programme through the village committees' coordinating body, which is the supreme authority at the cercle level.

This coordinating body is composed of network members and representatives of the village management, monitoring and activity assessment committees. It is responsible for developing partnerships between farmer collectives and partners (administration, technical services, elected officials, projects, programmes, nongovernmental organizations). It also oversees the development of strategies to mobilize the resources needed to plan, implement and monitor activities to guarantee the empowerment of various groups.

Since the 2012 rebellion in northern Mali, which led to the departure of the SoS programme and its development partners from Douentza, various farmers' organizations have assumed the task of implementing and monitoring activities. They have taken on the role of interface between the programme and the population through the implementation, monitoring and reporting of activities carried out by the programme and other displaced partners. This situation has allowed farming communities, who have nothing to gain from the conflict, to continue to benefit from the programme's support, consolidate gains and carry on with planned activities.

Networking

Currently, the strength of the eight community banks lies in the network that works in partnership with other community banks in southern Mali, where rainfall is higher than in Douentza and Mopti. This partnership allows them to carry out certain key activities to valorize and save farmer seeds, notably organizing seed fairs, multiplying seeds unsuited to the prevailing climate in other areas with a more favourable climate and exchanging seeds and advice to improve the productivity of different varieties. In terms of outputs, the most notable are the following:

- Farmers, both male and female, have appropriated this approach, which focusses on their knowledge, with regard to valuing and conserving agricultural biodiversity.
- Varieties that were not cultivated because of climate constraints are now produced in other locations where the climate is more favourable.
- Crops are more diverse because of the exchange of seeds and ideas among farmers during seed fairs, visits and exchange workshops.
- Farmers' knowledge is now preserved for future generations.
- Everyone, regardless of his or her position in society, has the right to access seeds to grow and feed their families and to contribute to the fight against food insecurity.

As of 31 December 2013, 178 farmers (100 men and 78 women) have been direct beneficiaries of these banks. Several challenges remain: consolidating self-sufficiency (now underway), setting up a sustainable strategy to boost the numbers of young girls and boys involved in bank activities and improving the literacy level of bank managers to ensure the appropriate use of management tools and the shared governance of bank activities.

23 Mexico

Community seed banks in Oaxaca

Flavio Aragón-Cuevas

Purpose and evolution

In the state of Oaxaca, Mexico, ten community seed banks have been in operation since 2005. The Sistema Nacional de Recursos Fitogenéticos para la Alimentación y la Agricultura provided funding for the first five (see Chapter 42), which were built by the Instituto Nacional de Investigaciones Forestales, Agrícolas y Pecuarias. The other five were constructed later with support from producer organizations and the Food and Agriculture Organization (FAO) of the United Nations. The main objective of these seed banks is in-situ conservation of the plant genetic diversity present in small farm plots (or milpas) as a strategy to address climate change and improve maize, bean and squash crops and general productivity at the farm level. On average, each bank includes 40 producers, for a total of 400 farmers participating in conservation and breeding of native seed.

Functions and activities

The seed banks have several functions: conserving plant diversity; promoting seed exchange among both member and non-member farmers; participating in local, state and national seed fairs; selecting seed in farmers' fields; participating as assistants and instructors in training courses; and reproducing seed of endangered or threatened species. Because crop diversity is high in Oaxaca, the community seed banks house a broad range of species and races (Table 23.1).

Most seeds in the collections are native species; others, such as Teocintle (*Zea mays* ssp. *parviglumis*) and some beans (*P. vulgaris* and *P. coccineus*) are wild species. The amount of seed stored depends on the amount provided by producers. A portion of each type of seed is kept in a place chosen by members of the bank to store all varieties of maize, beans, squash and other crops. A larger portion is stored in farmers' homes. Each seed bank member is required to store seeds of the varieties he or she grows in amounts equivalent to those planted. However, if risk of loss is high (for example, where frost, hailstones, hurricanes or drought are likely), the amount of seed stored is two or three times the amount planted. The effects of a natural disaster can thus be immediately mitigated.

Table 23.1 Species and races conserved in community seed banks in Oaxaca, Mexico

Location	Maize races	Bean species	Squash species
San Pedro Comitancillo	Zapalote chico	*Vigna* sp.	*Cucurbita argyrosperma C. moschata*
San Miguel del Puerto	Olotillo Tepecintle Tuxpeño Zapalote chico	*Phaseolus vulgaris*	*C. argyrosperma C. moschata*
San Marcos Zacatepec	Conejo Olotillo Tuxpeño	*P. vulgaris*	*C. argyrosperma C. moschata*
Santiago Yaitepec	Comiteco Mushito	*P. coccineus P. dumosus P. vulgaris*	*C. ficifolia C. moschata C. pepo*
San Cristóbal Honduras	Conejo Olotillo Pepitilla Tepecintle Tuxpeño	*P. vulgaris Vigna* sp.	*C. ficifolia C. moschata C. pepo*
San Agustín Amatengo	Bolita Pepitilla	*P. vulgaris Vigna* sp.	*C. argyrosperma C. moschata C. pepo*
Santa María Jaltianguis	Bolita Cónico Elotes occidentales Nal-Tel de altura Olotón	*P. coccineus P. dumosus P. vulgaris*	*C. ficifolia C. pepo*
Santa María Peñoles	Bolita Chalqueño Cónico Elotes cónicos Olotón Serrano Tepecintle Tuxpeño	*P. coccineus P. dumosus P. vulgaris*	*C. ficifolia C. pepo*
San Andrés Cabecera Nueva	Chalqueño Conejo Cónico Elotes cónicos Olotillo Tuxpeño	*P. vulgaris P. coccineus P. dumosus Vigna* sp.	*C. argyrosperma C. moschata C. ficifolia*
Putla de Guerrero	Conejo Olotillo Tuxpeño	*P. vulgaris Vigna* sp.	*C. moschata*

Because most of the producers involved in the seed banks plant less than 3ha, they store 20–60kg of maize seeds, 20–40kg of bean seeds and 1–2kg of squash seeds. Only 3kg of maize seeds, 2kg of bean seeds and 500g of squash seeds are stored in the community banks. When seeds are borrowed, the recipient farmer agrees to return twice the amount of the same material to the seed bank; the seed has to be selected in the field, then cleaned and dried for storage. Stored seeds are available to all bank members and farmers in the community and in neighbouring communities; however, only the bank's managers decide whether seed is to be sold or loaned to farmers who are not members.

Training in various areas is provided periodically as part of the bank's strategy for conserving and improving native seed. Emphasis is placed on seed conservation methods (in silos, barrels or hermetic plastic containers) and on mass seed selection (Plate 13). Each producer is responsible for selecting the best plants in the field. Selection starts from the onset of flowering and ends during harvesting when the best plants are tagged. Material from some of the community banks is used in participatory plant breeding. Maize races are also being characterized by morphologic traits and industrial quality.

Governance and management

Producers select a president, secretary and treasurer to manage each community seed bank. The duties of these officials include seed exchange and renewal, guaranteeing conservation of seed stocks, convening meetings and acting as liaison with the institution leading the project. A board of directors is elected for one to three years, depending on what is decided at the stakeholders' assembly.

Participation of women in seed bank activities in Oaxaca is very important. Women are involved in seed selection, conservation, exchange and use. Many are members of the boards and participate more actively than men in training courses and seed fairs, and in preparing traditional dishes.

Producers are given hermetic metal silos or barrels (with a storage capacity of 200kg) in which to store seed for planting and for stock. Farmers who participate in fairs receive diplomas and win prizes for high-quality seed, diversity or products they prepare.

Each accession stored in the seed bank has a passport containing data provided by farmers. This includes: characteristics of plant and fruit, areas to which the plant is adapted, recommended planting dates, traditional uses and agronomic advantages.

Technical aspects and assistance

Each year, farmers renew the seed stored in their homes to maintain viability of seeds in the community banks. In contrast, seed stored in tropical zones is renewed every other year and seed in banks in subtropical and temperate zones is renewed only every third year. Seed selection is carried out in the central part of each field to avoid contamination with varieties of neighbouring farmers. Once harvested, seeds are threshed and dried to 10 per cent humidity; they are then cleaned – to eliminate impurities, seed of different species and seed attacked by pests or diseases – and then stored in various sized hermetic barrels.

Financial resources are insufficient to carry out some necessary activities, such as morphologic characterization, ethnobotanical studies, artisanal seed production, regular training for producers and providing incentives to producers to encourage them to plant, select and conserve native seeds. One of the challenges faced by the community seed banks is sustainability, once government support is no longer available. To overcome this problem, as of 2013, community seed banks are being constituted as private limited rural production companies. This legal status gives farmers access to resources from the municipal, state or federal governments. Farmers have also been trained to continue conserving and selecting seeds on their own without external financial support. Several nongovernmental organizations (NGOs) participate actively in some of the banks in Oaxaca.

Achievements and sustainability

The community seed banks in Oaxaca have sensitized public opinion to the importance of conserving local species. Some seed banks have won prizes for diversity and quality of varieties and products at state seed fairs. Some have increased diversity by exchanging seed within the community and with producers from other seed banks. Several wild species of beans and maize have been rescued, for example, Teocintle. Seed is available throughout the year, but seed exchange takes place mainly just before planting during the rainy season. The community seed banks store materials with valuable traits in terms of tolerance to wind, drought, pests and diseases. Some native varieties have excellent nutritional quality and are well suited to both traditional and industrial uses.

Seed banks can operate independently once they are well established, if producers are conscious of the importance of their seeds, when conservation proves to be of benefit and when the banks are formed as legal entities. They must mobilize their own resources or find external funding to carry out their activities. Cooperatives should be established to organize consolidated sales of products produced by bank members. The Mexican government should establish a public policy to support the in-situ conservation of genetic diversity in community seed banks. This strategy can mitigate climate change and reduce threats posed by transgenic materials. Genetic resources legislation is also necessary to protect farmers' biocultural resources. Community seed banks in Oaxaca should be part of a national strategy for in-situ conservation of Mexico's plant genetic resources. Creation of other banks should be encouraged in areas close to indigenous and mestizo groups who are maintaining high levels of genetic diversity or threatened or endangered species.

24 Nepal
The historical Dalchowki community seed bank

Bharat Bhandari, Surya Thapa,
Krishna Sanjel and Pratap Shrestha

Purpose, activities and management

Established in 1994, Dalchowki is the site of Nepal's first community seed bank. Dalchowki village is about 25km south of Lalitpur district headquarters. Although not far from the country's capital, southern Lalitpur represents one of the most remote areas in terms of access to basic facilities and public services. The Dalchowki community seed bank was established through the Integrated Community Development Program (ICDP) implemented by USC Canada. Farmers in the area were growing several local varieties of cereals, pulses, oilseeds and vegetables. USC Canada, which was working with these communities, observed that some of the local crop varieties were in danger of disappearing because of the gradual introduction of improved and hybrid seeds along with chemical fertilizers and pesticides. The movement of farmers into nearby cities and generally poor seed management practices were contributing to the problem. ICDP decided to pilot a community seed bank in Dalchowki village district to address this issue by promoting seed security and the conservation of crop genetic resources. The main function of the seed bank was to collect, enhance and multiply seeds of local varieties. ICDP chose the community seed bank approach, as it was seen to be effective in terms of sensitizing, empowering and mobilizing communities and in promoting the use of local seeds and crop varieties.

The seed bank has been identifying custodian farmers in and around Dalchowki and mobilizing them to grow and conserve local varieties, particularly of broad-leafed mustard (rayo), radishes, small peas, faba beans and a perennial variety of local cauliflower. It has collected and conserved seeds of 17 varieties of seven cereals, 12 varieties of six legumes, six varieties of three oilseed crops and 22 varieties of 14 vegetables. In 2012, 70 farmers (37 women and 33 men) deposited seeds in the bank, and 21 farmers (14 women and seven men) 'borrowed' 1.1t of seeds to grow on their land. In addition, the seed bank has collected local varieties of finger millet to assess their diversity, and it has multiplied seeds with support from the 'Local initiatives for food security transformation' project implemented in the area by a nongovernmental organization (NGO) called Group of Helping Hands

(SAHAS) Nepal. The seed bank has also started to collect, evaluate and characterize rare and unique crop varieties with technical support from SAHAS Nepal, the national gene bank and USC Canada.

In addition to seed conservation, the Dalchowki community seed bank also produces and sells seeds of local crops, such as maize, rapeseed and some vegetables to meet local demand. It receives technical support from SAHAS Nepal and the District Agriculture Development Office in acquiring seed and maintaining its quality. The seed bank has established a revolving fund of US$2,050, part of which is used to provide small loans to its members and purchase seeds from group members. The seed bank has a mandate to buy seeds of rare crop varieties and store them for a year.

The Dalchowki Community Development Committee, made up of villagers and registered as a community-based organization, has overall responsibility for managing the seed bank. An 11-member executive committee elected by the general committee provides governance and management of the seed bank on a voluntary basis. Currently, 48 farming households are affiliated with the seed bank, and take part in organizing various activities. Seeds are distributed to members on the condition that they return twice the amount borrowed. The seed bank sells a small amount of seeds to outsiders at the current market price. The seed bank tries to maintain records of transactions with farmers, crops and varieties; prices are set by the executive committee. Income from the sale of seeds is not sufficient to cover the full cost of running the seed bank, but it helps with basic operational expenses.

During the past 19 years, the seed bank has had ups and downs. Although standards and rules were developed to increase community participation in management, implementation has not been effective because of limited technical and managerial capacities. Political unrest in the country has also greatly affected members' efforts to further develop and effectively manage the seed bank. In 2006, when armed conflict was resolved, the Dalchowki Community Development Committee re-established the executive committee and renewed its activities, including reviving the seed bank, with great enthusiasm. In 2009, an independent review of the community seed bank, carried out with support from USC Canada, recommended ways to strengthen management and operations. The report suggested ensuring a more dynamic and inclusive leadership and improving relations with other community groups, cooperatives, local government and other stakeholders.

Community seed bank members who are responsible for seed production are also responsible for selection and cleaning. The Dalchowki Community Development Committee organizes monitoring visits to ensure high-quality seed production. A community biodiversity register, documenting the traits, associated local knowledge and uses of all food crops, is maintained. It has been difficult to keep proper records of all seed transactions because of a lack of human resources. As the executive committee members are volunteers, they are unable to spend enough time keeping and updating records. To strengthen its functions and reach more farmers, the committee must develop workable guidelines to mobilize group and cooperative members to conserve rare crop seeds, maintain seed quality and manage information properly.

Support, networking and the policy environment

The Dalchowki community seed bank has received long-term support from USC Canada to develop its basic facilities and strengthen its capacity. Funds made available through the ICDP were used to purchase 1,000m² of land and construct two buildings: a community centre for holding meetings and training sessions, and the seed bank. The seed bank is a two-story concrete building with storage capacity for 28t of seed, four offices and kitchen facilities. USC Canada funding was also used to set up the US$2,050 revolving fund, which is used for management and operations, particularly for collection and distribution of local crop seeds, as well as to provide small loans to its members. The ICDP also supported the purchase of a hygrometer, thermometers and other materials necessary for seed storage and management. The ICDP's strategy was to make the seed bank sustainable through technical, financial and institutional empowerment. After the period of political unrest, the seed bank initiated collaborative arrangements with relevant NGOs, such as SAHAS Nepal and government agencies, such as the Lalitpur District Agriculture Development Office and the national gene bank operating under the Nepal Agriculture Research Council.

The Lalitpur District Agriculture Development Office has provided support for training farmers associated with the seed bank. In 2012, the seed bank established a partnership with the national gene bank and received technical and material support for the collection, documentation and conservation of seeds of rare and unique crops found in the area. The national gene bank also provided support for the establishment of a field gene bank for perennial crops. Despite all this assistance, there is still a need for better community support and mobilization of local resources to sustain and increase seed bank functions.

The seed bank collaborates with a local organic farmers' cooperative to market surplus seeds. It shares office space with the cooperative and is mobilizing financial resources for its members. The seed bank is also a member of the recently formed National Network of Community Seed Banks of Nepal.

The national policy environment has become more favourable for community seed banks. The Department of Agriculture has mainstreamed the banks in its plans and programmes as a strategy to increase access to high-quality seeds and conserve local crops. The recently amended National Seed Act and regulation has relaxed its provisions to allow registration of local crop varieties. The Dalchowki seed bank is currently preparing to register a local variety of broad-leafed mustard called Guzmuzze (Plate 14). The local government, particularly the Village District Committee and other formal and informal institutions, are taking a positive view towards helping the seed bank strengthen and expand its activities for the benefit of the larger farming community.

Achievements and prospects

The communities of Dalchowki, Sankhu and Chaughare have benefitted in many ways from the Dalchowki community seed bank. It has helped increase awareness about the value of, and the need to conserve, their local seeds and has taught them new ways to produce and manage healthy seeds. It has also encouraged farmers to use local crops and resources that reduce the need for external chemical inputs. The number of households saving their own farm seeds has increased significantly since the Dalchowki seed bank was established. However, there is still a need for a systematic assessment of the level of contribution of the seed bank in terms of promoting crop diversity and seed security.

Seed bank activities have been helpful in organizing farmers and promoting sustainable agriculture in the area. These farmers have adopted and continue to practice ecological farming. Recent activities of the Dalchowki seed bank, such as seed production and fund mobilization, are direct incentives for members and have led to improved access to quality seeds and credit. In 2012, the seed bank collected and distributed more than 6t of seeds of which 1t was of local crop varieties. Since the seed bank was established, there has been an increase in the diversity of crops, such as maize, millet, bean, rapeseed, soybean and pea. Women farmers play an important role in the seed bank; they have received training in seed selection, crop breeding and using diversity to adapt to stressful environments. About 60 per cent of women are engaged in seed production and selling, and this has contributed to their empowerment in the community.

Based on advice from support agencies and reflections on the past, the Dalchowki seed bank has developed a plan to operate as a resource centre, offering diversified services, such as training and workshops, and links with agro-ecotourism to help sustain its functions. The seed bank is benefitting from some financial support from the Dalchowki Village District Committee for maintenance of its physical resources. It also rents office space to a local cooperative and to SAHAS Nepal to generate some income. Since 2012, the seed bank has been producing seeds of maize, bean and rapeseed for sale and realizes a small profit margin of about 10 per cent. These revenue resources all together cover maintenance costs. To operate more successfully, the seed bank is still seeking additional support from SAHAS Nepal, USC Canada, the national gene bank, the District Agriculture Development Office and similar development organizations.

25 Nepal

The community seed bank in Tamaphok

Dilli Jimi, Manisha Jimi and Pitambar Shrestha

Purpose and evolution

Located in the eastern hills of Nepal, Tamaphok is one of the sites of a Local Initiatives for Biodiversity, Research and Development (LI-BIRD) project called 'Promoting innovative mechanisms for implementing farmers' rights through fair access to genetic resources and benefit sharing regime in Nepal'. Tamaphok is a geographic area governed by a village development committee, a political administrative unit in Nepal that is further divided into nine wards. A ward contains one or more small villages. The community seed bank was set up as a regional centre for seed conservation and sustainable use of agricultural biodiversity. It also served as a pilot project for implementing farmers' rights and an effective access and benefit-sharing mechanism for the use of genetic resources. From 2007 to 2011, various research, development and capacity-building activities were carried out, such as testing community-based biodiversity management practices, and a community seed bank was established at Mudhe, where a weekly market is held.

Tamaphok is also the name of a small village in the district, located several hours' walking distance from Mudhe over steep mountains. Despite the good intentions of the seed bank project leaders, residents of Tamaphok village found it difficult to deposit and collect seeds and take part in other seed bank activities. To address this situation, in 2010 a number of Tamaphok farmers, who were dedicated to maintaining crop diversity, decided to establish a separate community seed bank in the village. This case study describes that experience.

Awareness-raising activities, such as biodiversity fairs, field visits, village-level workshops, training and interactions facilitated by LI-BIRD helped the Tamaphok group members recognize the value of agricultural biodiversity for current and future seed and food security. As a group, they agreed to identify and document local varieties, associated information and traditional knowledge; to collect and multiply local seed varieties and planting materials and make them available to local communities; and to protect local varieties and preserve the associated traditional knowledge.

Functions and activities

The Tamaphok community seed bank performs multiple functions. Members regularly go on exploratory trips to identify and collect seeds of local varieties of cereals, vegetables and some medicinal plants. During these trips, they also keep their eyes open for new crops and varieties. The community seed bank maintains more than 100 local varieties: rice (16), maize (seven), finger millet (seven), wheat (one), barley (three), buckwheat (two), rapeseed and niger (three), cowpea (three), bean (three), pumpkin (five), cucumber (two), tree tomato (two), chili (six), brinjal or eggplant (two), pea (two), soybean (four), rice bean (four), black gram (three), sesame (two), leafy vegetables (four), spices (six), yam (two) and other vegetables (12).

Seeds are stored and farmers have access to them. Members of the seed bank distribute, grow and collect seeds of all crops and varieties in the seed bank annually. During distribution, the first priority is given to the general members who may choose seeds of their preference. If a member borrows 1kg of seed, he or she must repay 1.5kg. The executive members of the seed bank are responsible for regenerating seeds of the varieties not chosen by general members. Diversity blocks of major crops, such as rice and finger millet, are maintained each year and some vegetables and medicinal plants are grown at the periphery of the community seed bank's land.

Based on lessons learned from LI-BIRD's activities elsewhere in Nepal (see Chapter 34 for details), the seed bank has set up a community biodiversity management fund to generate income as an incentive for conservation. For example, the fund helps members undertake such income-generating activities as raising pigs and goats.

The community seed bank is part of the Biodiversity Conservation and Development Committee (BCDC), a village development committee-level farmers' organization that oversees biodiversity-related activities as part of an overall rural development strategy. The Tamaphok community seed bank receives about 20,000 Nepalese rupees (NPR; about US$200) annually from the BCDC for the village-level biodiversity fund. In practice, this support has been an effective incentive mechanism for members who take part in regenerating seeds stored in the community seed bank. Members are also involved in collecting monthly savings, generating revenues by growing vegetables on rented land and selling vegetable seedlings.

Awareness-raising activities include the establishment and management of diversity blocks of various crops. Finally, the seed bank's core team maintains records of local crop diversity and traditional knowledge in a community biodiversity register (Plate 15).

Governance and management

The Tamaphok community seed bank is managed by an executive committee made up of nine members (six women and three men). The executive committee has overall responsibility for seed collection, storage, cleaning, drying, distribution and regeneration of the seeds in the community seed bank. The bank has 92 members (from 76 of the 140 households in the village) organized into five groups including two women's groups. Initially, the executive committee was led by a man, but, in 2012, the leadership role was handed over to a woman to acknowledge the key role women play in the seed bank. In Tamaphok village, most residents are from the Yakkha ethnic group, which might contribute to the strong sense of unity and cooperation among them and their effective implementation of collective activities.

External support

Although the financial and material support provided by LI-BIRD was small, the knowledge it provided to the seed bank members was more important. So far, the Tamaphok community seed bank has received NPR 50,000 (about US$500) from LI-BIRD to build a temporary seed-storage structure. In addition, the District Agriculture Development Office, an extension agency, has provided 300 plastic jars of different sizes for storing seeds. Compared with the support provided to other community seed banks in Nepal and elsewhere, this is very modest. However, because the community is strong and cohesive, it has been able to establish and operate the community seed bank with this limited outside support.

In terms of knowledge gained by the community, a series of interrelated activities was organized by the Tamaphok Village Development Committee. A diversity fair, the community biodiversity register, setting up the diversity block, exposure visits, on-site and off-site training and informal interactions among farmers have all been instrumental in emphasizing the value of managing agricultural biodiversity among the seed bank members.

Benefits of the community seed bank

Although the Tamaphok community seed bank has only been operating for a short time and its 'to do' list is long, its members have already observed some benefits of having the seed bank in the community. Other than collecting and saving seeds from their own crops and trading with close neighbours, Tamaphok farmers previously had no other options for obtaining seeds and planting material. The community seed bank has decreased both social and physical distances, while greatly enhancing the knowledge associated with the seeds farmers are now using (i.e. source and quality). For example, the seed bank has recovered a traditional early-maturing, white-grained finger millet variety, Seta kodo. It has also introduced a new rice variety, Pathibhara, which is becoming very popular among the farmers because of its milling properties and palatability and the fact that it does well even when planted later than normal.

The community-based biodiversity management fund has created an incentive for members. They no longer have to go to a distant commercial bank for a small loan. Some members have increased their income by raising pigs obtained using funds from the community-based biodiversity management fund and from the monthly savings plan.

In addition, seed bank members have participated in training sessions, visits and workshops, taking advantage of these new opportunities to learn and share knowledge and ideas. This has led to greater curiosity about seeds and a change in the farmers' customary practice of keeping traditional knowledge 'secret', particularly that related to medicinal plants. The more open attitude is a welcome change and allows the farmers to make better use of their local genetic resources.

Looking ahead

The Tamaphok community seed bank believes in the saying 'small is beautiful'. It does not have ambitious plans that require large amounts of resources and great effort. Its members are confident that they can maintain the bank at its present level without external support. Currently, it generates income by selling vegetables grown in a rented plot and earns interest on loans made from monthly savings and the community-based biodiversity management fund. Members do not expect remuneration for the time they spend collecting seeds and working in the seed bank. They would like to become a legal entity and have plans to be registered as a farmer group with the District Agriculture Development Office. This would expand their interactions with other groups and, perhaps, also their resource base. An urgent need is for a permanent structure to store seeds safely and serve the community more reliably.

Acknowledgements

The authors would like to acknowledge the financial support provided by the International Development Research Center, Canada, through the project 'Promoting innovative mechanisms for ensuring farmers' rights through implementing access to and benefit sharing regime in Nepal' and The Development Fund, Norway, through 'Community-based biodiversity management South Asia Program' for establishing and strengthening the community seed bank at Tamaphok, Sankhuwasabha in Nepal.

26 Nicaragua

La Labranza no. 2 community seed bank – 'We are a network'

Jorge Iran Vásquez Zeledón

Purpose and evolution

La Labranza no. 2 community seed bank was established in 2007 to meet local farmers' need for seed at the appropriate time for planting. Seed loans provided by government institutions and local markets had failed in the past. Producers were overwhelmed by debt they had incurred to purchase seed and fertilizers. Farmers' mounting concerns over this situation coincided with an initiative started in 2000 by the Farmer to Farmer programme of the National Farmers' and Ranchers' Union (PCaC-UNAG from its Spanish name) in the region of Segovias to guarantee food security by rescuing local resources and creating community banks to conserve local seed.

The seed bank in La Labranza started with five families who stored their first seed stock in the home of one of the families, using sacks and silos provided by the owner. Each producer stored 2–11kg of maize and bean seeds (Plate 16). At the time, they agreed that 'even if we don't have anything to eat, that seed will not leave the bank', and that agreement has been honoured to date. Other families joined the group when they saw the results. After six years in operation, the seed bank now has 40 member families from La Labranza no. 2 and the neighbouring communities of Labranza no. 1, La Naranjita and San José (Plate 17).

Roles and activities

The community seed bank's main role is storing seed of local and domesticated varieties of staple grains produced by member farmers. Other functions include supplying seed during the planting season, promoting and conserving associated knowledge, developing technical capacities for seed management and fostering community organization. The community seed bank is a collective that encourages families to conserve their local varieties. The initial objective was to supply seed of local varieties to member families during the planting season. However, as the seed bank grew, founding families became self-sufficient and no longer required seed from the seed bank. They established their own family seed banks, which have now become a network. The seed bank transcends the needs of the community and benefits farmers in neighbouring communities.

The community seed bank currently holds seven maize varieties (Yema de Huevo, Amarillo Claro, Blanco Fino, Carmen, Pujagua, Pujagua Negrito and Pujagua Rayado) and four bean varieties (Colombiano, Estelí 90, Boaqueño and Guaniseño Amarillo), which were collected by the first member families as they were disappearing from the region. Maize varieties are for personal consumption and are used in many traditional dishes (atoles, pozol, rosquillas, rosquetes, pinol, pinolillo, tamales and nacatamales), but mainly for preparing tortillas. As of June 2013, the bank held 830kg of maize and 780kg of beans. The varieties, which are well adapted to and tolerant of changing climatic conditions, are recovering their importance and market value in the community and the region.

The seed bank is currently a collective that organizes promotional campaigns, documents farmers' experiences and carries out farmer participatory seed improvement and quality seed production. The PCaC-UNAG network supports the bank's activities by facilitating knowledge sharing and providing training and resources to improve the facilities. Bank users (23 women and 17 men) are maize and bean producers.

The community seed bank also plays a social role in that it improves and strengthens gender relations in the community. Doña Carmen Picado, a prominent member of the collective, says the bank stimulates family union: 'We men and women are fighting for the same cause; we are united by strong links. The 23 women and 17 men, we feel like one big family; we work together. Everyone cooperates.'

Women are very active in the seed bank and the group dynamics are unique. The board is composed mainly of women. Both men and women are responsible for paying their share.

There's no difference; there are men who are punctual and honest; the same with women. They don't come up with excuses. We give them the date when the grain will be ready and they come and pay. Some women are single and very responsible with their debts. There's no difference; both men and women request basically the same,

adds Carmen Picado, La Labranza no. 2 seed bank coordinator and farmer extension agent in the PCaC-UNAG project.

The challenge is to be sustainable over time.

We can't live just from hoping to get help. We need to make this sustainable ourselves, not let it down. It has to last and become an example for other communities. We need to have enough seed to sell, not be borrowing all the time,

explains Carmen.

Governance and management

President, secretary, treasurer and two support people make up the seed bank's coordinating committee; four of the members are women and two are men. The committee was elected by representatives of the 40 member families. They meet once a month, but if urgent matters arise they may get together as many as three times a month. Their main duties include coordination, shipping, receiving seed, establishing dates for receipt and shipping, recording demand before planting, ensuring that agreed conditions are met on delivery, coordinating postharvest activities, following up on members during the growing cycle and coordinating field days, fairs and assemblies.

They have established their own regulations. Loan requests are received in April, right before the first growing cycle (May to June). The committee scrutinizes these requests. An important factor they take into account – to ensure that the bank will recover its seed – is whether the requesting farmer is well known as an honest person. On receiving seed from the bank, the farmer signs a promissory note and a contract in which he or she agrees to return seed of the same quality that has been weighed, cleaned, dried and is free of mould. When it comes to seed loans, bank members have priority, but non-members are also granted loans when enough seed is available. Interest on loans is 50 per cent. The regulations include members' duties and rights and specify the conditions under which seed loans are to be repaid. To date, there has been very little commercial exchange; when seed is sold, the profit is used to purchase materials and equipment (sacks, weights, etc.) or seed varieties not already available in the seed bank.

Seed fairs, traditionally held in October, are excellent opportunities for residents of the Madriz, Nueva Segovia and Estelí – and, this year, Matagalpa – municipalities to share knowledge about agronomic and cooking characteristics and properties of the various species and varieties used for handicrafts. Fairs are organized once a year by the community, with the financial support of PCaC-UNAG and other organizations in the region. Approximately 1,000 people participate. Generally, the community seed bank's coordinating committee takes the lead, but all members of the community participate in the activities.

This collective is well known for its creative contests, with prizes awarded to the best artisanal and traditional foods prepared with local seed, as well as to cultural presentations, including dancing, poetry and music composed by farmers around the theme of local seed conservation and environmental protection.

The community bank is growing and surplus seed is being accumulated. If the seed bank is to venture into seed commercialization, it would have to revise its current organization to deal with an activity in which it does not have much experience.

Technical issues

The technical committee, with support from collaborating members, is in charge of seed handling. Farmers clean, select and dry the seed to the required moisture content for storage on their farms before delivering it to the bank. The process is carried out manually, as the farmers do not have hygrometers. Moisture content is assessed by biting the seed (if it breaks sharply with a cracking sound, then it is dry).

Varieties circulate constantly. As farmers meet the required conditions, they establish their own family bank and retain the best varieties for seed multiplication. In turn, the community seed bank acquires other varieties requested by new members; thus, there is constant renewal of material stored by the bank. Documentation is done by either recording experiences in writing, drawing on billboards or by organizing the information in passbooks coordinated by the national PCaC-UNAG network.

Assemblies, meetings, fairs, training courses and community social reunions are all mechanisms for interacting with bank users. Capacities are increased and skills are acquired and strengthened through formal and informal exchange and specific training courses. The most important technical challenge faced by the bank has to do with improving postharvest seed management, as humidity in the silos is still high.

Support, links and the institutional environment

To date, the only significant external support has been that from the national PCaC-UNAG network, which channels resources it receives from European nongovernmental organizations (NGOs). The most important of these is SWISSAID. In the past, the Finnish Siemenpuu Foundation, the Belgian Veco and the Nicaraguan Alexander von Humboldt Centre supported the establishment of the facilities of the central and family banks and training and experience-sharing activities. La Labranza collective, its network of family banks and its community seed bank are part of the national PCaC-UNAG network, which in turn is part of an alliance of organizations called Seeds of Identity, supported by SWISSAID. The bank and the community are not part of any other system or network.

There is no record of maintenance costs for the community seed bank. However, the cost of labour for constructing and managing the bank was covered by the community. The PCaC-UNAG network has collaborated in providing resources for infrastructure, equipment and knowledge-sharing and training events. The PCaC-UNAG foresees at least two more years of support.

The lack of policies to stimulate conservation of native genetic resources has resulted in the loss of varieties to genetic erosion and preference for only a few varieties of staple grains. Initiatives such as the Identity Seed Campaign Alliance are currently demanding enactment of a legal framework to promote and protect local varieties of seed. The alliance operates as a network to lobby those holding influential positions on the issues of local seed varieties and biodiversity. Members of the alliance include the Grupo de Promoción de la Agricultura Ecológica, the Alexander von Humboldt Centre, the Grupo de Incidencia en Seguridad y Soberanía Alimentaria, the Movimiento Agroecológico de

Nicaragua, the PCaC-UNAG and SWISSAID. The two latter organizations provide financial support to the alliance.

However, municipal bylaws are being considered for promoting and protecting local agricultural biodiversity. A legal framework could stimulate production and consumption of local varieties, as well as protect our national genetic patrimony and inspire the creation of innovative organizational forms among communities to safeguard these genetic resources. One important example is the community and family seed banks for conserving seed of local varieties.

Achievements and sustainability

Bank members view the establishment of the community seed bank as important in that it has brought together farmers into a solid organization: farmers help each other, are united and define their goals as a group; the community gains recognition nationally and internationally; and bank members feel they have gained independence. Initially, the group set out to restore two varieties; today, 11 have been rescued.

Overall, farmers feel that they do not have to look for seed outside the community. The families who started the group now have their own bank at home, and there is plenty of seed available. Farmers are more self-sufficient, and food quality has improved. According to Carmen Picado,

> Previously, people did not like yellow maize to make atole and tamales. Now they are trying it out and everyone says that yellow corn atole and tamales taste very good. The young ones are valuing again these typical foods which their parents had lost.

Excess seed is currently loaned to other communities. Quality seed is guaranteed, and farmers are advancing in participatory plant breeding to improve the variety known as 'Carmen'. Even though seed produced is competitively priced, which improves famers' incomes, the risk in the medium term is that low prices of staple grains will discourage small farmers from growing them.

Achieving sustainability without external aid is the biggest challenge faced by the community seed bank. The seed bank could venture in a more proactive way into local and national markets. However, a favourable legislative framework would be required to certify seed of local varieties produced by these small farmers and to acknowledge the role they play in conserving the national genetic heritage. It is feasible to belong to a national system that recognizes and respects small farmers' seed production systems, stimulates local exchange and considers diversity as a potential and not as a weakness. To become part of an international system, farmer groups must be familiar with management and distribution of information and materials and be able to sign agreements based on international treaties.

27 Rwanda

The Rubaya community gene bank

Leonidas Dusengemungu, Theophile Ndacyayisenga, Gloria Otieno, Antoine Ruzindana Nyirigira and Jean Rwihaniza Gapusi

The Rubaya community gene bank, located in the Rubaya sector of Gicumbi district in Northern Rwanda, is managed by the Kundisuka cooperative. It originated when a farmer by the name of Mpoberabanzi Silas and an agronomist working in the Rubaya sector recognized the need to preserve some of the genetic resources in the area that were being lost (e.g. several varieties of beans, peas, maize, wheat and sorghum).

Implementation of the project was supported by the staff of the Rwanda Agriculture Board (RAB) in cooperation with Bioversity International (Plate 18). The managing cooperative was created in September 2012 and consists of about ten members with Mpoberabanzi Silas as president. The community gene bank's storage facilities were constructed locally with support from Vision 2020's Umurenge Program and the Ministry of Local Government. Their main purpose is to store the region's priority crops (maize, wheat, beans and Irish potatoes), but farmers are free to use the facilities to store and conserve other seeds and planting material.

The community gene bank does not yet have a visible role in the community, for example, in seed production or participatory crop improvement, as it is still in its early stages. However, its members' vision is to invest in seed multiplication to make good-quality seeds available to the local community and regional gene banks. This will transform the enterprise into a business-oriented farmer cooperative certified by RAB.

Functions and activities

The community gene bank has three roles: conserving seeds of local crops; facilitating training in agricultural techniques; and propagating local varieties that are near extinction or are becoming less available as farmers turn to improved varieties. The community gene bank has begun collecting seeds from farmers in neighbouring villages and regenerating plant material that can be stored in the gene bank. In the beginning, it was confined to three small plots totalling 0.30ha, but it has now expanded to 15 plots (0.85ha) planted with varieties of beans, maize, garden peas, cow peas, Irish potatoes, sweet potatoes and sorghum.

Planting takes place at the beginning of each season. With support from the sector agronomist and RAB, farmers are able to monitor crops for pests, diseases and general growth. To ensure high-quality output, they adhere to good agricultural practices. RAB has provided support in the form of mineral fertilizer, which was added to farmyard manure. Normally, farmers have no access to such fertilizer: it is expensive and, therefore, there is no supplier in the area. RAB also offers technical support to farmers planting various varieties of beans and sorghum, including training in planting, weeding, pest and disease management, postharvest handling and storage. Such support is provided not only to the cooperative members but also to other farmers who have consolidated their small properties under RAB's Crop Intensification Program.

In the March–June 2013 planting season, crops grown by the cooperative for regeneration included beans (bush and climbing) in three plots, sorghum in three plots, Irish potato (Mbumbamagara) and sweet potato (Utankubura) in four plots, maize and peas in two plots. The average size of a plot was 0.15ha.

The sweet potato seeds were obtained from farmers, whereas sorghum seeds came from RAB and Irish potato seeds from the local market. After multiplication, the cooperative is planning to make these crop seeds available to other farmers. The community gene bank is playing a key role in the conservation and use of neglected and underused species, such as the local bean varieties, Kachwekano and Kabonobono, which are high yielding, but had been abandoned by farmers because of their susceptibility to disease.

The major challenge for the gene bank is drought. Lack of rain destroyed the crops in the first growing season, September–December 2012, partly due to late sowing. In addition, gene bank members have to cover operating costs, such as labour, land rental and agricultural inputs. The gene bank has two casual labourers who are paid 1,000 Rwandan francs (RWF) or about US$1.47 a day by the cooperative. They are cooperative members who choose to work seasonally on the common field for this salary. The cooperative hopes to increase its membership and envisions some form of community mobilization.

Similar to other cooperatives in the region, the one managing the community gene bank is governed by a committee composed of the president, vice-president, secretary, cashier and two advisors democratically elected by the cooperative members. The committee, which is made up of two women and four men, is working on guidelines for its officials. Cooperative members have agreed on a mechanism through which they have access to seeds and planting material in exchange for labour.

Technical issues and networking

High-quality seeds are selected in the field using ribbons attached to healthier plants, a traditional variety-selection method. Once harvested, cooperative workers label the selected seeds of different crops appropriately and store them separately. Currently, there is no formal system for documenting traditional knowledge and associated information about local varieties conserved at the community gene bank. Information concerning varieties, lots, planting dates, weeding dates, fertilizer application and harvesting dates for all varieties is kept in notebooks, carefully differentiated by activity and season. These notebooks are kept by the secretary of the cooperative. Committee members hold monthly meetings to discuss issues, but the chair can call an impromptu meeting in case of an emergency. Minutes are kept by the secretary. The community gene bank receives technical and moral support from RAB and the sector agronomist. Recently, it benefitted from a small grant from Bioversity International to buy shelves, plastic containers, bottles and pesticides.

The community gene bank collaborates with the Isonga Mw'Isango youth cooperative and is also linked to other farmer and public organizations at the national level, such as Caritas Rwanda, a nongovernmental organization (NGO) working in the agriculture sector, and RAB. Recently, the members of the cooperative visited a community gene bank in Uganda to share experiences and discuss gene bank management issues, including processes for procurement, preservation and storage of bean seed samples. During the visit, farmers from both countries engaged with breeders and other scientists in participatory evaluation of their climate vulnerabilities and coping strategies and, subsequently, determination of the traits desired for adaptation to climate change. They also conducted a participatory evaluation of the seeds in their possession to see which ones have those traits. Last, but not least, they explored a mechanism by which farmers can exchange varieties of seeds.

Policy environment and prospects

Rwanda's policy of land consolidation and focussing on one priority crop has had a negative impact on the activities of the gene bank because local varieties of crops cannot be grown freely by farmers. The government distributes seeds (improved varieties) and fertilizer to farmers as part of the crop intensification programme. However, the Rwanda Cooperative Authority provides advice to the cooperative committee members on how to balance between the prescribed varieties and their varieties of choice.

The community gene bank invested RWF 889,000 (about US$1,306) in setting up and maintaining its seed bank. This covered the cost of renting land, purchasing seed and fertilizers and paying for labour. The gene bank cannot operate without outside support because rent for land and the cost of agricultural inputs are high. To make the gene bank financially independent and sustainable, farmers need more financial and technical support so that they can expand their activities and increase production and profits.

Looking to the future, the community gene bank has established connections with RAB at the national level and Uganda's National Agricultural Research Organisation at the regional level to obtain technical support. The cooperative also needs to be strengthened in terms of management.

28 Sri Lanka

The Haritha Udana community seed bank in Kanthale

C. L. K. Wakkumbure and
K. M. G. P. Kumarasinghe

Establishment and functions

Traditionally, farmers in Sri Lanka have collected and stored seeds in their own homes using traditional simple but effective techniques and tools. Storage facilities include raised structures built outside the house on four timbers using clay, bamboo and paddy straw and used mainly to store paddy; one- or two-room structures inside the house; and racks above the stove. However, in the last three or four decades, as agriculture has become commercialized, these techniques and tools have been abandoned in many farming communities. Pressured by seed companies to adopt modern varieties and lacking support from the government to maintain local diversity, farmers have generally increased their use of introduced crops and improved varieties. This has led to a loss of crop diversity in many regions of the country. Fortunately, a number of custodian farmers in various farming communities continue to conserve some traditional and local cultivars in recognition of their sociocultural, ecological and economic value.

The community seed bank at Haritha Udana in Raj-ala, Kanthale, is one of five banks that are part of Sri Lanka's community-based biodiversity management project (Plate 19). This project was initiated and implemented by the Green Movement of Sri Lanka, a local nongovernmental organization (NGO), in collaboration with the Community-based Biodiversity Management Programme, South Asia, coordinated by Local Initiatives for Biodiversity, Research and Development (LI-BIRD) of Nepal.

The Haritha Udana seed bank was established in mid-2011. The community was well aware of the importance of local and traditional crop varieties and landraces to sustainable production systems and a nutritious, balanced diet. They also recognized the value of seeds as a resource and of their association with the local agricultural system. This knowledge provided a strong foundation for the establishment of the seed bank.

The community seed bank is governed by Haritha Udana, a community-based organization (CBO) established by the raja-ala farming community. Haritha Udana CBO is registered under the Kanthale divisional secretariat, the local administrative structure, and, thus, the seed bank has legal status. In the beginning, 35 households contributed to the bank, but now 80 member households and about 20 non-member households are benefitting from it, directly and indirectly.

The community seed bank provides space to store seeds of almost all annual crops and varieties available in the area, including grains, pulses, legumes, leafy vegetables, medicinal plants and selected fruit crops. Seeds are borrowed and returned to the bank by farmers. Based on the size of a member's home garden, the management team decides how much seed can be borrowed. The borrowers must return three times the amount borrowed. The major roles of the community seed bank have not changed since its inception. The bank is also providing local and traditional genetic resources, such as sorghum, finger millet and cowpea (*Vigna unguiculata*) for participatory crop improvement projects, in which farmers cultivate those crops to multiply and increase the availability of seeds.

Several people from Sabaragamuwa University, Kanthale agrarian service centre, the Prabavi CBO in Lunugamwehera and the Green Movement of Sri Lanka have received seeds from the bank to distribute among other farmers and to examine the morphologic differences in the varieties of paddy, sorghum, sponge gourd and green gram, among others. However, the national gene bank (Plant Genetic Resource Centre of Sri Lanka) has not yet obtained seeds or genetic materials from the community seed bank.

Governance, management and support

The executive committee of the Haritha Udana CBO has overall responsibility for managing the seed bank and delegating tasks and responsibilities to members. The members of the executive committee are elected annually by the members.

The executive committee is responsible for ensuring the quality of the stored seeds. However, seed selection, cleaning, storage and renewal are mainly carried out by women. In Sri Lanka, women traditionally assume these roles and, in general, are more actively involved in CBOs. Men are more involved in other types of livelihood practices, such as wage labour at construction sites, in and outside the villages. Currently, 66 women and 14 men belong to the Kanthale Haritha Udana CBO.

Individual community members may borrow seeds from the seed bank, but must return high-quality seeds from their home gardens and farms following established rules. The community seed bank uses glass and plastic bottles, clay pots and polythene bags for storing seeds. The type and size of the storage containers depend on the type of crop and the amount of seed.

All members of the CBO and all farming households in the community (within the village) have equal access to seed from the community seed bank. However, the CBO gives priority to those who are actively engaged in conservation and the sustainable use of agro-biodiversity. Such provision may encourage non-members to be associated with the CBO and become involved in local seed conservation activities. Currently, women are more active in such community-based activities in rural Sri Lanka than men.

The CBO keeps handwritten records of seed storage and exchange processes: mainly seed inflow and outflow. When seeds are received or provided to the community, an executive committee member or a delegate updates the records. She or he also keeps track of all the seed-storage containers, including crop information, variety, harvesting date and storage date to ensure smooth functioning of the seed bank. Monthly meetings, special meetings during project officers' site visits, face-to-face verbal communication, public notices in public places and telephone calls, when necessary, are used by the executive committee to interact with community members.

The Green Movement of Sri Lanka has provided technical, financial and moral support to the community seed bank, free of charge, since its inception. Government institutes, such as the Plant Genetic Resource Centre, the in-service training institute and the Kanthale seed farm have also provided technical and moral support so that the community can maintain, improve and expand the seed bank as a viable and sustainable seed resource centre. The Community-based Biodiversity Management Programme Sri Lanka provided initial monetary and non-monetary support, including training and capacity building. The money was mainly used to buy construction materials that were not available in the village. Other costs, such as land, labour, timber, etc., needed to set up the seed bank were contributed by the community.

Prospects

The results achieved so far have laid the foundation for reviving the community-based seed production that was lost due to agricultural modernization. However, the community seed bank is still at a very early stage.

The community seed bank is contributing to the sustainability of local and traditional agricultural biodiversity while helping to ensure food and nutrition security and improving livelihoods among the farming community in Raja-ala, Kanthale. To date, the farming community has achieved broader awareness and knowledge of the importance of agricultural biodiversity. For example, farmers are now more aware of the differences between mono-cropping and multi-cropping. The community seed bank plays a vital role in making the community aware of the importance of agricultural biodiversity, especially the younger generation. This awareness has motivated the community to search for, collect and cultivate different crops and landraces, varieties and wild relatives of the crops in their gardens. As well, they have revived traditional culinary methods used to prepare and cook food. The bank also supports the reintroduction of traditional and local crop varieties, neglected and wild crops – food and medicinal crops found in forest areas and natural vegetation – that were replaced by modern agriculture. Moreover, the community seed bank serves as an educational resource centre for the community in terms of sustainable agriculture and food security.

The community seed bank has also changed the attitudes of CBO members towards local and traditional landraces of crops and crop diversity. Nine landraces of paddy, almost all sorghum, yellow coloured green gram and pigeon peas have been restored as a result of the work of the bank. When exposed to the diversity of agricultural crops available in the area, most community members are interested in taking the initiative to achieve self-sufficiency in food for day-to-day life.

Seeds of the crops shown in Table 28.1, as well as bitter gourd, snake gourd and ridge gourd, are now available year round. The community is currently identifying future needs, seeking to increase the amount of seed stored, enlarging the storage facilities and improving the quality of the stored seeds for more effective use under unfavourable climatic and environmental conditions.

Intra-species and inter-species diversity of the crops in the area – mainly in the home gardens of the CBO members – has increased remarkably through the community seed bank and seed exchange mechanisms of the Haritha Udana CBO. Currently, the average number of crop species and medicinal plants in home gardens is about 45–50, a large increase from the 10–15 species of crops and medicinal plants farmers grew before the establishment of the community seed bank and the exchange process. Most member households cultivate at least two varieties of almost all crops in their home gardens.

Home gardens rich in agro-biodiversity provide the means to increase the diversity of food available for day-to-day consumption in the farming communities and to increase both food supply and the quality of the food. Before establishment of the community seed bank, people consumed 5–7 types of vegetables and fruits a week on average; now up to 12–15 species of

Table 28.1 Crop seeds available in the community seed bank

Crop	No. of varieties	Volume of annual transactions (g)
Yard-long bean	3	850
Cowpea	2	600
Black gram	1	2,000
Amaranth	2	100
Sward bean	1	1,250
Green gram	1	1,000
Bottle gourd	3	500
Tomato	2	150
Chili pepper (*Capsicum frutecens*)	5	100
Pumpkin	2	350
Cucumber	2	100
Okra (a.k.a. lady finger)	1	290
Sorghum	3	1,400
Wing bean	2	400

vegetables and fruits are consumed per week. The community seed bank has helped reduce day-to-day food expenditures by at least 15–20 per cent, and most members save about half the cost of vegetables and fruit. Furthermore, additional income is being generated through the sale of excess produce in and outside the villages and average household income is now about 900 Sri Lankan rupees (US$7) a month.

The Haritha Udana community seed bank is still growing and, to date, has made little impact on agricultural policy or farmers' rights. However, the visible outcomes from the community seed bank are expected to create an environment in which to address relevant policy issues. To maintain the community seed bank effectively and efficiently, the Haritha Udana CBO must have sufficient financial and non-financial resources. The community seed bank is a team effort that requires strong capacity building, human resource development and financial resources to reduce dependency on outside sources.

The challenges associated with the development of the community seed bank are the low level of technical and financial support, difficulties in finding competent resource people when they are needed and the unabated pressure from seed companies to move towards commercial agriculture. The absence of successful community seed bank models in the country also makes it difficult to find the right direction.

Recently, some members of the Haritha Udana CBO have moved away from the community seed bank. Awakened to the utility of having access to seeds that are not governed by the market, they have begun to maintain individual seed reserves at the household level. CBO members are concerned that this could reduce the synergy and group coherence of the CBO over time. Strengthening existing mechanisms to generate income, such as a community-based biodiversity management fund and community-based seed production, may ensure the viability of the community seed bank.

29 Trinidad and Tobago

SJ Seed Savers

Jaeson Teeluck and Satie Boodoo

Purpose and evolution

Our community seed bank, registered through our agricultural company, Agro plus 2007, Ltd, emerged because of many factors. One was concern over the need to preserve local germplasm. Another was the desire to be able to procure planting materials and supply farmers in the various communities with the varieties and species that do best under local conditions. The seed bank is now part of a private enterprise, SJ Seed Savers, which has pioneered all seed operations.

Because we live in a multi-ethnic society characterized by multicultural practices, for example, concerning traditional foods, we recognized from the beginning that the conservation and sustainable use of diverse crop varieties was central. Diversity of varieties and species is the core of our business. Some varieties that we maintain have been grown for many generations. Because of our concern over the preservation of landraces and open-pollinated varieties, all our research and development activities have been carried out in close cooperation with institutions, such as CABI International, whose library here in our country has helped us in our research.

Our seed bank was created to supply seeds to farmers and home gardeners, and we have made tremendous improvements in many areas. For example, we were able to improve seed storage by installing 'chillers' to stabilize seed moisture content, and we acquired a parcel of land to conduct trials and seed selection. We have been setting up farmers' groups and connecting farmers through our Facebook account. We are also a part of a civil society foundation that, since its inception in 2001, works with communities on such projects as backyard gardening for households.

The results have been excellent and include income generation, new working relations with new farming groups, and increased knowledge through cooperation with research agencies such as the Caribbean Agricultural Research & Development Institute (CARDI) at the university. We have worked with over 100 farmers in carrying out trials, and we provide part-time employment in growing and harvesting seeds for more than ten people.

In Trinidad, there are no gene banks; thus, preservation of genetic diversity is an uphill battle and it has become a lifelong passion and goal of our organization. We are interested in further education in seed development and research, and working with CARDI has offered us much hope for the future. As an organization, we involve women and men and young people. All our educational programmes are available to everyone involved in the seed bank.

Function and activities

The seed bank selects varieties of different species and grows them to supply farmers with seeds that are properly harvested for best quality. Appropriate chemical seed treatments and a storage system that involves the use of chillers make seed available throughout the year. Continuous germination tests are carried out to maintain viability. The bank uses materials of heirloom varieties of tomatoes, hot peppers (pimento) and various other chilies, melongene (eggplant), pumpkins, squash, beans, pigeon peas, bitter gourds and many more crops.

Due to changes in food culture, we have noticed that the flavours of landraces and heirloom varieties have become less popular. To some extent, we have been able to re-establish these varieties through our home garden projects, which are geared towards small-scale agriculture. In areas where employment for women is limited, backyard gardening projects help sustain households with food and also maintain a diversity of crops. We encourage the women to save some seeds and have organized short training courses in seed preservation for them. It has become evident to our seed bank that women in the community can play a pivotal role in ensuring the conservation of landraces and varieties that may not be in demand at present.

Each variety is labelled according to lot number and variety, and a logging system allows us to monitor and control how seeds are stored, selected and sold. We store some species that may not be for immediate use, but this germplasm is conserved for future development. Sometimes, it is used as stock material for grafting because of its exceptional resistance to pests and diseases.

Governance and management

The bank is organized by small committees made up of farmers and volunteers, each with a specific responsibility: land preparation, costing, growing seed crops, harvesting, packaging, etc. Overall management is our responsibility. Seed sales take place through SJ Traders, the commercial arm of our enterprise. SJ Traders is a company that supplies agro-chemicals, fertilizers and various consumables to farmers according to international quality standards for both chemical and biological commodities. A percentage of the profits and sales from SJ Traders is used to manage and operate SJ Seed Savers.

Because of the conservation work we are carrying out, we are recognized by CARDI, the main seed body in Trinidad in charge of crop development and plant breeding. Through this connection, we have been able to modernize our operations and become more successful through the introduction of seed thrashers and driers and a greenhouse to grow lettuce for seed production in a controlled environment that is not affected by rain. We also correspond with people with similar interests globally. SJ Traders finances our seed bank operation through sales of seeds to farmers and members of the community. We sometimes procure germplasm to develop a breeding programme that may be implemented in the future by SJ Seed Savers and collaborators.

There are no seed policies or laws in our country that apply to our work, except in relation to the import of seeds. Thus, we are free to work with what we have, develop our efforts and freely learn from others. However, we welcome assistance in whatever way that may be applicable to our situation.

Technical issues

Seeds are selected, cleaned, stored and renewed using many techniques; some are selected based on time to harvest or weather conditions. Some crops are grown in the greenhouse. Some are stored and parent lines are maintained. We rely on traditional cultural practices for seed gathering and manual harvesting. We have taught the women of our communities to harvest and select seed. Attached to SJ Seed Savers premises is our nursery.

We use various techniques to guarantee seed quality and run a continuous programme to test germination. We use a logging system that involves documenting seed stock varieties, regeneration requests from farmers and other related information and an accounting system to record financial operations. Our youth programme has provided us with extra hands, as we train youth in the importance of seed selection.

Currently, we are establishing a web site for SJ Seed Savers, and we are in the process of inputting data so that computers can be used, through a customized programme developed by our group, to monitor and control all facets of the seed bank. We are confident that the use of this technology will make our job easier by tracking varieties, scheduling and accounting in a transparent, easy to use manner.

Achievements and prospects

We have been able to select and supply over ten species of crop seeds, including tomato, sweet pepper, eggplant, okra, bitter gourds, cucumber, pumpkin and hot pepper, to over 100 farmers for a total of about 135kg of seeds. We have established a local chilling system for our seed-storage facility to maintain humidity at appropriate levels and store seeds as hermetically as possible. Through crop experiments, we have been successful in establishing varieties of pigeon peas, hot peppers, okra and other crops that do well under less than suitable conditions, e.g. drought, flood and other environmental factors.

Because of the increased availability of seeds to households in various communities, a surplus of food is now being produced, with improvements in quality as well as quantity. Households are now able to grow what they eat, eat what they grow and sell some of the produce. This is having a positive impact financially.

For now, financial stability and operational sustainability depend entirely on us, the two founders. However, because of the strong interest in our efforts, we decided to set up a new organizational structure for SJ Seed Savers that will allow us to operate more effectively. The organization includes a manager, assistant manager, secretary, assistant secretary, public relations officer, three trustees, committee members and ordinary members. We are now ready to work with other seed banks around the world and exchange new germplasm for research and development providing that we meet international standards, such as phytosanitary clearance from the necessary authorities. As an organization, we look forward to procuring and helping to procure the future of germplasm and genetic diversity.

Acknowledgements

We thank Bioversity International for giving SJ Seed Savers and, by extension, our island of Trinidad and Tobago the opportunity to let the world know about our enthusiasm and determination to perform this noble task of saving our landraces – and our world – for future generations while ensuring food sustainability and quality here and now.

30 Uganda

The Kiziba community gene bank

Mulumba John Wasswa, Rose Nankya,
Catherine Kiwuka, Joyce Adokorach, Gloria Otieno,
Marjorie Kyomugisha, Carlo Fadda and Devra I. Jarvis

Origin of the gene bank

The Kiziba community gene bank, located in Kabwohe, Kiziba parish, in the Sheema district of Uganda, was started in 2010. Focus group discussions and household surveys had revealed that some varieties of beans were becoming rare and others were no longer available in the area. Obtaining good-quality seed was also a problem, as most farmers relied on exchanges with fellow farmers, shops and markets. The lack of quality control among these sources was resulting in the rampant spread of seed-borne diseases in the area. Farmers also expressed a need for a facility where they could store some of the varieties that were less popular in terms of market, yield and taste, for example, so that they would be available in the future to meet unforeseen needs that may not be important at present. A series of meetings among farmers, Uganda's Plant Genetic Resources Centre and Bioversity International led to the realization that a community gene bank would solve these problems and provide farmers with a viable source of diverse, locally common bean seeds.

The seed supply journey

With technical support from Bioversity International and the Ugandan National Agricultural Research Organization and financial support from the United Nations Environment Programme's Global Environment Facility, farmers worked to save the seeds that formed the starting capital of the community gene bank. The first beneficiaries, about 100 farmers, returned twice the number of seeds borrowed from the gene bank, and that trend was repeated in the seasons that followed. By the end of 2012, 200 farmers had benefitted from the gene bank and, to date, 280 farmers have received varieties of common bean (*Phaseolus vulgaris*) seeds from the bank, with demand for some varieties surpassing the supply (Plate 20). The community gene bank management committee and the beneficiary farmers not only plant the seeds they receive from the gene bank, but also undertake careful observations of the varieties they plant to increase their knowledge and document the characteristics of the various common bean varieties – in the garden, in the store, in the market and 'in the mouth' (Tables 30.1 and 30.2).

Table 30.1 Characteristics of common bean varieties available in the gene bank

Variety	Farmer-preferred characteristics	Limiting characteristics
Nambale long (Kachwekano)	High market value, withstands adverse weather conditions, tasty, can be stored for long periods without being destroyed by weevils	Late maturing (four months to harvest)
Nambale short	High market value, withstands adverse weather conditions, tasty, can be stored for long periods (four months) without being destroyed by weevils	
Yellow short	Tasty, especially when cooked as katogo (mixture of beans, bananas, cassava or sweet potatoes), matures early (2.5 months), cooks quickly due to the soft testa (1.5 hours)	Susceptible to weevils
Kankulyembarukye purple	Tasty, especially when cooked as katogo, matures early (2.5 months), cooks quickly due to the soft testa (1.5 hours)	Susceptible to weevils
Kabanyarwanda	Grows well in poor soils, produces good soup, endures adverse weather	Small seeds
Gantagasize	High yielding, produces good soup, cooks quickly, seeds remain whole after cooking	
Kabwejagure	Good yields on poor soils, endures adverse weather	
Yelllow long	High yielding	Not marketable: poor cooking quality, produces slimy soup, spoils overnight
Kiribwaobwejagwire	High yielding, can be stored for long periods without being attacked by weevils (four months)	Long cooking time due to the hard testa (four hours)
Kanyamunyu	High yielding, can be stored for long periods without being attacked by weevils (four months)	Long cooking time due to the hard testa (five hours)
Kakurungu	Tasty, matures early (2.5 months), cooks quickly due to the soft testa (1.5 hours)	Susceptible to weevils
Kanyebwa	Tasty, matures early (2.5 months), cooks quickly due to the soft testa (1.5 hours)	Susceptible to weevils
Kayinja	Tasty, matures early (2.5 months), cooks quickly due to the soft testa (1.5 hours)	Susceptible to weevils
Mahega short	Matures early (2.5 months)	
Kahura short	Matures early (2.5 months)	
Kahura long	Can be stored for long periods without being attacked by weevils (four months)	Long cooking time due to the hard testa

Table 30.2 Ten most preferred varieties from the gene bank and their characteristics as ranked by farmers (5 highest rank, 1 lowest)

Variety	Type	Marketability	Taste	Cooking time	Early maturity	Pest resistance	Endurance in heavy rainfall	Drought tolerance	General acceptability	Total score
Kahura	Landrace	5	5	4	4	3	3	3	5	32
Kaki short	Landrace	5	5	4	3	4	3	3	5	32
Kanyebwa	Landrace	5	5	5	4	3	2	3	5	32
Yellow short	Landrace	5	5	4	5	2	3	3	5	32
Kankulyembarukye purple	Landrace	5	5	3	3	3	3	4	5	31
Katosire	Landrace	5	5	3	3	5	2	3	5	31
Nabe 14	Modern	5	5	3	3	3	3	3	5	30
Kabwejagure	Landrace	5	5	4	2	3	2	3	5	29
Kanyamunyu, long and short	Landrace	3	4	1	4	5	4	4	3	28

Through a series of training sessions, farmers learned about the life cycle of bean weevils and now endeavour to time the harvest and dry the seeds to minimize damage before they are treated and stored in the gene bank.

Initially, the gene bank operated smoothly, with the volume of seed increasing steadily every season. However, in July 2012, the pattern of rainfall and sunshine began to change and affected the growth of beans. Some varieties died out completely. For others, the total harvest amounted to about 10 per cent less than the amount sowed (Figure 30.1). This occurred at the Kabwohe, Nakaseke and Kabale sites as well as at the national gene bank at the Plant Genetic Resources Centre in Entebbe. From the initial 49 varieties, the gene bank's capital dwindled to only 35. Fourteen varieties did not survive the 2012 planting season, possibly because they were unable to adapt to the changes in the weather.

Among the 14 varieties that did not survive were the climbing beans that had been brought from the Rubaya site, a different agro-ecological environment with a higher elevation. Their loss might have been partly due to the fact that Kiziba farmers do not like climbing beans, as they must be staked and this is seen as an extra burden in terms of both labour and funds to buy stakes. The gene bank management committee is monitoring and documenting the situation to establish the real cause of the disappearance. Farmers have expressed

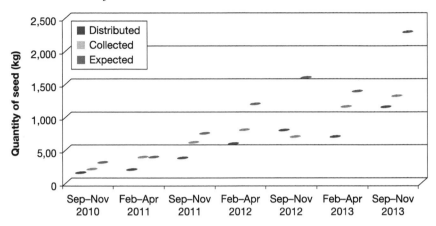

Figure 30.1 Quantities of seed distributed and collected by season since the gene bank was established

concerns about weather vagaries, especially long droughts and short rainy seasons, and how this will affect their community gene bank. Irrigation would help, but is too expensive for the majority of farmers in this area.

Operations

The gene bank is governed by bylaws developed by the Kiziba beneficiary community. It is staffed by a management committee composed of the gene bank manager, records manager, distribution manager, quality assurance manager and four 'mobilizers'. The management committee operates on a voluntary basis, which may be limiting in terms of motivation, particularly with the increased workload resulting from the steady increase in seed turnover. The manager is in charge of overall functioning of the gene bank; the records manager keeps the records; the quality assurance manager ensures that good-quality seed is brought, preserved and stored; and the distribution manager is in charge of distributing seed. The mobilizers are responsible for ensuring that farmers get seed from the gene bank and repay a portion of their harvest. Farmers not only have access to a diversity of common bean varieties, but they also benefit from training carried out by the committee with support from the National Agriculture Research Organization and Bioversity International. Among other agronomic practices, farmers learn how to produce good-quality seed and how to handle seeds after harvest.

After distributing seeds at the beginning of each planting season, members of the management committee, led by the quality assurance manager, monitor farms to ensure that the recommended agronomic practices are followed. Farmers must adhere to these practices; however, some are unwilling to do so, while others fail to harvest enough seeds to return to the bank because of poor soil and bad weather. In a few cases, seeds have been rejected by the management committee because they were of poor quality. Sorting seed is a responsibility of the farmers and the distribution manager, who then records the amount of seed returned; the gene bank will only accept clean seeds.

The management committee ensures that seed deposited in the gene bank is stored properly and preserved using locally made organic materials, mainly cow dung, which is burned and ground to powder before being applied to the bean seeds at a rate of 25g per kilogram of beans. Because the effectiveness and shelf life of this preservation technique was not known, the management committee was prompted to work with the Plant Genetic Resources Centre and Bioversity International to investigate how it works. The committee has expressed interest in receiving more information about seed preservation and storage.

Governance

The gene bank is currently functioning as a community-level initiative managed by members of the community with technical oversight and guidance from Bioversity International and the Plant Genetic Resources Centre. Members of the gene bank management committee are appointed by general consensus of community members at their annual general meeting and serve for a two-year renewable term. The parish chief presides over the election of the committee. The general meeting is held at the end of a planting season, after harvest and return of seeds to the gene bank, to let all farmers know how much seed has been returned to the gene bank and to agree on the quantity to be given out the following season. Farmers apply for seed through the mobilizers two months before planting time and the beneficiaries are approved by the management committee. The quantity distributed depends on quantity returned.

Costs for establishment

Construction of the gene bank cost US$4,633, and furnishing it cost US$612. Another US$3,312 was needed to cover the costs of the meetings that initiated the idea and brought it to reality, to train farmers in how to run the gene bank and for capacity building. These funds were provided by Bioversity International through the National Agriculture Research Organization with support from the United Nations Environment Programme's Global Environment Facility and the Swiss Development Corporation. Operation of the gene bank is still on a voluntary basis, but discussions are underway to see how a business arm can be established to generate income from the sale of some of the seeds and still maintain the original idea of supplying free seed to small-scale farmers.

Links and networking

This initiative has come a long way and is now attracting attention in neighbouring districts. The National Agricultural Advisory Services have asked the Kiziba group to supply seeds to the surrounding areas of Buhweju and Mitoma and to help other farmer groups set up similar facilities elsewhere in the region. This presents an opportunity for collaboration, although it is also a challenge, as the quantity of seed produced at the moment is not sufficient to satisfy the demand in Kiziba. The group has discussed the need to work on a sound strategy for increasing seed production without sacrificing quality. They are expecting to receive more technical support during a transition to a medium-scale business operation, while maintaining the free seed service for small-scale farmers. The group wishes to strengthen its capacity for business planning and management, financial management and marketing strategies, among other functions.

The farmers have had discussions with officials from the Integrated Seed Sector Development Programme, an organization that develops commercially sustainable local seed businesses and explores possibilities for collaboration. In recognition of what the gene bank is doing, its manager was elected to represent the Sheema district in the Uganda southwestern region multistakeholder seed platform. The community gene bank staff work closely with the national gene bank in Entebbe, with the Plant Genetic Resources Centre providing technical guidance. The centre keeps duplicate accessions of the Kiziba varieties as well as linking the gene bank with international support, such as that received from Bioversity International. In a bid to create visibility and more opportunities for collaboration, the Kiziba community gene bank group has also started participating in functions, such as exhibitions on International World Food Day and at diversity fairs.

Policy and legal environment

The gene bank is registered at the district level as a seed-producing group and operates under various policies, but the draft national agricultural seed policy (2011) that is currently being reviewed will be the major policy influencing its operation. The seed policy defines the modalities by which the seed industry should be regulated and the roles of various players in the industry, including farmers. The Seed and Plant Act (2006) is the legal framework that provides for the promotion, regulation and control of plant breeding and variety release, seed multiplication and marketing, seed import and export and quality assurance of seeds and planting materials. The Seed and Plant Regulations (2009) provide guidelines for enforcement of the act. The International Treaty on Plant Genetic Resources for Food and Agriculture and the Multilateral System also stipulate ways in which the gene bank can be linked to the international system of access and benefit sharing. The members of the Kiziba community gene bank have expressed enthusiasm about collaborating and benefitting from connections with other parts of the world.

Achievements

The gene bank started with 100kg of seed, but, in three years, it has distributed over 3,000kg of good-quality common bean seed. Its coverage has also expanded: from fewer than 100 farmers in 2010 to 280 farmers in 2013 and the demand for seed surpasses the supply of some varieties.

The member farmers have also benefitted from a number of capacity-building initiatives, including training in general bean production, postharvest handling, sorting, preservation and pest and disease control. They have also started learning about business management in a bid to expand the gene bank and become an enterprise.

The group has shared knowledge, information and experience with farmer groups involved in seed activities elsewhere: for example, the Kakindu Farmers' Association from Mityana, Uganda, and the Kusinduka Farmers' Cooperative from Rubaya, Rwanda. In addition, their awareness of issues surrounding the International Treaty on Plant Genetic Resources for Food and Agriculture has increased and they have learned how they can exchange germplasm with farmers operating community gene banks in other countries.

Sustainability and prospects

The gene bank can be sustainable if it becomes a profit-making enterprise. For example, the farmers are looking to raise funds from the sale of seeds and by teaching other groups who want to engage in seed production in the same manner. Links with other organizations may provide more opportunities for the gene bank to evolve further. Exposure to the Multilateral System is also an opportunity for the gene bank to collaborate with other countries, increase crop diversity and receive technical and financial support.

31 United States of America

Native Seeds/SEARCH

Chris Schmidt

Purpose and core operations

The southwestern United States and northwestern Mexico (the 'Greater Southwest') form an arid region of immense natural and cultural beauty, rich indigenous agricultural traditions and among the greatest food security challenges in North America. Recognition of the accelerating erosion of the region's unique cultural and agricultural diversity led to the formation of Native Seeds/SEARCH in 1983 by a dedicated team of private citizens. A nongovernmental organization (NGO) based in Tucson, Arizona, Native Seeds/SEARCH works to improve regional food security and sovereignty through the preservation, documentation and promotion of the Greater Southwest's adapted crop diversity and associated cultural knowledge, using a combined strategy of ex-situ and in-situ conservation and targeted public education.

At the heart of the organization's work is an active programme of ex-situ conservation, anchored by its seed bank and a 24ha conservation farm. The seed bank collection holds 1,900 accessions of domesticated crops and wild relatives, representing the agricultural and ethnobotanical legacies of over 50 indigenous peoples from the region as well as Hispanic communities and Anglo settlers. With their unique adaptations to the harsh conditions of the arid southwest, the crop varieties conserved and distributed by Native Seeds/SEARCH are characteristically tolerant of drought, heat and poor soils. In this era of climate change and desertification, such varieties will take on ever-increasing global importance. Many of these varieties, along with their unique genetic traits and the cultural roles they embody, were on the verge of extinction before Native Seeds/SEARCH began its collection.

The majority of the collection consists of landrace or local varieties and is dominated by maize and multiple species of beans (*Phaseolus*) and squash (*Cucurbita*). In total, over 100 plant species are represented, including some promising but neglected crops such as Sonoran panic grass (*Panicum sonorum*). Seeds are stored at the seed bank in a 56m² cold room (7°C and 25 per cent relative humidity) for short-term storage or in an 11m² freezer (−18°C) for long-term storage. They are regenerated periodically at the conservation farm using standard techniques to maintain genetic diversity and purity. The Native

Seeds/SEARCH farm has also traditionally been the source for most of the seed stock that the organization has distributed and fulfills important research and education functions.

Recognizing that crop diversity has little value if it is not used and that the evolutionary processes that promote continuous crop diversification and adaptation are essential to the long-term resilience and sustainability of any agricultural system, Native Seeds/SEARCH actively distributes seeds from the collection to farmers and gardeners throughout the Greater Southwest and beyond. Currently, over 50,000 packets are distributed annually, in addition to limited bulk quantities for farm-scale operations. The distribution of landrace material from the collection is supplemented by heirloom varieties of crops that are not traditional to the southwest but are frequently sought by growers in the region. This strategy results in additional revenue to support the organization's conservation work, an increased diversity of crop species available locally and enhanced opportunities for public outreach.

Native Seeds/SEARCH distributes seeds through several channels. They are sold through a retail store in Tucson (which also serves as an important interface between the organization and the public), through an online store, a catalogue and via wholesale distribution through local grocery stores and nurseries. One of the most important programmes operated by Native Seeds/SEARCH is the Native American Free Seed Program, in which seeds are provided free of charge to Native people in the region to support indigenous agriculture and share the benefits of the broader use of the region's indigenous crop diversity. Approximately 5,000 seed packets are distributed annually through the Free Seed Program. Native Seeds/SEARCH also donates seeds to educational, nutritional or community development projects throughout the region via its Community Seed Grant programme.

Access to diverse seeds is not sufficient in itself to build a robust regional seed system. Another prerequisite is knowledge of how to grow and use the crops and how to save seeds and apply simple breeding practices to promote crop adaptation and improvement. Native Seeds/SEARCH, therefore, devotes a great deal of its energy to public education. The organization's flagship educational programme is Seed School, a week-long course in strengthening individual and community capacity for building resilient seed systems (Plate 21). Native Seeds/SEARCH also provides public education through a free lecture series, public tours of its seed bank and farm and presentations at a diversity of venues.

Governance and support

Native Seeds/SEARCH is governed by a volunteer board of directors that provides direction to the executive director, who is responsible for overseeing the fulfillment of the organization's mission and for supervising staff, which at the time of this writing includes 16 people spread across conservation, distribution, development, education and administrative functions. In addition to paid staff, the organization relies heavily on volunteer support from the community. Volunteers assist with many aspects of farm grow-outs, as well as seed cleaning and packaging at the seed bank and various tasks at the retail store and elsewhere.

Native Seeds/SEARCH draws its financial support from many directions. It operates as a member-supported NGO, and contributions from members (currently numbering about 3,000 households) and non-members alike account for about a third of its revenue. An additional third of the revenue is derived from sales of seeds, southwestern food products, Native crafts and related products. The remainder of the organization's financial needs is met by grants from private or corporate foundations, tribal communities or government entities.

Successes and future directions

Native Seeds/SEARCH has had many notable successes in its first 30 years of existence. Perhaps most obviously, the creation of the seed bank collection resulted in the preservation of a substantial number of unique crops, many of which were on the verge of permanent loss and would likely otherwise be extinct today. Not only was this diversity buffered from loss, but it has been documented, made more broadly accessible and, in many cases, returned to the communities from which it originated. Perhaps less tangible but no less important, the pioneering work of Native Seeds/SEARCH is an example of a regional seed model that has provided inspiration for efforts elsewhere and has brought the importance of crop diversity to increased public attention in the southwest and beyond.

Several successful past and current projects demonstrate the breadth of Native Seeds/SEARCH's activities and impact. Through its Sierra Madre project, it worked closely with the Rarámuri people of the Sierra Madre Occidental of northern Mexico to support their traditional livelihoods, including their rich agricultural systems. Native Seeds/SEARCH was also instrumental in establishing a botanical reserve in Arizona dedicated to the in-situ preservation of wild chilies (*Capsicum annuum*), the first reserve of its kind in the United States. It also founded the Traditional Native American Farmers' Association, which networks and supports the work of Native farmers in the United States. The Desert Foods for Diabetes project provided education on the benefits of wild and domesticated desert foods from the southwest for people suffering from obesity or diabetes, and the Diné Cultural Memory Bank produced an educational programme to teach Diné children about their people's traditional agricultural crops and practices. Native Seeds/SEARCH recently established the first 'seed library' (a small community seed bank with free exchange of seeds) in Arizona and provided seeds and education to help get others started in the region, including a sophisticated network in eight public libraries in Tucson. Native Seeds/ SEARCH has also been instrumental in the recent revival of a local heritage wheat variety called White Sonora, which is contributing to the re-establishment of a local grain economy in southern Arizona.

In many ways, the model for regional seed security that Native Seeds/ SEARCH developed has proved to be successful, but much remains to be done. The organization has operated under a centralized model of seed production and distribution, which, while efficient and effective in some respects, fails to fully engage the entire community in the management of the region's crop diversity and, therefore, does not achieve the full potential for adaptation and resilience. Furthermore, the increasing demand for the desert-adapted seeds stewarded by Native Seeds/SEARCH is putting a strain on the ability of the organization to produce an adequate quantity and diversity of seeds. In combination, these and other considerations stress the need for a more decentralized, community-driven approach to regional seed production, distribution and education, with robust mechanisms for seed backup and exchange. We envision an integrated network of community seed banks and seed libraries in the region, with Native Seeds/SEARCH providing a valuable supporting role, and with a strong community of empowered custodian farmers forming a solid foundation.

32 Burundi

Community seed banks and the Welthungerhilfe programme in Kirundo

Christian Ngendabanka, Godefroid Niyonkuru, Lucien D'Hooghe and Thomas Marx

Purpose and evolution

The Welthungerhilfe programme in the province of Kirundo in northern Burundi was concerned about the availability of seeds during the planting season. Farmers lost many seeds because of poor storage at the household level, theft was also common and some farmers tended to sell their seeds when faced with a cash shortage. The result was that many families did not have anything left from their own harvest and had to count on external sources of new seeds to plant. Building on an existing seed multiplication programme and personal experience, Welthungerhilfe's project leader and country director initiated the establishment of seed banks. The dual-purpose structures are used as storage facilities during harvest, but mainly as seed banks. Part of the harvest is stored to ensure there is enough for the next planting season, and usually a portion is sold to traders. The stores are called Ikigega rusangi in Kirundo, which means community granaries (Plate 22).

Welthungerhilfe developed the plan for construction of the storage facilities and a training programme for their management. This plan and approach later inspired other organizations (the Alliance 2015 Partner of Welthungerhilfe Concern International, the Belgian Technical Cooperation and the European Union's support programme in Burundi, Programme Post-Conflit de Développement Rural) to invest in seed banks as well. Several seed banks have been built, and the local government is starting a support programme for them. At first, fewer than 50 farmers participated in each seed bank, and only a few crops were stored. However, numbers have increased significantly: now, 300–1,000 farmers are involved at each of 14 seed banks, which are still being used as initially planned and designed. Recently, seed banks have been formally registered at the level of a notary.

Construction of an equipped 15m by 10m seed bank and a 10m by 10m germination storage area currently costs about 20,000 Euros (EUR; about US$27,740). These funds were provided by the Welthungerhilfe project with co-financing from Germany's Federal Ministry for Economic Cooperation. Operation and maintenance costs are estimated at 5 per cent of the value of stored seeds or about EUR 1,000 per season for each seed bank. Seed banks are currently functioning without further direct financial support from Welthungerhilfe.

All members pay a one-time subscription fee. This fee differs from seed bank to seed bank, ranging from 1,000 to 5,000 Burundi francs (about US$0.65–3.23). Seed bank members must contribute 5 per cent of the quantity of seed they store, and this is sold by the management committee to cover operating costs. Welthungerhilfe's administrative and monitoring costs are not paid by the community.

Functions and activities

The seed banks store both food and seeds to ensure food security and make seed available for the next season. Another aim is to guarantee proper conservation and protection against theft. The seed banks store beans, maize, rice, potatoes, sorghum, onions and cassava. Potatoes and onions have been newly introduced to the region, and special storage areas have been built for those two crops.

The seed banks have an important indirect impact: they contribute to regulating seed and food prices for smallholder farmers. This became particularly apparent in 2011 when local government prohibited the sale of staple food crops to traders to ensure that farmers conserved their crops for personal use and kept a minimum reserve of seeds. This had a major impact on the seed banks; they experienced a 40 per cent increase in use in 2011, which was sustained in the following years. The 14 seed banks currently store about 500–700Mt.

All seeds come from local crops. Farmers store some of their harvest in the seed banks to ensure that they have seeds for the next planting season. The banks play a very important role in the communities' food and seed production systems. Over time, more seeds have become available as crop yields have increased. The quality of seeds has improved compared with those stored at the individual level; for example, the rate of weevil infestation has decreased considerably as proper fumigation is carried out at the banks.

The seed banks also have a teaching function: farmers come together at the seed bank facilities and exchange experiences. A challenge remains in terms of maintaining good management of the stored products and the facilities.

Support

In the beginning, the communities received financial and technical assistance to build the seed banks. The management team received training in management and operation of the facilities, fumigation materials, basic furniture and stationery, administrative training and grants for income-generating activities. After the seed banks were established, support was reduced to monitoring visits and refresher training courses. Welthungerhilfe staff provide further capacity-building support as follow up and fund improvements to the structures as new developments occur in the region.

At the moment, the seed banks maintain informal contacts and exchange experience mainly among themselves, as farmers have limited opportunities to communicate beyond their own communities. However, Welthungerhilfe has created links with regional organizations and crop research institutes. Recognition of the seed banks at the national level is a result of their connection with Welthungerhilfe. The Burundian government has taken the first steps towards supporting the organization of farmers into cooperatives by putting in place the necessary laws and regulations, and this has had an impact on the seed banks (see below). At the moment, there is no formal relation with the national gene bank.

Management and collaboration

All seed bank members are smallholder farmers, who have access to the facilities in their location. No distinction is made between women and men. In Burundi, there are no specific roles for women and men in agriculture. In some cases, husband and wife work together in the field; in other cases, only the woman works in the field. Size of the land is an important factor: when the holding is less than 0.8ha, which is the case for 20 per cent of the farmers in Kirundo, the woman of the family usually works the land and the man works elsewhere, e.g. as a daily labourer for large landowners or as a small trader on a bicycle. Burundian society is progressing, and more attention is being paid to gender issues.

Withdrawing stored food and seeds from seed banks is based on a code of conduct consisting of rules defined by the members themselves when the seed bank is first established. At some seed banks, members opted for a requirement that both husband and wife be present when a withdrawal is made or, at least, written authorization of the absent spouse. This rule was a solution to the locally widespread practice of polygamy. Men with two or more wives (usually two, of which one is unofficial) often withdrew the harvest of the older wife to give to the younger one. There were also allegations that men would remove goods to sell for money to buy drinks, without the knowledge of their wives.

The seed banks contain both stockpiles belonging to individual members and stockpiles per crop designated for the overall management of the seed bank. Records of the stored material are kept by an elected committee.

Under the guidance of an elected management committee, members carry out daily operations with backup from Welthungerhilfe staff. Members use word of mouth to keep informed and to organize regular meetings. The challenge of dealing with embezzlement and mistrust among members and management has affected some of the community seed banks. Currently, all banks are officially registered as cooperatives, and this 'official character' is expected to contribute to improving governance by the management teams. Welthungerhilfe continues to advocate policies and laws that will make the seed system more supportive of smallholder farmers. It recently asked the ministry in charge of cooperatives to recognize the management structures of the seed banks, as Welthungerhilfe had been involved in their setup and training of the management committees.

Welthungerhilfe cooperated with the Institut des Sciences Agronomiques du Burundi (ISABU) on trials of various varieties of potatoes, which eventually resulted in the choice of one variety that was then promoted in the region by providing plants to farmers who would grow and multiply them. Currently, some farmers still produce potatoes although in small quantities. The seed banks were designed with a second storage area especially devoted to germination of potato seeds; however, the dryers are mainly used to dry onions produced through another Welthungerhilfe project. With ISABU involvement, Welthungerhilfe supported continuation of the potato production activity by linking some of the farmers who had been propagating the plants with private farmers in other provinces who were already advanced in the production of potato seeds.

The International Crops Research Institute for the Semi-Arid Tropics, based in Nairobi, provided the Welthungerhilfe programme with improved seeds of groundnut, pigeon pea and *Elusine* (grass species), which are better adapted to dry spells and have short growing cycles. Field trials were conducted by Welthungerhilfe, and the seed banks were used to store seeds. Currently, some farmers are producing the groundnut variety.

The Celian Zonal Research Centre is a research institute based in Tanzania for the introduction and promotion of yam, another drought-resistant crop that has shown encouraging results during field trials. This crop is not well known in the Kirundo, although more and more farmers are growing it. The produce is not stored in our seed banks, even though there is no special need for protected storage for this type of plant. According to our agronomist, yam has much more potential in this region than potatoes.

Welthungerhilfe has also cooperated with the Food and Agriculture Organization (FAO), ISABU and the Catholic Relief Service in the introduction of plants resistant to cassava disease (mainly mosaic virus) in the region.

Policy and legal environment

The Direction Provincial d'Agriculture et Élevage (DPAE) in Kirundo provided assistance to the Welthungerhilfe programme in terms of sensitization of farmers regarding the establishment of community seed banks. It also helped during the establishment of the seed bank management committees. In all its projects, Welthungerhilfe collaborates closely with DPAE field personnel: agricultural extension workers, of whom there is one per 'hill', the smallest administrative unit in Burundi; and agronomists, of whom there is one per 'commune'.

The new Burundian national agriculture policy (Plan national d'investissement agricole, 2012–2017) highlights the importance of the agricultural sector and smallholder farmers in Burundi in ensuring food security and reducing poverty. Support to farmer cooperatives is one way to improve agricultural productivity and improve the flow of food to markets. Seed banks could benefit from this support. To date, Kirundo has one of the only approved provincial investment plans for the agricultural sector. Construction and support for seed banks are part of this plan and the budget is earmarked at EUR 1.875 million (EUR 125,000 for each of the 15 units); this amounts to 2.7 per cent of the total agricultural investment budget for Kirundo.

At present, people at all Welthungerhilfe-built seed banks have had training in how to set up a registered cooperative or at least a registered association, e.g. training on the constitution, membership, benefits, rights and obligations. All units have already submitted a plan for their particular structure and have introduced written regulations endorsed by a notary. They are now waiting for government approval of their registration. Welthungerhilfe has been cooperating closely with the Burundian Ministère du Développement Communal in the establishment of seed banks and the training of their members to become an officially registered cooperative.

Achievements and prospects

In general, as a result of the seed banks, crop diversity has increased; potatoes and onions, which are new to the region, are now grown. The banks' facilities and the seed multiplication programme make seed available all year round. The food supply for member households has increased, as has the quality of food. Although we have not made precise calculations, the income of member households has likely increased as a result of the efforts of the community seed banks. Involvement of the cooperative movement at the provincial level is likely to further strengthen the banks. The new Burundian agricultural investment plan gives us hope that investments in agriculture will increase. The national plan focusses on boosting small farmers' capacity to ensure national food security. In this context, further investments in capacity building among farmers, in agricultural infrastructure and in building a network could lead to a national (or even international) system of seed banks – although not in the short term.

33 Honduras

Community seed banks established by local agricultural research committees

Orvill Omar Gallardo Guzmán,
Carlos Antonio Ávila Andino, Marvin Joel
Gómez Cerna, Mainor Guillermo
Pavón Hernández and Gea Galluzzi

Background

In Honduras, community seed banks are closely related to the local agricultural research committees (Comités de Investigación Agrícola Local or CIALs), which were introduced by the Centro Internacional de Agricultura Tropical (CIAT). A CIAL is a group of men and women who are interested in engaging in collaborative research to improve crop management and productivity and to find solutions to the general challenges surrounding agricultural activities in their communities. The so-called 'young' CIALs are recently established groups of 12- to 20-year-olds who have come together to receive hands-on training to improve their agricultural management skills. In the 1990s, two organizations began working with the CIALs: the Fundación para la Investigación Participativa con Agricultores de Honduras (FIPAH) and the Programa de Reconstrucción Rural (PRR). Currently, 151 CIALs are in operation throughout the country; 117 with the support of FIPAH and PRR.

CIALs were initially conceived as a way for communities to participate in agricultural research and focussed mainly on improving productivity by introducing new management technologies and methods. The work of FIPAH and PRR was kick-started by funding from the International Development Research Centre in Canada, in collaboration with the University of Guelph (Canada) and World Accord (a nongovernmental organization (NGO)), respectively. Since 1998, FIPAH has been receiving support from USC Canada through its Seeds of Survival programme (Chapter 37). By the end of the decade, Norway's Development Fund had begun to provide support (Chapter 35), and the government of Honduras allocated some funding for technology diffusion and crop diversification. Over time, other organizations have become interested in using the CIAL approach. Among them are CARE, through its food security and economic development programme (Promoción de la Seguridad Alimentaria y Desarrollo Económico en las Cuencas) in the Choluteca and Negro river watersheds, and the Escuela Agrícola Panamericana Zamorano (EAP-Zamorano); these two programmes manage a total of 34 CIALs.

Participatory plant breeding

By the end of the 1990s, the CIALs began to get involved in a participatory bean-breeding programme, evaluating improved lines obtained from EAP-Zamorano and CIAT. The objective was not only to improve yields but also to broaden this commodity's genetic base to withstand the environmental disasters that had affected production and conservation of local plant genetic resources (primarily Hurricane Mitch in 1998). In tests, most introduced lines were found to be less adapted and less productive compared with the local varieties they were meant to replace. Therefore, the focus of participatory research turned to locally available landraces; material was recollected from several areas, characterized and introduced into the breeding programme. In this way, the breeding effort gradually evolved into a broader programme that encompassed issues related to conservation and use of agro-biodiversity.

Early on in the process of collecting and characterizing local varieties, the importance of conserving and documenting this material became evident to maintain a broad genetic base for plant breeding. A decision was made to conserve seed at different levels: at the community level in each CIAL or group of CIALs and in regional backup centres managed by FIPAH and PRR experts in collaboration with farmers and volunteers. This gave rise to the seed bank component of the programme.

The first community seed bank was established in 2000 in the CIAL of the Mina Honda community in the department of Yoro, where the community had been concentrating on breeding beans and had released a successful improved variety, Macuzalito, from crosses between the landrace Concha rosada and an improved line supplied by EAP-Zamorano. Based on the interest shown by other CIALs, new banks were established. To date, 11 community seed banks supported by FIPAH (Santa Cruz, La Patastera, La Laguna de los Cárcamos, Cafetales, San José de la Mora, Agua Blanca, Los Linderos, Ojo de Agua, Barrio Nuevo, El Águila and Maye) and two supported by PRR (El Palmichal and Nueva Esperanza) are in operation (Plate 23). Three regional backup seed banks have been established in Yorito (Yoro); San Isidro (Francisco Morazán); and La Buena Fe (Santa Barbara).

Network of seed banks and their operation

The seed banks differ in size and capacity, depending on the size of the CIAL they are associated with, but they tend to have a common minimum infrastructure and equipment. They are operated by the CIAL's management committee and follow the same basic model. Their main role is to maintain seed reserves of the local varieties that have been included in breeding efforts and are frequently planted by farmers in the area. Smaller samples of the original landraces collected in the region are also kept, especially those that are still being used. Other materials are maintained in regional backup banks that fulfill a more conservation-oriented role.

The Santa Cruz CIAL in Yorito has six active members and its seed bank is relatively small; it conserves local bean and maize landraces and is mainly dedicated to reproducing and distributing improved maize varieties – Chileño, Negrito, Capulín, Capulín cycle 2, Guaymas and Santa Cruz – mainly to local farmers.

Although it focusses on maize and beans, the Ojo de Agua CIAL in the municipality of Jesus de Otoro (department of Intibucá) conserves a broader diversity of genetic material, including species such as runner beans (*Phaseolus coccineus*) and lima beans (*Phaseolus lunatus*), several cucurbits (including numerous types of 'pataste' [*Sechium edule*]) and a few forage crops. The seed bank also maintains samples of fruit produced by trees introduced and maintained on the back patio of CIAL coordinator Don Claros. His family values conservation of agricultural biodiversity and also uses the seed bank to raise awareness of the importance of diversity in a healthy diet.

In both seed banks, small amounts of seeds of landraces that are less used are stored in glass jars. Large amounts of the landraces that are more actively used by farmers are stored in metal silos or clay containers. Seed is mixed with ashes, chili peppers or garlic to protect it from diseases or with cedar resin to protect it from weevil attack.

Reserves kept in community seed banks are available to both CIAL members and other farmers. Seed is distributed by loan, sale or exchange. Loans are used when requesters are CIAL members or people who are trusted to return seed in good condition, at least from the phytosanitary point of view. In this case, the borrower is required to return one-and-a-half times the amount borrowed. These seed repayments are generally used or sold as grain, as CIAL members prefer to have full control over stock in terms of its genetic integrity and phytosanitary health.

Although regeneration of bean landraces is a task widely shared among CIAL members, reproduction and re-establishment of maize seed is closely linked to maize 'guardians' (see Box 33.1). A guardian is someone recognized by the community as a natural conservationist who is given the responsibility of reproducing seed of a specific maize landrace (or improved landrace) year after year, trusting his or her capacity to select the best seeds and enough ears of maize to be representative of the landrace's genetic diversity. This is particularly important in a crop in which a high proportion is cross-pollinated.

Community seed banks in the CIALs receive support from the regional, backup bank in terms of regeneration of materials, especially those that form the base collections but are not actively in use by farmers and, thus, communities have less incentive and resources to keep reproducing. Regional banks also receive direct requests for seed from farmers and have played an important role in supplying seed in emergency situations, such as after the intense rainfall that caused the loss of over 60ha of maize in La Majada community (Comayagua) a few years ago. The regional banks provide slightly longer-term seed

---

Box 33.1 Don Santos Herrera and Don Claros Gomez, maize guardians

For several years, Don Santos has been the guardian of the local variety Capulín for the CIAL of Santa Cruz. In 2013, he passed this responsibility over to another guardian, because he had been assigned the task of reproducing the product of the second cycle of a landrace's line that had been improved through mass selection by CIAL members. To avoid contamination with other varieties, his plot – located at the top of a mountain in Santa Cruz county – is isolated from other maize plots. Don Santos visits his plot at least once a day to check on the plants. Under CIAL's guidelines, Don Santos has to select at least 200 ears in each cycle (from a 500–1,000m^2 plot or a quarter of a manzana, the local unit of land measurement) to preserve the diversity of this landrace and avoid inbreeding.

Don Claros is the coordinator of the Ojo de Agua CIAL in the county of Jesús de Otoro; the CIAL's seed bank is right in front of his house. Don Claros' family's interest in conservation is evident not only in their work with maize (in this case the Matazaneño landrace, whose height has been reduced by a metre over five years of participatory selection), but in the diversity of their orchard and garden. When Don Claros arrived in the region many years ago, farmers were unsure whether they could grow maize or beans with sufficient yields to guarantee their food security or have a surplus to sell. They were dependent on an unreliable potato production and marketing system. Don Claros' determination and the technical support provided by FIPAH through the CIAL enabled the introduction of these crops, thus strengthening food security for the whole community.

---

conservation under safer and more controlled conditions. The regional bank managed by PRR and the association of CIALs of Lake Yojoa has a seed conditioning system that maintains a constant temperature of close to 18°C and a relative humidity of 12–14 per cent. Under these conditions, regeneration of accessions can be programmed approximately every 2.5 years.

Regional banks have also forged important links with other institutions and regional and international banks. Both PRR and FIPAH are members of the national association for organic agriculture (Asociación Nacional para el Fomento de la Agricultura Ecológica). FIPAH collaborates with the International Maize and Wheat Improvement Centre, EAP-Zamorano and other regional banks, such as that of the Centro Agronómico Tropical de Investigación y Enseñanza (CATIE). FIPAH and CATIE have signed an agreement to repatriate vegetable germplasm from CATIE's germplasm bank and include it in community conservation and breeding programmes.

Documenting collections

Community seed banks in the CIALs maintain a simple documentation system on sheets of paper on which they record the site where each material was collected or obtained, the name of the farmer who contributed the seed, the collection date, the altitude of the site where it was collected and the average reported yields. Also recorded are seed loans and sales and data on the user. Regional banks have more elaborate databases, including, for example, morphological data for accessions that have been characterized. Information on traditional uses of each variety is not recorded as this information is part of the community's oral traditions. Criteria have not been established for managing and distributing information on the collections to third parties, and there is great interest on the part of FIPAH and PRR in correctly managing issues related to access, benefit-sharing and farmers' rights with respect to the community seed banks.

Capacity building and public awareness

Information on community seed bank initiatives is mainly transmitted informally among communities and CIALs, although there have also been efforts to spread the word through radio programmes. Both FIPAH and PRR regularly organize agro-biodiversity fairs where seed bank members present their collections, exchange seeds and offer typical dishes prepared with the conserved materials. Each year, CIAL members involved in seed bank activities receive training focussed on crop diversity conservation and management and crop breeding, and they now have advanced knowledge of the basic concepts of population genetics and selection. Recent training efforts have been devoted to the introduction of a landscape approach to conservation, encouraging farmers to conserve forest patches and the habitats of the wild species from which crop plants have been derived.

Impact, sustainability and future plans

Through the agro-biodiversity programme, FIPAH has promoted conservation of maize and bean landraces in 80 communities. PRR estimates that, since June 2011, it has distributed bean seed to more than 5,000 farmers and maize seed to more than 2,500, both through the central bank and the CIAL-based banks. Women have been important beneficiaries of this effort, as they generally make up 50 per cent of CIAL members. Community seed banks currently operate with support from FIPAH and PRR, who in turn still receive support from USC Canada, the Norwegian Development Fund and World Accord. A seed multiplication and commercialization programme – for traditional and improved landraces – has been envisioned to guarantee sustainability of the agro-biodiversity programme over time. With some initial external support, small seed enterprises could be created, linked to the CIALs, and quality labels for seed produced by the CIALs could be developed and registered. The plan for the future is to explore maize and bean diversity in new areas of the country and to expand the programme to include other crops and develop specific protocols and approaches. There is also an interest in improving and integrating the banks' documentation systems to develop a national database of maize and bean landraces and locally improved varieties.

Institutions, policies and legislation

Institutional recognition of agro-biodiversity conservation and use initiatives has been slow and is still very limited. Only recently, thanks to FIPAH's advocacy, has there been a change in attitude among decision-makers: FIPAH and PRR are now members of the national seed committee, which enables them to participate in discussions on how to develop systems for registering and commercializing seed of improved landraces through the CIALs. FIPAH and PRR are also members of the recently re-established (2012) national plant genetic resources commission (Comisión Nacional para los Recursos Fitogenéticos) and of national networks on climate change.

In general, it will be important to devise an appropriate legal framework to protect farmers' rights, especially if CIALs begin to register and sell seed from locally improved landraces as an incentive and a mechanism for financing the conservation activities of the local seed banks. To date the main incentive that has kept communities firm in their conservation activities has been their success in stabilizing food production and generating surplus grain for the market. However, younger generations need further incentives if they are to continue being involved in this important activity for the conservation and sustainable use of Honduran agricultural biodiversity.

34 Nepal

LI-BIRD's approach to supporting community seed banks

Pitambar Shrestha and Sajal Sthapit

Purpose and evolution of support

Kachorwa in Bara district in Nepal's central terai or plains is one of three sites of a research project entitled 'Strengthening the scientific basis of in-situ conservation of agricultural biodiversity in Nepal', implemented collaboratively by Bioversity International, the Nepal Agricultural Research Council (NARC) and Local Initiatives for Biodiversity, Research and Development (LI-BIRD) between 1997 and 2006. From 1997 to 2002, various awareness-raising activities and research were conducted at the project sites to sensitize local farming communities to the importance of agricultural biodiversity. The participatory approach that was used resulted in the enthusiastic involvement of many community members. However, despite increased awareness in the farming community, the loss of local rice varieties continued unabated in Kachorwa: from 33 in 1998 to only 14 in 2003. After much soul searching by the project team and extended consultations with the farming community, the Bara community seed bank was established as a pilot project (Plate 24). Managed by the local farmers, its aim was to halt the rapid loss of local varieties and to recover lost varieties. The success of the seed bank can be measured in terms of the large increase in the number of local varieties now available in the community: 80 in 2010 (Shrestha et al., 2010).

To make the community seed bank functional and sustainable, an extra effort was made to empower farmers. An organization of farmers, called the Agriculture Development and Conservation Society (ADCS), was established and registered at the district administration office. The purpose of this organization was not only to promote the community seed bank, but also to function as a nodal organization for agriculture and biodiversity research and development at the village level. By mid-2014, ADCS had about 400 members, of whom 362 were women.

With the establishment of ADCS, members started searching for and recovering lost varieties by visiting neighbouring villages and districts when crops were mature to be able to easily identify varieties. They were motivated to collect local varieties partly because some members were already involved in participatory plant breeding of rice in which local varieties were used as a parent, and these efforts were leading to good results in the form of improved varieties. Farmers named one of the promising varieties Kachorwa 4 combining their village name and the fact that it was variety line number 4. Members of ADCS now produce seeds of this variety every year and have been generating revenues for both the producers and the organization. This variety is now being registered with the National Seed Board of Nepal.

ADCS has two strategies to maintain its conservation work: it grows all local varieties in a diversity block each year under the control of the organization to ensure a regular return of seeds to the community seed bank; and it keeps a small amount of seed of each variety in the community seed bank as a reserve that is replenished after each harvest.

ADCS has been operating a community biodiversity management fund to make the conservation work sustainable and to support members' economic activities at the household level. Starting with 75,000 Nepalese rupees (NPR; about US$1,000 at the time) in 2003, by mid-2014, the fund had grown to about US$10,000. Each year, about 100 members receive a small loan from this fund to support income-generating activities, such as rearing livestock or maintaining a small shop. ADCS charges 12 per cent interest, which is lower than other sources. The borrower does not need collateral and has a year to repay the loan. ADCS also lends seeds of local varieties to its members, who pay back 150 per cent of the amount borrowed after harvesting the crop. Members also commit to growing at least one rare local variety conserved in the community seed bank.

In addition to conserving local varieties and operating the community biodiversity management fund, ADCS encourages its members to practice monthly saving. This strategy mobilizes social capital to generate financial capital. By mid-2014, the amount of members' savings had reached US$48,500. Each year, almost all members request a loan for production and consumption purposes. A few years ago, ADCS was registered as a cooperative to allow it to operate the saving and community biodiversity management funds legally.

ADCS produces and sells seeds of a few improved varieties that are in high demand in the area. This helps members earn income by selling seeds from their harvest. ADCS provides storage and processing of the seeds for a fee. Neighbouring farmers benefit by being able to buy seeds close by at a low price compared with other sources.

Because of all these successful activities of the ADCS, the Kachorwa community seed bank has become a centre of attention among farmers' groups and organizations working in the field of on-farm management of agricultural biodiversity in Nepal.

Based on the success of the seed bank at Kachorwa, LI-BIRD introduced the community bank as a major intervention in other agricultural biodiversity management projects, such as the 'Western terai landscape complex project' supported by the Global Environment Facility (six cases), the Community-based Biodiversity Management Programme supported by The Development Fund (six cases) and 'Promoting innovative mechanisms for ensuring farmers' rights through implementing access to and benefit sharing regime in Nepal' supported by the International Development Research Centre, Canada (two cases). Later, under the Community-based Biodiversity Management South Asia Programme supported by The Development Fund, LI-BIRD assisted nongovernmental organizations (NGOs) in Sri Lanka to introduce community seed banks there as well (five cases) (Chapter 28). In Nepal, about 2,000 farmer households have access to various local seeds from the 15 community seed banks that collaborate with LI-BIRD (Shrestha et al., 2013b; Chapter 25).

Functions and activities

In areas of Nepal where production potential is high, only a few farms maintain a wide diversity of local varieties of staple crops and some vegetables and fruit. However, many local varieties are still valued for their taste, agro-ecological niche specificity, ritualistic use and food culture, biotic and abiotic stress tolerance, better storage and a longer fruiting period providing households with a more extended supply of vegetables. Once local varieties with these traits disappear, their reintroduction will be difficult, as farmers – not the formal seed sector – are the sources of seeds of these varieties. Thus, the main goal of community seed banks supported by LI-BIRD is to ensure on-farm management of local varieties of selected crops and their availability to farmers.

A community seed bank first gathers information and seed samples of local varieties by organizing a diversity fair (Adhikari et al., 2006) or carrying out participatory four-cell analysis to identify the status of local crop diversity (Sthapit et al., 2006). The information is used to identify common, unique and rare local varieties and, based on this, seeds are collected and a distribution plan is developed. Regular regeneration of seeds is carried out by establishing diversity blocks (Tiwari et al., 2006) and also by distributing seeds to seed bank members. In addition to conserving local varieties, community seed banks have also engaged in the production and marketing of some improved varieties for which there is high demand locally. The seed banks consider this a way to provide services beyond their members, increase the incomes of seed-producer farmers and generate some operating revenues.

Community seed banks have included a number of cereal crops (rice, wheat, finger millet, maize, barley, buckwheat and minor millets), vegetables (sponge gourd, pumpkin, ridge gourd, bottle gourd, taro, elephant foot yam, yam), pulses (cowpea, bean, soybean, broad bean, horse gram, pigeon pea and field pea) and oil seed crops (rapeseed, lean seed and sesame) in their collections. So far, the 15 community seed banks supported by LI-BIRD have conserved more than 1,200 local varieties of these crops, which amounts to about 10 per cent of what is conserved in the National Agriculture Genetic Resources Centre (national gene bank). Many of these crops fall into the category of neglected and underutilized species.

When seeds are stored in a community seed bank, records are kept of the details of collection and the properties of the variety. To continue regeneration of the collections, community seed banks employ three strategies: distribution of seeds among members and non-members, establishment of diversity blocks for major crops and retention of small amounts of seed at the bank as remnant stock.

Based on the principle of conservation through use, seeds and planting materials are regenerated in small areas or multiplied in larger plots depending on local demand. Seeds are normally distributed on loan or sometimes sold to members and non-members both within and outside the village. At the community seed bank at Kachorwa, seed production and the sale of a variety of rice produced through participatory plant breeding (Kachorwa 4) are regular activities. In other cases, varietal enhancement also takes place with technical support and guidance from LI-BIRD. For example, improvement of Kalonuniya and Tilki aromatic rice varieties is carried out in Shivagunj, Jhapa and Rampur Dang.

Rural farming communities in Nepal face multiple challenges. A strong farmers' institution like a community seed bank can also function as a forum for local problem-solving and collective action. Some community seed banks also provide additional services to community members. For example, every community seed bank supported by LI-BIRD has been operating a community biodiversity management fund (Shrestha et al., 2012; 2013a), which can be loaned at a low rate of interest to finance production activities. This fund has not only created opportunities for seed bank members to increase their income, but it has also been a way to generate revenue for the seed bank in the form of interest.

Support

LI-BIRD, as a facilitating organization, offers support to farming communities for the establishment and management of a community seed bank. This involves several steps, beginning with creating awareness through various participatory methods, such as informal discussions, village workshops, diversity fairs and a site visit. These activities help raise awareness among farming communities of the value of genetic resources for current and future use and provide a general idea of the status of local agricultural biodiversity, which is necessary for planning community seed bank activities. Through its various projects, LI-BIRD also provides financial support for developing the necessary physical infrastructure (seed store, meeting room, seed-storage structures, wooden racks, seed cleaning and drying materials, etc.). LI-BIRD considers empowerment of seed bank members a key to success and sustainability. Hence, training and capacity-building activities are designed to cover not only technical aspects of seeds and community seed bank management, but also local institution management and governance. Its work includes developing local resource people and ways to generate local financial resources for maintaining the seed bank when there is no support from external agencies. In addition, LI-BIRD facilitates the process of linking the community seed bank with local government, extension offices and the national gene bank.

Networking

At the latest count (2013), there were 115 active community seed banks in Nepal, located across the country from terai to high hills and from east to west. Most are supported by international organizations or NGOs, but a few are funded by the government. They can be grouped into three types: those that deal only with local varieties; those whose main function is to conserve local varieties, and also to regenerate and distribute seed of modern varieties; and those that primarily supply high volumes of modern varieties of seeds (Chaudhary, 2013). At the first national workshop on community seed banks in 2012, participants reached the consensus that a true community seed bank should engage in farm management of local varieties. They also concluded that, although Nepal has a large number of community seed banks, sharing of knowledge and resources has not occurred, except in a few cases where farmers' groups and practitioners have visited each other's seed bank.

In March 2013, a national workshop for farmers and groups involved in establishing and managing community seed banks in Nepal was held at Kachorwa. It concluded with the formation of an ad hoc committee to set up a national network of community seed banks. A detailed procedure is yet to be developed, but the committee intends to provide a platform for learning and sharing among community seed banks; facilitate the exchange of seeds and planting materials; prepare a national catalogue of genetic resources conserved by community seed banks; facilitate a process of linking community seed banks with the national gene bank; represent community seed banks in national fora when necessary; and facilitate incorporation of the conservation of plant genetic resources into the activities of community seed banks that are not already doing this. LI-BIRD staff are helping the new national network become a well-functioning organization.

Policy and legal environment

To fulfill its obligation as a party to the Convention on Biological Diversity, the government of Nepal developed the National Biodiversity Strategy 2002 and drafted an Access to Genetic Resource and Benefit Sharing bill. Similarly, as a member country of the International Treaty on Plant Genetic Resources for Food and Agriculture, it has drafted a Plant Variety Protection and Farmers' Rights Act. In addition, an agro-biodiversity policy has been in place since 2007.

Remarkably, none of these legal documents discusses the term 'community seed bank'. It was only in 2008/09 that the government of Nepal endorsed the concept of a community seed bank in the budget speech of that year. The government envisioned that seed banks would improve access to quality seed for small and marginal farmers. An operational guideline was prepared by government staff for piloting new community seed banks in 17 districts. However, this document focusses mainly on increasing the seed replacement rate of improved varieties to increase food security and pays little attention to the conservation and sustainable use of plant genetic resources. Although a step in the right direction, it does not, in the view of most community seed banks in the country, offer much concrete support (for a more detailed discussion of policies affecting community seed banks in Nepal, see Chapter 41).

Sustainability and prospects

One of the challenges for community seed banks is to develop mechanisms for sustaining their activities without support from external agencies. In the case of those supported by LI-BIRD, this is an important agenda item right from the beginning. Community seed banks that are completely self-sustaining do not yet exist in Nepal, but a number of practices have been tested with good results. For example, a locally managed fund, established with contributions by (donor) project funds and the community, has been established for every LI-BIRD-supported seed bank, and this has been effective in generating some financial resources. Some of these seed banks have generated income by integrating the production and sale of seeds of improved varieties to farmers beyond the community. Some seed bank members have agreed to grow one variety each, while others have introduced the idea of a diversity block managed by a farmers' group or a village. Both strategies are helpful in terms of minimizing costs. Linking community seed banks with local government, line agencies and the national gene bank is another way in which LI-BIRD is addressing sustainability.

Acknowledgements

The authors would like to acknowledge the financial support provided by Bioversity International for initiating the community seed bank in Kachorwa, Bara, in 2003, the first one in the history of LI-BIRD. We also thank funding agencies, such as The Development Fund (Norway), the United Nations Environment Programme's Global Environment Facility, the United Nations Development Programme's Western Terai Landscape Complex Project and the International Development Research Centre (Canada), for their support in establishing and strengthening community seed banks in Nepal.

References

Adhikari, A., Rana, R., Gautam, R., Subedi, A., Upadhyay, M., Chaudhary, P., Rijal, D. and Sthapit, B. (2006) 'Diversity fair: promoting exchange of knowledge and germplasms', in B. Sthapit, P. Shrestha and M. Upadyay (eds) *On-farm Management of Agricultural Biodiversity in Nepal: Good Practices*, Nepal Agricultural Research Council, Khumaltar, Lalitpur, Nepal; Local Initiatives for Biodiversity, Research and Development, Pokhara, Kaski, Nepal; and Bioversity International, Nepal, pp25–28
Chaudhary, P. (2013) 'Banking seed by smallholders in Nepal: workshop synthesis', in P. Shrestha, R. Vernooy and P. Chaudhary (eds) *Community Seed Banks in Nepal: Past, Present, Future. Proceedings of a National Workshop, 14–15 June 2012, Pokhara,*

Nepal, Local Initiatives for Biodiversity, Research and Development, Pokhara, Kaski, Nepal, pp130–139

Shrestha, P., Shrestha, P., Sthapit, S., Rana, R. B. and Sthapit, B. (2013a) 'Community biodiversity management fund: promoting conservation through livelihood development in Nepal', in W. S. de Boef, A. Subedi, N. Peroni, M. Thijssen and E. O'Keeffe (eds) *Community Biodiversity Management: Promoting Resilience and the Conservation of Plant Genetic Resources*, Routledge/Earthscan, London, pp118-122

Shrestha, P., Sthapit, S. and Paudel, I. (2013b) 'Community seed banks: a local solution to increase access to quality and diversity of seeds', in P. Shrestha, R. Vernooy and P. Chaudhary (eds) *Community Seed Banks in Nepal: Past, Present, Future. Proceedings of a National Workshop, 14–15 June 2012, Pokhara, Nepal*, Local Initiatives for Biodiversity, Research and Development, Pokhara, Kaski, Nepal, pp61–75

Shrestha, P., Sthapit, S., Paudel, I., Subedi, S., Subedi, A. and Sthapit, B. (2012) *A Guide to Establishing a Community Biodiversity Management Fund for Enhancing Agricultural Biodiversity Conservation and Rural Livelihoods*, Local Initiatives for Biodiversity, Research and Development, Pokhara, Kaski, Nepal

Shrestha, P., Subedi, A., Paudel, B. and Bhandari, B. (2010) *Community Seed Bank: A Source Book* (in Nepali), Local Initiatives for Biodiversity, Research and Development, Pokhara, Kaski, Nepal

Sthapit, B., Rana, R., Subedi, A., Gyawali, S., Bajracharya, J., Chaudhary, P., Joshi, B. K., Sthapit, S., Joshi, K. D. and Upadhyay, M. P. (2006) 'Participatory four-cell analysis (FCA) for understanding local crop diversity', in B. Sthapit, P. Shrestha and M. Upadhyay (eds) *On-farm Management of Agricultural Biodiversity in Nepal: Good Practices*, Nepal Agricultural Research Council, Khumaltar, Lalitpur, Nepal; Local Initiatives for Biodiversity, Research and Development, Pokhara, Kaski, Nepal; and Bioversity International, Nepal, pp13-16

Tiwari, R., Sthapit, B., Shrestha, P., Baral, K., Subedi, A., Bajracharya, J. and Yadav, R. B. (2006) 'Diversity blocks: assessing and demonstrating local diversity', in B. Sthapit, P. Shrestha and M. Upadyay (eds) *On-farm Management of Agricultural Biodiversity in Nepal: Good Practices*, Nepal Agricultural Research Council, Khumaltar, Lalitpur, Nepal; Local Initiatives for Biodiversity, Research and Development, Pokhara, Kaski, Nepal; and Bioversity International, Nepal, pp29–32

35 Norway's Development Fund

Supporting community seed banking practices

Teshome Hunduma and Rosalba Ortiz

Climate change is predicted to have major impacts on subsistence small-scale farmers in the developing world, but these impacts are likely to be complex and locally specific. For subsistence farmers and their communities, the risks are diverse – drought, flood and crop and animal diseases are some of the anticipated changes affecting agriculture (Morton, 2007). To ensure long-term food security in the context of these increasing risks, it is crucial to strengthen the adaptive capacity of vulnerable food producers in developing countries.

As part of the response to these challenges, the Development Fund has established a programme on agro-biodiversity and climate change adaptation. It emphasizes sustainable natural resource management and agriculture practices adapted to local conditions. Also part of the programme are strengthening community knowledge of vulnerability risk assessment, planning, local governance and implementation of measures to reduce vulnerability.

Today's food production is increasingly dependent on a narrow genetic base, which reduces farmers' choice of crops and makes them more vulnerable. One of the key strategies in the Development Fund's programme is to work with farmers and their organizations to conserve, use and develop agricultural biodiversity on farm. Food security and the capacity of farming systems to adapt to a changing climate depend not only on sustainable crop diversity, but also on the ability of farmers to make use of traditional knowledge and innovation. In this regard, the Development Fund is supporting initiatives, such as community seed banks and participatory plant breeding, as ways to increase on-farm genetic diversity and local seed security.

Purpose and evolution

The community seed bank emerged as a collective approach to strengthening local capacity to conserve, use and develop crop genetic resources. It provides two important benefits to farm communities: it ensures both the availability of good seeds and genetic variability of crops so that they can adapt to changing growing conditions. These two functions are best achieved through a collective approach as individual households have limited capacity to store high-quality seeds or maintain a large variety. In practice, a group of farmers produce and store seeds in larger quantities to ensure their availability at the right time. They also keep diverse types of seeds in smaller quantities to ensure conservation of genetic material for use in plant breeding to develop particular varieties for special needs now and in the future. The overall result has been increased local seed security. The approach has been spearheaded by many local civil society organizations in partnership with the Development Fund and working with organized farmer groups. The size and scale varies from location to location, but the model is similar. One necessary feature is collaboration with other stakeholders working on conservation and development of genetic resources, such as breeding institutions, universities and national gene banks.

Through its regional programmes, the Development Fund has supported 62 community seed banks that have benefitted about 21,000 smallholder households in Asia, Africa and Central America. These seed banks also provide services to non-member farming households and communities (see Table 35.1). Not all 62 are operating well, and some are relatively new (those in Bhutan and Malawi), but, overall, they offer important conservation and seed security services.

The community seed banks serve three major functions:

- *Provide access to germplasm:* Most gene banks are located far from farming communities, making it difficult for farmers to gain access to their collections. In addition, centralized gene banks have long-term conservation objectives and usually do not keep the large quantities of seeds required to fulfil farmers' short-term needs, for example, in the case of a natural catastrophe.
- *Make diverse, high-quality seeds available:* Variation in the quality of seeds in the informal seed system and the inability of the formal seed system to provide diverse seeds to poor farmers continue to be a challenge in poor countries. Community seed banks focus on germplasm collection, conservation, participatory plant breeding, participatory variety selection and community-based seed production and distribution.
- *Make up for the inadequate coverage of the formal seed supply system:* The formal seed sector (government and private industry) does not meet the demands of smallholder farmers; for these farmers, the system still dominates. For example, in Ethiopia (IFPRI, 2010) and Nepal (Joshi et al., 2012), the formal seed sector contributes less than 10 per cent of the national seed supply. Community seed banks strengthen the informal seed supply.

Operations

During the last decade, seed bank practices have evolved in terms of crops covered, activities and management. In the beginning, restoration of crops from gene bank collections and farming communities was the main activity. This was done through seed multiplication on land that was either rented by the seed bank or offered by members. After multiplication, seeds were distributed by loan and through sales at a local price.

Table 35.1 Community seed banks currently supported by Norway's Development Fund

Country and region	Partner organization(s)	Year established	No. CSBs	No. FGBs	Organizational platform	Access Communities	Access Households	Main crops targeted
Ethiopia Oromia region, East Showa (Ejere and Chefe Donsa)	Ethio–Organic Seed Action (EOSA)	1997	2		Run by legally registered farmer conservator associations.	15	1,142 Indirect benefits to over 2,000 households	Teff, emmer wheat, durum wheat, chickpea, lentil, grass pea, field pea, faba bean, barley, flax, fenugreek, some spices
Amhara region, North Showa (Ankober and Siya Debir)		1997	2		Set up through a Global Environment Fund project; since 2001, supported by IBC to some extent. Not fully operational. EOSA is reorganizing them with DF support.	8	239 maintained as members	Barley, durum wheat, naked barley, emmer wheat, oat, field pea, flax, faba bean, lentil, sorghum, grass pea, chickpea, some spices
Southern region, SNNP (Gunjuru, Andegna Akulu, Wita, Cigado, Shey Amba Qleni, Gozo Boma Shash, Beayde and Mino)		2010	8		New and set up with the regional government budget and technical support from EOSA. EOSA is reorganizing them with DF support.	8	472 household members	Barley, durum wheat, emmer wheat, field pea, flax, faba bean, lentil, maize, sorghum, grass pea, enset, chickpea, root crops, spices

Malawi Northern Malawi (Rumphi)	Biodiversity Conservation Initiative and Find Your Feet	2008	14	Community managed with the support of local DF partner. The area development committees and village development committees play an important role in management, mobilization and supervision.	14 village development committees	13,440	Bambara nut, ground nut, maize, beans, sorghum, pearl and finger millets, sesame, pigeon pea, okra, amaranths, cow pea
Guatemala Chiantla, San Juan Ixcoy, Aguacatán and Todos Santos Cuchumatan	Asociación de organizaciones de los Cuchumatanes (Asocuch)	2008–2010	7	A famer seed committee runs each bank. The seed committees are linked to farmer cooperatives, which are associated with a larger network of cooperatives: Asocuch. Asocuch provides support through local promoters.	15	680	Maize, beans, wheat, legumes, potatoes
Honduras Taula B, Concepción Sur, Jesús de Otoro, La Iguala–Lempira and Monte Verde in San Francisco de Opalaca	Fundación para la Investigación Participativa con Agricultores de Honduras (FIPAH)	2004–2009	6	Run by farmer research teams associated with regional farmers' associations, with FIPAH providing technical support.	6	370	Maize, beans, legumes, tapioca, chayote, taro

(Continued)

Table 35.1 (Continued)

Country and region	Partner organization(s)	Year established	No. CSBs	No. FGBs	Organizational platform	Access Communities	Households	Main crops targeted
Nicaragua Pueblo Nuevo–Estelí, Unile, Somoto and Cayantu Totogalpa	Federación de Cooperativas para el Desarrollo	2010	3		Run by a seed committee, which is linked to a farmers' cooperative.	7	100	Maize, beans, sorghum, millet, Jamaica, nitrogen fixing beans
Bhutan	National Biodiversity Centre, natural resources and renewable research centres, district offices of the Department of Agriculture	2009	4		CSBs are managed by Farmer Field School graduates in each of the four districts with support from local extension agents (technical backstopping) and the National Biodiversity Centre.	10	More than 300	Rice, maize, buckwheat, millet, legumes
Nepal	LI-BIRD	2009	6	54	Managed by village development committee level farmers' organization called Biodiversity Conservation and Development Committee.	6	More than 2,000 annually	Rice, wheat, maize, vegetables (cucurbits, beans, cow pea, etc.), root crops, spices

Philippines	Local government units, agricultural colleges and universities, farmers' organizations	1996	3	Managed by farmers' groups (FFS graduates) together with agricultural colleges and SEARICE.	17	500	Mainly rice and maize
Thailand	Joko Learning Centre (JLC), Agriculture Land Reform Office, Alternative Agriculture Network, local government units (tambon)	1996	7	Managed by farmers' groups and supported by JLC, schools in some areas and tambon administration in other areas.	60	1,800	Rice, maize, legumes (mungbean, yardlong bean, pigeon pea, etc.), vegetables (eggplant, luffa, pumpkin, chilies, tomatoes, etc.)

Note: CSB = community seed bank; DF = Development Fund; FFS = farmer field school; FGB = field gene bank; IBC = Institute of Biodiversity Conservation; LI-BIRD = Local Initiatives for Biodiversity, Research and Development; SNNP = Southern Nations, Nationalities and People's region.

Other activities included variety rehabilitation (purification and restoration of varieties whose qualities had deteriorated), participatory plant breeding and participatory variety selection (Plate 25). These activities are undertaken by farmer groups with technical support from relevant institutions. Linking conservation with economic incentives has become important during the past few years, and some members of community seed banks are becoming organized in seed grower associations for local seed production and marketing (e.g. in Ethiopia and Guatemala).

In terms of crop coverage, most of the pioneer work has been done on cereals, pulses and oil crops; however, work has also expanded to accommodate other crops, such as potatoes in Ethiopia and chilies in Thailand. More and more farmers are forming cooperatives as a way to engage in the seed market. Another activity that has received increasing attention is the documentation of traditional knowledge of local plant genetic diversity to protect it from disappearing or being misappropriated; for example, in Nepal, seed banks keep 'community biodiversity registers'.

Services

The Development Fund's partners promote various community seed bank activities in different countries. Some are highly specialized in the collection, regeneration, distribution and maintenance of local crop diversity and documentation of the associated information and traditional knowledge, while others are engaged in variety improvement, seed production and marketing of improved farmers' varieties and modern varieties released from public research institutions.

The main services seed banks provide include:

- *Stable local seed supply:* Being close to the growers, community seed banks ensure the availability of enough good planting materials for poor farmers at the right time.
- *Conservation:* Small samples of crop varieties are collected and conserved in community seed banks to ensure that planting material is available, especially varieties that are endangered. Such samples are multiplied for conservation and for use in participatory variety improvement.
- *Emergency relief:* Seeds are stored in large quantities by organized groups of farmers to ensure that planting material is available to members through a loan system and to non-members through sales at the local price. During emergency situations, e.g. crop failure due to drought, hail or flood, the community seed bank serves as a source of planting materials for the community.
- *Variety development:* Community seed banks serve as a meeting place for the exchange of knowledge and skills in the management of plant genetic resources in general and in varietal improvement in particular. They provide a venue in which organized farmers' groups can conduct participatory plant

breeding and participatory variety selection using their own collections and advanced lines from public research institutions to develop varieties more adapted to their needs.

- *Local seed business:* Community seed banks allow farmers jointly to produce high-quality seeds that can be marketed. This can generate income and ensure the sustainability of community seed bank activities.

Women are closely involved in Development Fund-supported activities at the grassroots level: as selectors, preservers and traders of seed. In many farmers' groups, women are well represented and even outnumber men. However, there are still challenges in terms of women assuming leadership and decision-making roles given that they are often less vocal because of cultural norms that limit their mobility, education and self-confidence.

Policy and legal environment

In most countries where the Development Fund is active, the policy and legal environment is not very supportive of local seed systems. Some countries, such as India and Ethiopia, have farmers' rights acts or provisions, but implementation may not be evident. In many cases, smallholder farmers are not allowed to produce or market seeds; in others, the laws are too restrictive, e.g. seed certification laws based on criteria of the formal seed system for distinctiveness, uniformity and stability. Seed policies that are not supportive of local seed systems affect the availability of funding and technical support from governments. On the positive side, the Development Fund is working towards the legal registration of community seed banks. This step is important in terms of managing funds, seed marketing in some countries and gaining recognition and support from local government and other stakeholders.

The Development Fund has some experience with networking. South–south exchanges within and between countries allow the sharing of experience and knowledge, not only at the partner nongovernmental organization (NGO) level, but also among farmers' groups within a country. Although links between stakeholders involved in Development Fund projects at the national level are generally good, networking among the farmers' organizations that support community seed banks has been weak. Furthermore, it has been difficult to gain the support of the institutions that are developing and revising policies and regulations in the seed sector.

At the international level, the governing body of the International Treaty on Plant Genetic Resources for Food and Agriculture (ITPGRFA) is a relevant platform for the Development Fund and its partners. The Development Fund wrote a report about community seed banking practices that was distributed at the 4th session of the governing body meeting in Bali (Development Fund, 2011). The report reached delegates from over 120 countries as well as observers from many international and civil society organizations. Some of the points made were the need for governments to:

- Establish and/or support community seed banks as part of their obligation to implement farmers' rights and other provisions of the ITPGRFA, such as sustainable use and conservation of crop genetic diversity. Parties should support the up-scaling of community seed banks to reach as many farmers as possible, especially in marginalized areas.
- Integrate community seed banks with broader programmes on agricultural biodiversity, where the local seed banks should serve as a storing place for results of participatory plant breeding and participatory variety selection, and make such results accessible to farmers. Seed banks should also be venues for seed fairs for farmers to exchange and display their seed diversity.
- Include community seed banks in governments' agricultural development strategies as a vehicle for adaptation to climate variability. Agricultural extension services would provide the best institutional infrastructure to embark on a scaling up of local seed bank experiences to a national level.
- Revise seed regulations and provisions on intellectual property rights to seeds to ensure farmers' rights to save, use, exchange and sell farm-saved seeds.
- Redirect public subsidies from promoting modern varieties to fund the abovementioned activities.

Sustainability

Some of the key elements needed to ensure sustainability are strengthening the technical and organizational skills of farmers' groups and collaborating with stakeholders in the various countries. The latter are institutions supporting farmers on issues related to organization (e.g. the offices of cooperatives), seed-related policies and regulations (e.g. seed control and certification) and technical skills (e.g. research institutes, gene banks, seed quality and marketing control units).

Policy work related to plant genetic resources is also important. The Development Fund works with networks at various levels – local, national and international – to promote smallholder farmer friendly policies and the realization of farmers' rights. In this regard, the Development Fund's policy and advocacy work draws on the practical results of the community seed banks it supports.

Technical training of stakeholders is important to increase knowledge and skills in such activities as germplasm collection and short-term conservation, participatory variety selection, high-quality seed production and distribution, as well as financial management and local governance.

Apart from the financial support channeled through the Development Fund, a local fund is established and managed by the farmers' group managing each seed bank. Income sources are the sale of seeds to non-members in the community when there is a surplus, contributions from local governments and registration fees. Long-term economic sustainability could be ensured by establishing local seed businesses. Nonetheless, care should be taken to promote diversity instead of narrowing the genetic base by focussing on a few varieties and crops. Table 35.2 shows examples of how seed banks in Ethiopia are working towards sustainability.

Table 35.2 Strategies for ensuring the sustainability of farmer-led community seed banks in Ethiopia

Strategy	Examples
Financial sustainability	
Develop local seed businesses and other micro-enterprises to generate income	Initiatives include beekeeping, fruit production, membership fees and rental of meeting rooms/office space. A new community seed bank built in Ejere with Development Fund support is set to provide services as a centre for both national and international training sessions and conferences.
Enhance financial management skills	The community seed banks have bank accounts and undergo annual government audits of their finances; they are working to strengthen financial systems further in light of an increasing diversity of initiatives (youth/women's groups, soil and water conservation, etc.).
Diversify sources of financial support	Engage in seed production and marketing as well as feed supply.
Use local materials and construction techniques	The community seed banks are constructed using local materials to ensure lower costs.
Organizational sustainability	
Register farmers' groups as cooperatives or other legally recognized entities	At the community seed bank in East Showa, some farmers' groups are legally registered as seed producers. The Ejere group is one of four farmers' organizations that have won government awards at the national level: the prize was a tractor with full accessories, which will be used to provide services at the local level enabling the association to generate income.
Enhance women's leadership and participation	All programmes encourage women's leadership and ensure that their skills and knowledge within the community are valued. Strong women's leadership also helps motivate other women to become involved.
Engage young farmers and youth in activities	In all programmes, specific strategies have been developed to engage school children, youth and young farmers, including support for youth-specific farmer research teams and young farmers' productive activities (seed production and beekeeping) as well as collaboration with local schools.
Collaborate and partner with local government, agricultural extension services and other institutions	Community seed banks in East Showa have established links with local and national government agencies (extension and environment development) and research organizations in terms of participatory variety selection, genetic diversity study, on-farm conservation, germplasm introduction and seed production.

Challenges and prospects

From our work over the years, we have learned that community seed banks have brought important crops and varieties from national gene banks back to farmers' fields, distributed seed to farmers after natural catastrophes, made high-quality seeds available to farmers, secured the seed demands of poor farmers who cannot afford to buy seeds from traders, conserved crop diversity and increased farmers' income through seed sales and community biodiversity management funds.

However, there remain many challenges. Among them are: lack of policy and technical support; lack of markets for farmers' varieties; inadequate capacity and knowledge about marketing seeds among farmers; inadequate storage facilities; lack of human resources for group work during peak seasons; inferior seed quality; late distribution of seeds and late payment of seeds loaned; as well as high dependence on NGOs or a few dedicated farmers.

The main challenge, however, is at a higher level than the community. Government agricultural policies that prioritize a few high-yielding varieties still work against community seed banking objectives. Funding, research and government extension services are focused on improved varieties and ignore local seeds, and the training and orientation of development/ extension agents gives them little appreciation of the need to support local seed diversity.

There is also an impression among farmers that their traditional varieties are inferior because of the push to use modern varieties, and this may contribute to erosion of genetic resources and loss of related traditional knowledge.

Despite these challenges and based on ongoing debates and recognition of the role of plant genetic diversity for local food security and climate change adaptation, we are optimistic that governments may increase their support to community seed banks. We have already observed this in Ethiopia, Nepal and several countries in Central America. We also hope that the international community will continue to support the objectives of the ITPGRFA and that community seed banks become a key approach to the management of plant genetic resources. A step in the right direction could be made if the Global Crop Biodiversity Trust – which collects, conserves, characterizes and evaluates wild and weedy relatives of crops – would consider collaborating with the civil society organizations that support community seed banks.

References

Development Fund (2011) *Banking for the Future: Savings, Security and Seeds*, Development Fund, Oslo, Norway, www.planttreaty.org/sites/default/files/banking_future.pdf, accessed 17 July 2014

IFPRI (International Food Policy Research Institute) (2010) *Seed System Potential in Ethiopia: Constraints and Opportunities for Enhancing Production*, International Food Policy Research Institute, Washington, D.C., USA, www.ifpri.org/sites/default/files/publications/ethiopianagsectorwp_seeds.pdf, accessed 17 July 2014

Joshi, K. D., Conroy, C. and Witcombe, J. R. (2012) *Agriculture, Seed, and Innovation in Nepal: Industry and Policy Issues for the Future*, International Food Policy Research Institute, Washington, D.C., USA, www.ifpri.org/sites/default/files/publications/ Agriculture_seed_and_innovation_in_Nepal.pdf, accessed 17 July 2014

Morton, J. F. (2007) 'The impact of climate on smallholder and subsistence farming,' *PNAS*, vol. 104, no. 50, pp19680–19685, www.pnas.org/content/104/50/19680. full.pdf, accessed 17 July 2014

36 Spain

The seed network, Resembrando e Intercambiando

Members of the Red de Semillas

The Spanish seed network, Red de Semillas: 'Resembrando e Intercambiando' (re-sowing and exchanging) is a decentralized organization of a technical, social and political nature that has been active for the last 14 years. In April 1999, a small group of people involved in the organic agricultural, ecological and rural development movement in Spain organized a workshop in Madrid on agricultural biodiversity issues in which they laid the foundations of the organization. Later, in 2005, a non-profit association was established and nowadays, the seed network is an informal federation that brings together 26 local seed networks that are distributed throughout Spain (Red de Semillas, 2008). The members of the Red de Semillas are farmers and farmer organizations, technicians, agricultural experts, supporters of responsible consumption, local action groups, university staff and students, activists in ecological movements, researchers and other groups and people interested in developing a different agri-food system. The main objectives are the reintroduction of local, traditional and farmers' varieties, inspired by an agro-ecological framework (Altieri and Nicholls, 2000), the concept of food autonomy and the central role of family farming. The aim is to help coordinate activities among the various local seed networks and promote their participation at national and international levels.

Specific objectives are to:

*   support and facilitate conservation and use activities carried out by farmers;
*   facilitate and support access, production and exchange of seeds among farmers;
*   raise public awareness about the importance of agricultural biodiversity in the agri-food system;
*   promote local and traditional varieties among consumers;
*   create employment in rural areas through seed production and trading at a local level;
*   reclaim the development of public policies intended to facilitate farmers' rights to conserve, use, exchange and sell their own seeds;
*   ban genetically modified crops from the Spanish agri-food system.

These objectives are accomplished by the local seed networks and also by working groups of the Red de Semillas. These groups are focussed on topics such as national and international seed regulations, traditional knowledge, microenterprise management and organization, seed exchange, national and international relations and communication.

Working at the local level

To develop an integrated approach to working with local varieties, it is essential to include farmers and consumers in all activities. These actors are closely linked and a collective effort is needed to improve the use of local, traditional and farmers' varieties. Seed networks are the structures that create space to develop such joint activities.

Recovery of traditional knowledge

The Red de Semillas develops various research projects at the local and national levels. One area is the recovery of traditional farmers' knowledge about the management of local varieties. The people who know about the production and use of local varieties are the farmers who have been working with them for many years. Members of local seed networks interview farmers to recover their knowledge related to traditional varieties. The information is synthesized and a report is prepared to share the results. Those most interested in these reports are farmers who want to work with local, traditional and farmers' varieties. This is an example of farmer-to-farmer learning.

Participatory work in describing, testing and evaluating local varieties

In 2011, the local seed network in Andalusia carried out an in-depth study of local traditional knowledge. Seventy small farmers were interviewed, and the network subsequently published guides to the management of 50 varieties of four vegetables and seven fruit trees (Red Andaluza Semillas, 2011a, 2011b; Sanz García, 2011).

This type of research is very important because there is a dearth of information about local and traditional varieties in terms of morphology of the plants, uses and production. To encourage more people to use these varieties – both farmers and consumers – there is a need for sound technical information. In Andalusia, a group of seven farmer-researchers, with technical support from the local seed network, is carrying out research on variety descriptions, on-farm testing and evaluation of the crops in terms of yield and resistance to diseases and pests under organic conditions (Red Andaluza Semillas, 2012). Through participatory action research they have prepared protocols for the description of 15 vegetable species, discussed the most important elements to take into account in the research and the most appropriate vocabulary to use and interacted with consumers to find out what information is important to them.

Training and counselling

The Red de Semillas organizes and delivers many training activities. Each year they hold workshops aimed at farmers in several regions. The main topics include seed production (vegetables, cereals, fruits), traditional preparation, and uses and management of community seed banks and seed exchange networks. In terms of counselling, the Red de Semillas provides advice, at local and national levels, to farmers who want to start producing and selling their own seeds. This includes instructions about administrative requirements and procedures.

Seed exchange networks

Farmers in Spain used to exchange seeds of local varieties with their neighbours, but nowadays this practice is in decline. In general, Spanish farmers no longer save seeds. Seed exchange networks are mechanisms to help farmers obtain seeds of local and traditional varieties through a revival of exchange practices. Interested farmers donate seeds to the exchange network and they are pooled in a collection, as in a seed library. Farmers who have shared seeds can obtain seeds from the collection in return. In Andalusia, the local network has built an exchange system that in 2013 had 400 members and more than 300 varieties available (Red Andaluza Semillas, 2013). Exchanges can be carried out by regular mail or directly at seed-exchange workshops that the network organizes.

Consumption

Farmers need to sell their products to be able to continue producing; thus, consumers are the cornerstone in the conservation and use of local varieties. Based on this insight, the Red de Semillas carries out a large number of activities that involve consumers. The objective is to raise public awareness about the importance of local varieties in the agri-food system and to promote the consumption of these varieties. The main methods the seed network uses to reach consumers are:

- informative conferences in universities, schools, women's associations, etc.;
- information points in schools, local markets, consumers associations and small shops (the latter two are very important allies for developing local food production and short supply chains);
- tasting activities where consumers are invited to sample local varieties and provide their evaluation.

The tasting sessions have two objectives. The first is to find out which varieties are favoured by consumers: because they are sweeter, they have a better smell, etc. This information helps farmers identify varieties that consumers like and this stimulates marketing. The second aim is to help consumers reflect on their sensations while eating. People tend to eat without thinking, and it is important to teach our minds and bodies to think about our senses: touch, smell, sight and taste.

Knowledge transfer: publications

The Red de Semillas publishes information about its research, projects, reflections, conclusions and methods. All these publications are available free on the network's web site, which operates under a creative commons licence (www.redsemillas.info). The objective is to share knowledge and experience.

Internal workshops for reflection

Each year the Red de Semillas organizes an internal workshop for reflection. This is a three-day meeting, held in Madrid in winter, in which representatives from all the local seed networks participate. This annual meeting includes the following events:

- a one-day training workshop on a topic suggested by the local networks, such as seed health, management of seed exchange networks, etc.;
- two days of meetings during which members reflect on and discuss:
    - political issues related to agricultural biodiversity: seed law, seeds in organic agriculture, farmers' rights, etc.;
    - internal aspects of the organization;
    - development of the tasks of the working groups;
    - other technical and political topics.

Cultivated biodiversity fair

This is the Red de Semillas' main open event. At the cultivated biodiversity fair, local varieties are displayed, debates and conferences are held and contacts are established among farmers, researchers, consumers and local residents (Plate 26). Each year the fair is celebrated in a different region, and all the local seed networks participate, enjoy and work together for three days. In 2013, the Red de Semillas held its 14th fair.

'Cultivate diversity. Sow your rights'

Since 2009, the Red de Semillas has been engaged in a political campaign (www.siembratusderechos.info) to demand a change in the public policies related to the conservation and use of local varieties and seed production. This is a long-term effort that so far has not led to any concrete policy or legal changes. 'Cultivate diversity. Sow your rights' is focussed on:

- demanding a legal framework that allows farmers to produce and sell their own seeds – this means respect for farmers' rights to save, use, exchange and sell farm-saved seeds and propagating material;

- demanding strong support from public administrations for the task of recovery of our cultivated heritage;
- visualizing the importance of small farming and organic production systems, the use of local varieties, the recovery of traditional knowledge and local culture;
- fighting against an agriculture of patents and genetically modified organisms.

The main impact of the campaign has been to link several Spanish organizations working on such related topics as organic farming, ecology and rural development and focus the collective work on defending local varieties and farmers' rights.

Building alliances

The Red de Semillas is working hard to build an international movement. The network participates as an active member of a European organization called Let's Liberate Diversity (www.liberatediversity.org), which brings together various seed networks from European countries such as France, Germany, Italy, Spain, Switzerland and the United Kingdom. The network also collaborates with international platforms, such as the International Movement of Organic Agriculture (www.ifoam.org) and No Patents on Seeds! (www.no-patents-on-seeds.org) and has good relations with seed networks in Latin American countries, such as the Mexican organization Red de Alternativas Sustentables Agropecuarias (www.redrasa.wordpress.com) and the Latin American Agro-ecological Movement (www.maela-agroecologia.org).

References

Altieri, M. and Nicholls, C. I. (2000) *Agroecología: Teoría y práctica para una agricultura sustentable*, Programa de las Naciones Unidas para el Medio Ambiente/Red de Formación Ambiental para América Latina y el Caribe, Mexico DF, Mexico, www.agro.unc.edu.ar/~biblio/AGROECOLOGIA2[1].pdf, accessed 3 September 2014

Red Andaluza Semillas Cultivando Biodiversidad (2011a) 'Fichas de saber campesino. Vol. I', www.redandaluzadesemillas.org/IMG/pdf/Ficha_Saber_Campesino_RAS _31ago2011.pdf, accessed 3 September 2014

———— (2011b) 'Guía de conocimiento sobre utilización y manejo tradicional ligadas a las variedades autóctonas. Vol. I', www.redandaluzadesemillas.org/IMG/pdf/ guia_RAS_calidad_baja.pdf, accessed 3 September 2014

———— (2012) 'Informe: Descripción de variedades tradicionales andaluzas en fincas agroecológicas de Sevilla, Córdoba, Cádiz y Málaga', www.redandaluzadesemillas. org/IMG/pdf/121231_Memoria_RAS_Descripcion_VVLL_HEx_P-V_2012.pdf, accessed 9 January 2014

———— (2013) 'Red de Resiembra e Intercambio de variedades locales de cultivo: listado existencias Banco Local. Otoño – Invierno 2013', www.redandaluzadesemillas. org/IMG/pdf/130530_listado_banco_local_rei_temporada_o-i-2013.pdf, accessed 3 September, 2014

Red de Semillas (2008) 'Dossier de la Red de Semillas "Resembrando e Intercambiando"', www.redsemillas.info/wp-content/uploads/2008/06/dossier-rds.pdf, accessed 9 January 2014

Sanz García, I. (2011) 'Estudio sobre conocimiento campesino en relación con el manejo de las semillas en una comarca de interés agroecológico: la sierra de Huelva', Master's thesis, Universidad Internacional de Andalucía, Baeza, Spain, www.redandaluzadesemillas.org/IMG/pdf/Conocimiento_campesino_en_relacion_con_el_manejo_de_las_semillas_en_la_sierra_de_Huelva-Sanz.pdf, accessed 3 September 2014

37 USC Canada's experience in supporting community seed banks in Africa, Asia and the Americas

Sarah Paule Dalle and Susan Walsh

From famine to feast

In over two decades, USC Canada's support for community seed supply systems has grown from a seed recovery programme responding to drought and genetic erosion in Ethiopia, to a global programme focussed on promoting food security and food sovereignty through the sustainable use of agricultural biodiversity. USC Canada is a nongovernmental organization (NGO) based in Ottawa. Originally founded in 1945 as the Unitarian Service Committee of Canada, USC has worked internationally for over six decades to support communities in a variety of rehabilitation and development initiatives. In light of the success of its Seeds of Survival programme described in this chapter, since 2007, USC Canada has focussed all its efforts on supporting food and livelihood security through agro-ecological approaches, with specific attention to the conservation and sustainable use of agricultural biodiversity, including seed systems.

Community seed banks have been a central feature of this work. They serve as incubators of community resilience, where communities not only store seeds and germplasm, but also carry out experimentation and innovation around seeds that can handle the vagaries and extremes of climate change. Equally important, community seed banks are helping farm communities organize around their rights and their interests in production that is affordable, productive and respectful of the integrity of their landscapes and plant genetic resources.

Throughout this journey, USC Canada has learned many things from the women and men farmers and partner organizations who are leading these initiatives. One of the key lessons has been the importance of sustained support and careful accompaniment to cultivate leadership, a sense of ownership and organizational mechanisms in the farming communities that manage community seed banks. As these experiences accumulate, our programmes are increasing efforts to spread the work to the national level, through both targetted training and collaboration with other institutions and policy work. Efforts to integrate work on vegetable seed security into the programmes; to enhance market development and income-generation opportunities; and to ensure gender equality and youth engagement are also current areas of focus. Research and impact assessments will also give us a better understanding of the factors that facilitate long-term sustainability and will be valuable in guiding future work.

The early days

USC Canada's support for community seed banks began in Ethiopia in the late 1980s in the wake of one of the world's worst famines in the previous decades. This major centre of the origin and diversity of crop genetic resources was confronted with more than a hunger crisis; after repeated poor harvests because of drought, farming families in the Wollo and Tigray regions of the north had lost many of the seed varieties that had sustained their farming systems and culture for generations. The shortage of seed material was so widespread that families could not easily obtain desired seeds through exchange with relatives and neighbours or on the market. Nor were well-intentioned humanitarian aid initiatives the solution: seeds distributed to farmers were not well adapted to the specific growing conditions of the area and performed poorly, not only in terms of grain yield, but also in terms of the diverse agronomic, cultural, economic and other selection criteria of small-scale farmers (Teshome et al., 1999). Serious loss of Ethiopia's on-farm crop genetic resources and weakening of farmer-based seed systems was also occurring elsewhere in the country, because of displacement by modern varieties, land shortages and conflict, among other reasons (Tsegaye, 1997; Worede et al., 1999; Tsegaye and Berg, 2007).

Two visionaries, Dr. Melaku Worede, director of Ethiopia's national gene bank, the Plant Genetic Resources Centre in Addis Ababa (now named Ethiopian Institute for Biodiversity Conservation), and Pat Mooney, researcher and activist with the Action Group on Erosion, Technology and Concentration (ETC Group), formerly the Rural Advancement Fund International, embarked on a mission to rescue genetic material for future harvests. They convinced John Martin, the director of USC Canada, to support an ambitious initiative: the Seeds of Survival (SoS) programme. Financial support provided by USC was backed by funding from the Canadian International Development Agency and private donations from the Canadian public and family foundations.

Launched in 1989, SoS set out to work in partnership with farmers to rebuild the indigenous seed system. Using ex-situ materials obtained from the national gene bank and tirelessly scouting out seed reserves still held by farm families, scientists from the national gene bank collaborated closely with a network of over 500 farmers in North Shewa and Wollo to multiply on farm as many varieties as possible of sorghum and locally adapted maize. These varieties were re-integrated into the local seed systems by participating farmers and distributed to thousands of farmers who were hardest hit by the droughts in North Shewa, Wollo and Tigray. Similar work was initiated in the wheat-producing systems in East Shewa, helping farmers re-introduce varieties of durum wheat, chickpea, fenugreek and vetch that had been almost entirely displaced by introduced modern varieties (Tsegaye and Berg, 2007). An innovative approach to participatory crop improvement emerged, with farmers and scientists working together to develop 'enhanced' farmers' varieties, adding specific characteristics of interest to farmers, while maintaining the broad genetic diversity and integrity of the variety (Worede et al., 1999).

Taking root

Between 1989 and 1997, thousands of farmers benefitted from this effort and regained access to a diversity of precious genetic resources that were well adapted to their heterogeneous farming conditions and diverse cultural and economic needs. One of the key lessons learned was that seed security and genetic diversity were crucial for food security. Yet, with national agricultural development strategies primarily focussed on supporting commercial production through high-input technologies, few plans were in place to backstop and strengthen the resilience of farmer-based seed supply systems.

Based on the SoS experience, an integrated approach to strengthen the security of farmer-based seed systems and promote the on-farm conservation of Ethiopia's plant genetic resources began to emerge. Community seed banks were proposed as a key strategy to empower communities to conserve their plant genetic heritage, while providing a backup seed source to strengthen household seed saving and exchange practices (Feyissa, 2000; Worede, 2010). This was combined with participatory crop enhancement and farmer innovation to support ongoing adaptation and diversification of cropping systems to meet emerging needs and challenges.

To share the lessons learned from the SoS programme, between 1990 and 2006, USC Canada supported over a dozen international training workshops, which provided conceptual and field-based training on the conservation and sustainable use of plant genetic resources to nearly 300 development practitioners, farmers and scientists from 29 countries. An SoS small-projects fund was established to promote community-based food and seed security initiatives (many led by SoS trainees), while technical assistance, South–South exchanges and networking sustained ongoing learning and exchange among SoS initiatives that were developing in various parts of Africa, Asia and Latin America.

As a result of these efforts, community seed banks began to be established in USC programmes from 1995, initially in Mali (Chapter 22), Ethiopia and Nepal (Chapter 24) (Feyissa, 2000; Bhandari et al., 2013; Goïta et al., 2013), and eventually spreading to 16 countries with direct USC support (Table 37.1). Although many of these countries represent centres of origin and diversity for a range of grain, tuber, root, vegetable, pulse and oil crops, the specific programme and country context in which community seed banks have been developed varies substantially. These include programmes focussed on farmer-led agricultural research and strengthening of seed systems (e.g. Ethiopia; Honduras (see Chapter 33); Cuba); programmes with a major emphasis on land rehabilitation and livelihood diversification (Bolivia, Nepal, Timor Leste, West Africa); and even one programme (Bangladesh) that builds on an initiative aimed at life-skills development with adolescent girls. As of 2013, USC Canada

Table 37.1 Community seed banks (CSBs) and field gene banks (FGBs) currently supported by USC Canada, 2013*

Country (region)	Partner organization(s)	Year CSB work began	Supported by USC CSBs	FGBs	Organizational platform of CSB	Access to CSB Communities	Households‡	Main crops targeted by CSB/FGB	Programme context
Africa									
Ethiopia (Kalu and Woreilu districts, South Wollo)	Ethio–Organic Seed Action	1997‡	5	0	CSBs in two districts are run by a legally registered farmer conservator association (FCA), with a total membership of >1,800. The nine-member executive of each FCA manages the CSB operations in collaboration with local subcommittees at satellite locations.	18	1,955	Field crops, including sorghum, teff, pearl and finger millets, emmer wheat, durum wheat, chickpea, lentil, grass pea, field pea, mung bean, fenugreek	CSBs and associated participatory varietal selection are a central organizing feature of the programme. Income generation with youth and women's groups, soil and water conservation and other initiatives are organized through the CSBs. Ethio-Organic Seed Action has replicated this work in other parts of the country.

(Continued)

Table 37.1 (Continued)

Country (region)	Partner organization(s)	Year CSB work began	Supported by USC		Organizational platform of CSB	Access to CSB		Main crops targeted by CSB/FGB	Programme context
			CSBs	FGBs		Communities	Households†		
Mali (Douentza and Mopti cercles)	USC Canada-Mali	1995	8	1	Six CSBs are managed by an inter-village committee with representatives from each member village; day-to-day operation is coordinated by a six-member management team. Two CSBs are run by legally recognized farmers' cooperatives.	32	6,072	Pearl millet, sorghum, rice, fonio, maize, cowpea, bambara groundnut, peanut, fonio, sesame, hibsicus, okra, chili, cotton, gourds, watermelon, African eggplant, garlic, sweet potato, manioc, sugarcane, banana	CSBs integrated to strengthen seed security and promote crop diversification in the Sahel. CSBs complement work on land rehabilitation, market gardening, agro-forestry and support to farmers' organizations. Experience developed in the Douentza region has inspired other SoS initiatives in West Africa.
Mali (Safo and peri-urban Bamako)	CAB Demeso	2008	1	1	The CSB is managed by Dunka Fa farmers' cooperative (250 members), the FGB by a women's group (about 100 members).	14	1,655	Sorghum, maize, pearl millet, rice, groundnuts, cowpea, taro, banana, okra, sweet potato, quinqueliba, cotonier	Main programme focus is promotion of agro-forestry and income generation through support to farmers' cooperatives and women's groups in peri-urban Bamako.

Location	Organization	Year						Crops	
Burkina Faso (Djibo)	Association pour la protection de la nature, Sahel	2002	9	3	CSBs are run by the development committees of each village. Two people are assigned to oversee day-to-day operations at each CSB.	12	786	Sorghum, maize, pearl millet, fonio, cowpea, bambara groundnut, peanut, sesame, okra, hibiscus, manioc, sweet potato, sugarcane	Programme initially focussed on participatory land rehabilitation. CSBs integrated to strengthen seed security and promote crop diversification, as part of broader land rehabilitation.
Senegal (Podor)	Réseau Africain pour le Développement Integré	2007	2	1	CSBs and FGB are run by management committees assigned by the district (commune) in which they are located.	2	358	Sorghum, pearl millet, maize, cowpea, tomato, squash, African eggplant, banana	CSBs integrated to strengthen work on seed systems, including promotion of a vegetable seed farm run by a farmers' organization.

Asia

Location	Organization	Year						Crops	
Nepal (Lalitpur district)	Dalchowki Community Development Committee (DCDC)	1998	1	0	Managed by DCDC, a legally registered community-based organization with participation of 16 farmers' groups.	16	>100	Cereals, legumes, oil crops, vegetables	Support for CSB and related participatory varietal selection and crop diversification. Work is underway to develop stronger linkages between the CSB and farmer groups, national gene bank and other institutions in Nepal for long-term sustainability.

(Continued)

Table 37.1 (Continued)

Country (region)	Partner organization(s)	Year CSB work began	Supported by USC — CSBs	Supported by USC — FGBs	Organizational platform of CSB	Access to CSB — Communities	Access to CSB — Households†	Main crops targeted by CSB/FGB	Programme context
Nepal (Makawanpur and Sarlahi districts)	Parivartan	2006	1	3	CSB is run by Ramibas Organic Agriculture Cooperative Society (153 members); the FGBs are run by local farmers' groups.	4	350	Cereals, legumes, oil crops, vegetables, taro, yam, banana, mango, guava	Riverbank rehabilitation and support for sustainable, agro-biodiversity based livelihoods, through crop diversification in field and home gardens, improved quality of seeds, organic practices, soil and water conservation and cooperative development.
Bangladesh (six districts in northwest)	USC Canada–Bangladesh (with nine local NGOs)	2011	9	0	CSBs are based at adolescent resource centres, which have a total membership of 4,455 youths. CSB management committees are composed of eight youths, two adults and one representative of the partner NGO.	33	2,033	A variety of vegetable crops	Promotion of diversified home garden production, with specific emphasis on young farmers. Builds on prior work supported by USC on life-skills training with adolescent girls at adolescent resource centres.

Timor Leste (Aelieu and Manatuto districts)	Resilient Agriculture and Economy through Biodiversity Action (RAEBIA Timor Leste, formerly USC Canada–Timor Leste)	2007	10	0	Each CSB is managed by a farmers' group, which stores seeds used for collective activities and manages a revolving seed fund.	10	869	Maize, beans, rice	Watershed management and livelihood diversification, including promotion of agro-forestry, home gardening, aquaculture/fishing and income generation activities. CSBs help support diversification of food production.

Americas

Honduras (Yoro, Intibucá and Francisco Morazán)	Fundación para la Investigación Participativa con Agricultores de Honduras (FIPAH)	2001	13	5	Eleven CSBs are each run by a farmer research team (137 members in total); the remaining two are co-managed by regional farmers' organizations.	98	679	Maize, beans and other legumes, taro, chayote, banana, sugarcane, manioc	Through youth and adult farmer research teams, FIPAH uses a participatory approach to on-farm conservation of farmer seed varieties, secure seed supply through seed reproduction and sale, participatory plant breeding, community-run seed banks, cooperative grain storage systems and collective enterprise development.

(Continued)

Table 37.1 (Continued)

Country (region)	Partner organization(s)	Year CSB work began	Supported by USC CSBs	Supported by USC FGBs	Organizational platform of CSB	Access to CSB Communities	Access to CSB Households[†]	Main crops targeted by CSB/FGB	Programme context
Cuba (ten of 15 provinces)	National Institute of Agricultural Sciences (INCA)	2000¶	95	Part of CSBs	CSBs are run by families with a keen interest in conserving crop diversity.	56	1,000–1,800 annually borrow seed from CSBs	There are 77 crops including cereals, legumes, vegetables, condiments, fruit trees, tubers	The Program for Local Agricultural Innovation is an innovative farmer-scientist research programme that has brought seed diversity and security to over 50,000 rural farmers in Cuba. Includes promotion of agro-biodiversity, ecological farming practices, knowledge-sharing and farmer-scientist collaboration.
Bolivia (northern Potosí)	Programa de Desarrollo Integral Interdisciplinario (PRODII)	2008	10	Part of CSBs	CSBs are run by families with a keen interest in conserving crop diversity.	Data not available. Germplasm held in CSBs is disseminated through seed fairs and farmer–farmer exchanges		Andean tubers (potato, oca, ullucus), maize, wheat, faba bean	Support for sustainable, agro-biodiversity-based livelihoods, through crop diversification, soil and water conservation and postharvest transformation, cooperative farmers associations, marketing and sales

Country	Organization	Year	Description	Crops	Notes
Canada (national)	Seeds of Diversity Canada (SoDC)	2014	SoDC houses a community seed collection at Everdale Farm, Ontario, which facilitates exchange of seed between and among Canada's national gene bank and over 1,000 SoDC members across the country. In collaboration with USC Canada, work is currently underway to support community seed libraries across Canada to increase public access to diverse seed materials.	Field crops and vegetable seeds of potential interest to farmers and either unavailable on the commercial market or not available in sufficient quantities to be useful to growers	The Bauta Family Initiative on Canadian Seed Security is USC Canada's application of its SoS programme in Canada. The nationally coordinated and regionally driven programme works with producers, researchers, civil society organizations and relevant industry and government partners to increase the production, conservation and spread of regionally adapted, biodiverse, ecologically grown Canadian seed.

*Other countries where CSBs have been supported by USC in the past include Lesotho, Malawi, Ghana, India and Indonesia.

†Unless otherwise noted, number refers to households that have access to CSBs based on membership or as a resident of a village that supports the CSB.

‡Initial funding for the CSBs in Ethiopia was provided by a grant from the United Nations Global Environment Facility to the Ethiopian Institute for Biodiversity Conservation (national gene bank), and subsequently continued by Ethio-Organic Seed Action with USC support in 2002.

¶USC contributed financial support to the Program for Local Agricultural Innovation from 2007 to 2012, and is currently contracted by INCA to provide ongoing technical support and networking to the programme.

is actively supporting over 150 community seed banks in ten countries of Africa, Asia and Latin America, and in 2014 will begin supporting community seed libraries across Canada, as part of the Bauta Family Initiative on Canadian Seed Security (www.seedsecurity.ca/en/).

Farmer led and multifaceted

Models of community seed bank organization vary from one country and locality to another. In all cases, USC partners with a local organization (usually an NGO) that supports and works directly with community seed bank initiatives. Although functions and roles vary, they generally include the following components.

Germplasm conservation

Most community seed banks include storage space for a collection of crop varieties used in participatory varietal selection and plant breeding programmes and as a backup in case of major crop failure. These collections generally focus on farmers' varieties from the region, but seeds obtained from seed fairs, agricultural research stations and other sources are often included as well. Community seed banks ensure that collections are renewed on a regular basis, either through ongoing participatory varietal selection activities or by specific members.

Seed access

A major function is to provide adaptable seed materials to community members who are facing seed shortages or who wish to experiment with new crops or varieties. 'Revolving seed funds' are the most common solution: seeds are borrowed, planted and paid back at harvest time, usually with interest at a rate determined by the community or members. The seed fund may be built up by purchasing seed from local farmers at harvest time, by members contributing a portion of their seeds or cash or by establishing seed multiplication plots managed by participating villages or farmers' groups. In a few cases, seeds are sold rather than loaned, particularly when surplus seed is made available to non-members. In Mali, community radio has been used to advertise the availability of surplus seed to attract purchasers from surrounding villages. In Bolivia, seeds are disseminated primarily at district seed fairs, but occasionally individual farmers purchase seeds from a community seed bank, particularly when their household stock has been lost due to crop failure.

Backup seed storage

Community seed banks can operate as a backup for household-level seed saving and storage. Members sometimes also store some of their own seed supply in the community seed bank. This can be advantageous in terms of distributing risk, for example, in case of fire or other damage to household seed stocks. The backup seed-storage service is generally limited to members of the cooperative or farmer group that manages the seed bank, but in some cases the privilege is also extended to vulnerable groups in the community. For example, in Burkina Faso, female-headed households are allowed to store seeds in exchange for helping to maintain the premises; and in the Douentza and Mopti regions of Mali, resource-poor families who do not have a granary can store seeds in the seed bank for a small fee.

Participatory crop enhancement

Community seed banks can play a key role in introducing, evaluating and selecting crops and varieties from seeds obtained at seed fairs, exchanged with other institutions or communities or generated through the breeding activities of farmers themselves. This is done through farmer-led participatory varietal selection, in which both women and men farmers work with programme technical staff and other scientists or extension workers over several seasons to assess the adaptability of new crop varieties to local conditions. Farmers' own selection criteria – such as grain yield, biomass production, disease resistance, storability, milling quality and nutritional value – are used to assess the results (Teshome et al., 1999).

For instance, in Harbu, Ethiopia, farmers have selected several varieties of drought-resistant pearl millet, previously unknown in the region, which can be integrated into their cropping pattern in years when long-maturing varieties of sorghum fail. This provides an interesting complement to fast-maturing sorghum varieties, which are usually difficult to store, thus helping to increase grain availability in low-rainfall years. In Ethiopia, as well, seed multiplication plots have been established in local farmers' fields to multiply seed chosen after several seasons of participatory varietal selection. These seeds are then made available to community seed bank members through the revolving seed fund and disseminated more widely through farmer–farmer exchanges and networking with other agricultural actors. (See also, the Nepal Dalchowki and Honduras case studies, Chapters 24 and 33 respectively.)

Knowledge exchange and training

Community seed banks can serve as key knowledge-exchange and learning spaces through training sessions, seed fairs, farmer–farmer exchanges, visits by schoolchildren, development workers and others, and even popular theatre presentations. These events range from local training in production and the use of biopesticides, for example, to international events, such as a field visit to East Shewa, Ethiopia, by participants of the Wheat for Food Security in Africa International Conference (October 2012).

Some community seed banks have been designed to play a special role as knowledge hubs and have specific infrastructure or resources to support this role, including rooms or shaded outdoor areas for meetings, training sessions or other events; demonstration plots where soil and water conservation, terracing, agro-forestry or other agro-ecological techniques are tried and showcased; and resource centres or libraries holding information on the crop genetic resources held by the seed bank. In Ethiopia, plans are underway to develop a multimedia 'knowledge library' linked to the community seed banks and supported by USC (Worede, 2010); this would help support a range of training and knowledge-exchange activities.

Income generation and other initiatives

Many of the farmer groups and cooperatives that run community seed banks have developed income-generating activities to create livelihood opportunities and other benefits in the community. The Dunka Fa cooperative in Safo, Mali, has built an onion storage facility so that cooperative members' produce can be held until prices are favourable (usually a few months after the harvest). Seed production and marketing is also being developed in a number of community seed banks. (For further examples, see the Honduras case study, Chapter 33.)

Networking

As initiatives mature, there is increasing effort to promote networking among community seed banks at both local and regional scales. For examples, see the Mali and Nepal case studies (Chapters 22 and 24, respectively).

Gender considerations

Women play crucial roles in seed saving. They often have the main responsibility for this task in their households and communities and retain specialized knowledge of the culinary, storage and other postharvest characteristics of plant genetic resources (Howard, 2003). Community seed banks and their work related to seed systems can thus be a strategic entry point for increasing the value of women's knowledge and contributions, addressing women's priorities and needs relating to agricultural production and providing an area where women can play a greater leadership role within their families and communities. A few key approaches have been employed by USC to promote gender-equitable spaces.

Valuing women's knowledge, crops and production spaces

From the early days of the SoS programme, women's knowledge related to seed saving and agricultural production has been recognized and valued (Tsegaye, 1997). Both women and men have been actively involved in participatory varietal selection and plant breeding, and their selection criteria, including both agronomic and postharvest characteristics, are valued.

Most community seed banks supported by USC also focus on a wide range of crops, helping to address the needs of women who, in some contexts, have specific responsibilities for certain crops or production spaces (e.g. home gardens). In West Africa, for example, seed bank crops include cowpea, bambara groundnut, hibiscus and okra, which are generally grown by women. Support for tree nurseries and field gene banks has also contributed to strengthening access to germplasm for home gardens in Timor Leste, Nepal, Cuba and elsewhere. In Bangladesh, community seed banks focus specifically on native vegetable seeds as part of a broader programme aimed at empowering adolescent girls through involvement in home gardens.

Despite these achievements, in many USC programme countries, a number of introduced vegetable crops (such as carrot, tomato and cabbage) are still grown, and farmers must rely on purchased seed, often imported from Europe or elsewhere. Although some initiatives in USC Canada programmes promote local seed saving and production (e.g. a vegetable seed farm supported in Podor, Senegal), this is one area that requires more attention in the future.

Promoting women's participation and leadership

In most USC-supported community seed banks, there is a good gender balance in terms of membership and leadership – in many cases, as a result of ongoing monitoring and gender awareness-raising by USC and other community actors.

For example, until recently only 22 per cent of registered seed bank members in Ethiopia were women, reflecting the fact that membership was accorded on a household basis and typically registered under the name of the male household head. However, the farmer conservator associations that run the seed banks launched a campaign to attract more women members by establishing individual rather than household-level memberships. This move appears to be the result of a participatory gender equality review process supported by USC to encourage communities to assess how to enhance gender equality within the programme (Dalle and Stefov, 2013), as well as ongoing gender-awareness training by field staff and local government agencies. Support for women's and youth groups has also helped increase interest in the community seed banks and stimulate more active participation, as has the emergence of some strong women leaders within the farmer conservator associations.

In Honduras, a recent study found that participation in the Comités de Investigación Agrícola Local (CIALs) has contributed to notable improvements in gender equality and empowerment of women, by providing a space where men and women are able to challenge unequal gender roles (Humphries et al., 2012a). This shows that collective action around food and seed security has the potential to contribute to broader social change – a strategy that is actively pursued in USC-supported programmes.

Policy influence

Community seed banks provide important fora for rural communities and farmers' organizations to interact and learn about broader trends and policies that can affect local seed and food security, to craft policy changes that reflect farmers' concerns and priorities and to open negotiations with policymakers and other actors at local and national levels. The partner NGOs play an important role in facilitating this process, which also serves to inform the national and international policy efforts that these NGOs undertake, often in collaboration with larger farmers' organizations and other civil society actors.

In recent years, the CIALs in Honduras have been reflecting on what they view as equitable benefit-sharing in relation to the participatory plant breeding varieties in which they have invested years of labour and skill to develop. They see this as a first step towards engaging in open dialogue on ownership rights with governmental and nongovernmental collaborators (Humphries et al., 2012b). The Foundation for Participatory Research with Honduran Farmers also successfully convinced the government to convene a Committee on Plant Genetic Resources for Food and Agriculture to develop mechanisms to fulfill Honduras' obligations under the International Treaty on Plant Genetic Resources for Food and Agriculture. These initiatives are particularly crucial in light of Honduras' 2006 free-trade agreement with the United States, under which farmers' plant genetic resources and knowledge are considered patentable commodities (Humphries et al., 2012b). USC-supported programmes in West Africa are similarly involved in the regional Coalition for the Protection of Africa's Plant Genetic Patrimony to engage communities, farmers' organizations and policymakers in issues related to the conservation of plant genetic resources.

In a few countries, provisions to support and promote community seed banks have been included in national legislation, regulatory frameworks and agricultural development programmes (see the policy case study for Nepal, Chapter 41). In Timor Leste, USC Canada's partner, Resilient Agriculture and Economy through Biodiversity Action (RAEBIA), has participated in a steering committee to guide the country's draft national seed policy (2013), which makes explicit note of the value of community seed banks.

USC is also supporting initiatives to establish community seed banks more broadly. In recent years, USC-supported programmes have worked to share their hands-on, decades-long experience with a broad range of actors at the local and national levels and, increasingly, are providing technical expertise and training to governmental, civil society and academic institutions to integrate the lessons USC has learned into their own practices. In Ethiopia, for example, Ethio-Organic Seed Action (EOSA) field staff and expert farmers from established community seed banks have helped Wollo University develop participatory varietal selection trials on campus, allowing local farmers, students and faculty to learn from one another in a novel way. EOSA is also providing technical support and guidance to the Southern Nations, Nationalities and People's Regional Government to establish community seed banks in eight districts, all with government funding. EOSA frequently receives requests from government agencies and NGOs for technical advice on seed system-related work.

Last but not least, USC Canada makes every effort to assist its partners and, when feasible, selected women and men farmers, to participate in international fora, the three most prominent being the International Treaty on Plant Genetic Resources for Food and Agriculture, the Committee on World Food Security and the International Convention on Biological Diversity.

Sustainability

As farmer-led and managed institutions, community seed banks generally inspire a strong sense of ownership and pride among the farmers' organizations and communities who benefit from them – a feature that can help sustain these initiatives into the future. However, USC's experience has shown that this sense of ownership, along with the organizational skills and mechanisms needed to sustain a community seed bank, require time to develop and must be cultivated carefully.

A case in point comes from Mali, where after the withdrawal of USC Canada–Mali's support from the village of Badiari (Douentza cercle), the community seed bank continued to operate independently. A strong sense of community ownership had been established, and the management committee had developed clear organizational mechanisms to sustain operations. In contrast, in the village of Ouornion (Mopti cercle), the community seed bank ceased to operate when USC's funding for the project ended earlier than expected, only three years after it had been established. In both cases, USC eventually re-engaged with the communities, and provided additional support to help upgrade infrastructure, which had begun to deteriorate, and, in the case of Ouornion, to rebuild the organizational skill and community support needed to relaunch the seed bank.

In all USC-supported community seed banks, farmers are working with USC partners to develop tailor-made strategies to sustain the financial and organizational viability of these farmer-run institutions (Table 37.2). In Timor Leste, only modest financial resources are required to sustain the seed banks and the focus is primarily on building organizational capacity, including engagement of young farmers. For more complex seed bank operations, significant effort is being invested in generating financial resources to help maintain them, to strengthen financial management skills of the farmers' organizations and to diversify funding. In all cases, a favourable policy environment, as well as strong capacity among accompanying agencies to facilitate farmer-led approaches, are particularly important in the long run.

Acknowledgements

We warmly thank and acknowledge all USC Canada's partner organizations (Table 37.1), who provided valuable data and insights that were essential to preparing this chapter. Any errors or omissions, however, are the sole responsibility of the authors.

Table 37.2 Strategies for building the sustainability of farmer-led community seed banks

Strategy	Examples
Financial sustainability	
Development of micro-enterprises and other mechanisms to generate income	Many seed banks are developing the capacity to produce and sell seeds. Other initiatives include beekeeping, fruit production, establishment of membership fees and rental of meeting rooms and office space.
Capacity building to enhance financial management skills	Most farmers' organizations and cooperatives are receiving support to build financial management skills. In Ethiopia, the seed banks have bank accounts, undergo annual government audits and are working to strengthen financial systems in light of an increasing diversity of initiatives (youth/women's groups, soil and water conservation, etc.).
Diversification of sources of financial support	In Nepal, seed banks have obtained financial support from government agencies (district agricultural and livestock offices, national gene bank).
Use of local materials and construction techniques	Most seed banks make use of local materials and construction techniques; this enhances the capacity of local communities to maintain the infrastructure in the long run.
Organizational sustainability	
Registration of farmers' groups as cooperatives or other legally recognized entities	Several village-based seed banks in Mali have chosen to form cooperatives, institute membership contributions and use savings/credit funds to generate financial resources for the seed bank and its members. Legally registered cooperatives can also access certain government programmes.
Enhancement of women's leadership and participation	All USC programmes encourage women's leadership and ensure that their skills and knowledge are valued and contribute to seed bank management. Strong women's leadership encourages other women to become involved, broadening the seed bank's support base.
Engagement of young farmers and youth in activities linked to the community seed bank	In several programmes, specific strategies have been developed to engage schoolchildren, youth and young farmers. These include support for youth-specific farmer research teams (Honduras), young farmers' productive activities (Timor Leste, Bangladesh, Ethiopia) and collaboration with local schools (Ethiopia). Youth-specific programmes are expected to engage more young farmers in seed bank management and activities.
Collaboration and partnerships with local government, agricultural extension services and other institutions	All USC-supported seed banks have established links with local and national government agencies and research institutions; this has enhanced knowledge and understanding in these institutions of the farmer-led approach of the seed banks and, in several cases, has led to provision of material, technical or financial support to the seed bank.
Transformation of USC Canada offices into national NGOs and other organizational development of partner NGOs	USC has supported the establishment of national NGOs to take over its field operations; this helps diversify funding sources and has increased access to national programmes, networks and coalitions. USC has also invested in various organizational development initiatives of partner NGOs, including strengthening of financial management systems, support for gender equality reviews, staff capacity building and professional development and leveraging funding from other donors to support seed banks.

References

Bhandari, B., Hamal, M., Rai, J., Sapkota, D., Sangel, K., Joshi, B. K. and Shrestha, P. (2013) 'Establishment and present status of Dalchoki Community Seed Bank in Lalitpur, Nepal,' in P. Shrestha, R. Vernooy and P. Chaudhary (eds) *Community Seed Banks in Nepal: Past, Present and Future*, Local Initiatives for Biodiversity, Research and Development, Pokhara, Nepal, pp 47–58

Dalle, S. P. and Stefov, D. (2013) 'Monitoring & evaluation as a learning process: USC Canada's experience in Bridging Gaps,' in D. Buckles (ed.) *Innovations with Evaluation Methods: Lessons from a Community of Practice in International Development*, Canada World Youth, Montréal, Canada, pp46–52

Feyissa, R. (2000) 'Community seed banks and seed exchange in Ethiopia: a farmer-led approach,' in E. Friis-Hansen and B. Sthapit (eds) *Participatory Approaches to Conservation and Use of Plant Genetic Resources*, International Plant Genetic Resources Institute, Rome, Italy, pp142–148

Goïta, M., Goïta, M., Coulibaly, M. and Winge, T. (2013) 'Capacity building and farmer empowerment in Mali,' in R. Andersen and T. Winge (eds) *Realising Farmers' Rights to Crop Genetic Resources: Success Stories and Best Practices*, Routledge, New York, USA, pp156–166

Howard, P. L. (2003) *Women & Plants: Gender Relations in Biodiversity Management and Conservation*, Zed Books, London, UK

Humphries, S., Classen, L., Jimenez, J., Sierra, F., Gallardo, O. and Gomez, M. (2012a) 'Opening cracks for the transgression of social boundaries: an evaluation of the gender impacts of farmer research teams in Honduras,' *World Development*, vol 40, pp2078–2095

Humphries, S., Jimenez, J., Gallardo, O., Gomez, M., Sierra, F. and Members of the Association of Local Agricultural Research Committees of Yorito Victoria and Sulaco (2012b) 'Honduras: rights of farmers and breeders rights in the new globalizing context,' in M. Ruiz and R. Vernooy (eds) *The Custodians of Biodiversity: Sharing Access and Benefits to Genetic Resources*, Earthscan, London, UK, and International Development Research Centre, Ottawa, Canada, pp79–93

Teshome, A., Fahrig, L., Torrance, J. K., Lambert, J. D., Arnason, T. J. and Baum, B. R. (1999) 'Maintenance of sorghum (*Sorghum bicolor*, Poaceae) landrace diversity by farmers' selection in Ethiopia,' *Economic Botany*, vol 53, pp79–88

Tsegaye, B. (1997) 'The significance of biodiversity for sustaining agricultural production and role of women in the traditional sector: the Ethiopian experience,' *Agriculture, Ecosystems and Environment*, vol 62, pp215–227

Tsegaye, B. and Berg, T. (2007) 'Genetic erosion of Ethiopian tetraploid wheat landraces in Eastern Shewa, Central Ethiopia,' *Genetic Resources and Crop Evolution*, vol. 54, pp715–726

Worede, M. (2010) *Establishing a Community Seed Supply System: Community Seed Bank Complexes in Africa*, Food and Agriculture Organization, Rome, Italy

Worede, M., Tesemma, T. and Feyissa, R. (1999) 'Keeping diversity alive: an Ethiopian perspective,' in S. B. Brush (ed.), *Genes in the Field: On-farm Conservation of Crop Diversity*, Lewis Publishers Inc., Boca Raton, USA, pp143–164

38 Zimbabwe

The experience of the Community Technology Development Trust

Andrew T. Mushita, Patrick Kasasa and Hilton Mbozi

Purpose and evolution

The 1991/92 drought that ravaged southern Africa and was declared a national disaster in Zimbabwe was instrumental in the establishment of community seed banks in our country. Most farmers lost their traditional crop varieties in the drought. The Community Technology Development Trust (CTDT), in consultation with government agencies and farmer communities, decided to initiate an intervention that would prevent further losses to farmers' plant genetic resources, prevent genetic erosion, act as a risk aversion measure against the effects of climate change and vulnerability and conserve local crop varieties on farm. It aimed to help farmers enhance cultivation of local, drought-tolerant crops, including sorghum, pearl millet, groundnuts, cowpeas and local vegetables.

In 1998, with financial support from Norway's Development Fund, CTDT established three community seed banks on a pilot project basis in Uzumba-Maramba-Pfungwe, Tsholotsho and Chiredzi districts (see Table 38.1). The community contributed local building materials, and the Ministry of Agriculture's Institute of Engineering provided the technical design. The

Table 38.1 Types of germplasm in community seed banks in three districts, 2013

Crop	Number of varieties		
	Uzumba-Maramba-Pfungwe*	*Tsholotsho*	*Chiredzi*[†]
Sorghum	17	12	7
Pearl millet	5	6	2
Groundnuts	6	4	4
Bambara	9	6	5
Maize	4	3	3
Cowpeas	12	16	8
Rapoko	4	2	2
Total	57	49	31

*Currently, 500kg sorghum, 100kg rapoko and 300kg pearl millet seed are in bulk storage. The seed was left last year as a strategic reserve in case of drought or other calamity.
†Because of recurring drought in Chiredzi, no substantial amount of seed has been accumulated in the seed bank.

community seed banks aimed to promote knowledge and seed exchange, local experimentation by farmers and community germplasm conservation. They are seen as a collective framework and institutional platform for making decisions about crops to cultivate, seeds to produce and locally adaptive germplasm to conserve. As such, they are a mechanism to implement farmers' rights as defined by the International Treaty on Plant Genetic Resources for Food and Agriculture.

Functions and activities

Each community seed bank measures 12m by 5m and is divided into five rooms (Plate 27). Two serve as seed-storage areas and are insulated with a 1m-thick concrete ceiling to maintain a constant room temperature. The rooms have shelves to protect accessions from pests. The accessions are labelled alphabetically by farmer's name. There is bulk storage for seed that is multiplied in the field. The facilities also contain an office and a meeting room.

Germination tests are conducted every two years to assess seed viability. Seed with a germination rate below 65 per cent is distributed to trained farmers for regeneration. A study carried out in 2008 showed that small grain crops can be stored for at least a decade.

To increase awareness of agricultural biodiversity conservation and management, diversity within crop species and the role of exchange of germplasm, seed fairs are held annually at each community seed bank and bi-annually at the national level. Initially organized by CTDT in collaboration with the farmers' management committee, these events are now planned by community seed bank committees. During seed fairs, farmers are encouraged to display their crops, and prizes are awarded based on number and range of crops on display, seed quality and presentation. The seed fairs provide a forum for farmers to meet, discuss and exchange seeds, knowledge and their experience with old and new crops and to exchange information about local-level seed production. Seed fairs also make it possible to evaluate the level of diversity within the community and assess and monitor genetic erosion. Seeds are also acquired at the fairs to increase seed bank collections.

Governance and management

Community seed banks are managed by local farmers with support from CTDT and government agencies. The community elects a management committee responsible for the coordination and management of all seed bank activities. The committee operates under a constitution drafted by farmers with guidance from CTDT. It is made up of a chair, vice chair, secretary, vice secretary, treasurer, security, vice security and five other members. Duties include the regulation and control of seed moving in and out of the seed bank, checking for pests, recommending and supervising fumigation of the building and conducting germination tests.

All members of the community who deposit seed in the general storage rooms have equal access to the seed. Farmers are issued a membership card that allows them to deposit seed in the general or family collection sections. They are required to produce the card each time they need a service from the facility. Member farmers are expected to be active and take part in seed fairs and training.

Seeds in the general storage room belong to individual members and are used by them free of charge. This acts as a seed reserve in case of drought, flood or any other catastrophe. The seed in the bulk storage room is sold to anyone who wants seed. However, non-members, especially the most vulnerable such as elders and orphans, may also be given seeds on the recommendation of the management committee – a social commitment made by the seed bank.

The seed bank committee works closely with CTDT field officers and local agricultural extension (AGRITEX) officers to register participating farmers. New collections are added to the community biodiversity register kept at the seed bank office, and the following information is recorded: name of the farmer, identification or registration number, village name, ward number/name, crop name, variety, date of collection, accession number, shelf number, germination rate, quantity of seed collected and the name of the person receiving the material. This information is also kept at CTDT head office as a backup system. CTDT has produced a community seed banking manual for technical staff.

Women, who play a key role in household food security, participate in seed bank activities and make up at least half of the 12-member management committee. Because of socioeconomic and cultural norms and values, women are mostly involved in communal farming and, thus, contribute mainly to selecting seed in the field and after harvest, cleaning and depositing seeds, participating in seed fairs and general cleaning of the building. Youth participation is still minimal; only those engaged in conservation agriculture bring their seeds to the community seed bank. Youth are not much interested in farming, and most look towards formal employment opportunities in the cities.

Seed selection and management

Collecting and cleaning seeds is largely carried out by farmers who are supervised by the seed bank management committee with guidance from two AGRITEX officers and a CTDT staff person. Collection of seeds is done in individual households by farmers who have been trained in seed handling. When the crop is ready for harvesting, women do most of the seed selection, both in the field and after harvesting. What farmers consider good quality may vary: for example, size of grains or kernels, colour or drought tolerance. Seed destined for storage is taken through a winnowing or cleaning process to remove deformed seed, dust and dirt. Seeds are sun-dried at homesteads to reduce the moisture content to about 11 per cent. Farmers test for acceptable dryness by breaking the grain with their hands or teeth. Germplasm is stored either in plastic bags or tins. The management committee inspects all seed material before storage. When approved, seeds are placed in air-tight bottles, which are mainly provided by CTDT.

Regeneration of seed with low germination rates is facilitated by the management committee; this technical procedure empowers farmers in seed management methods. There is no rule about how much seed a farmer should return to the seed bank at the end of the growing season; however, the management committee encourages farmers to bring back twice as much as they withdrew. The CTDT field officer and management committee monitor deposits and withdrawals from the seed bank by recording pertinent information. The CTDT officer works in close consultation with the management committee, AGRITEX and the government agriculture department but is also part of the farming community.

Seed multiplication activities have deliberately targeted open-pollinated varieties of such crops as sorghum, pearl millet, cowpeas and maize. Farmers have received training on seed multiplication and seed production methods. Farmers in Tsholotsho and Uzumba-Maramba-Pfungwe are linked to seed companies (Seed Co and Agri-Seeds) from which they receive foundation seeds. In the 2009/10 season, they produced 185t of improved pearl millet, 120t of improved sorghum and 85t of improved quality cowpea seed. Communities in these districts also participated in crop-improvement programmes, such as participatory plant breeding and participatory variety selection. Four maize varieties stored in the community seed banks are products of such programmes. CTDT developed advanced maize lines that were given to farmers at field schools to develop further during the 2009/10 agricultural season.

Implications of the Seeds Act for community seed banking

The Zimbabwe Seeds Act regulates production of high-quality seeds by corporate seed companies for both domestic and export markets. However, a new seed variety can only be registered and marketed commercially after its distinctiveness, uniformity and stability (DUS) and value for cultivation and use (VCU) have been determined by a variety-release committee. The DUS and VCU tests delay the release of new varieties and the system is very expensive. The need for seed certification and standardization make it nearly impossible for smallholder farmers to trade their seed. Intellectual property rights are an issue when farmers want to sell their materials outside the defined borders of the communities. National seed laws prohibit farmers from selling any farm-saved seed. However, they are allowed to multiply farm-saved seed under the auspices of community seed banks, which provides them with a window of opportunity. The established seed banks are able to carry out on-farm seed multiplication and exchange between and among themselves as they are linked to the national gene bank.

Technical support and cooperation

Technical support is provided through training. In Tsholotsho, for example, the International Crops Research Institute for the Semi-Arid Tropics trained

CTDT and AGRITEX officers in crop improvement. The national gene bank also trained the same officers in germplasm collection, recording, processing and storage. AGRITEX is always on the ground working closely with seed bank management committees. CTDT provides technical back-stopping to both field officers and the committees. CTDT has also trained all committee members in leadership and seed bank management. Exchange visits (look-and-learn tours) have been organized to allow committee members to share information and ideas including best practices in plant genetic resource management. CTDT receives funds from OXFAM-NOVIB and the International Fund for Agricultural Development.

The seed bank committees have a close working relationship with the national gene bank. CTDT field officers, AGRITEX officers and committee members (the core seed bank management team) were trained by national gene bank staff in germplasm collection, documentation of collected materials, seed treatment and storage. The national gene bank also collects samples from community seed banks for its own collection, its officials participate in seed fairs and it repatriates germplasm to farmers for regeneration. Local farmers participate in germplasm collection for the national gene bank, and, in Tsholotsho, the national gene bank has occasionally paid a small amount of money (US$1 per kg of seed collected) to individual farmers.

Farmers consider that the issue of benefit sharing requires more attention. CTDT has conducted several awareness-raising meetings on access and benefit sharing. At the community level, this issue is complicated. In Chiredzi, for example, farmers indicated that there was no mechanism for obtaining royalties from the use of materials collected by researchers or outsiders. Women felt that this kind of benefit should be given individually rather than to chiefs or other traditional leaders.

Policy and legal environment

Currently there is no specific policy or legal framework to support community seed banks, apart from general support through the extension service, but there have been discussions on the need for comprehensive farmers' rights legislation. A proposed framework will cover the establishment of community seed banks interacting closely with the national gene bank and the South African Development Community (SADC) regional gene bank. Currently, a subcommittee has been established to work out details to be presented to the cabinet and, once approved, a draft law will be prepared for presentation to parliament.

In terms of moral support, the Government of Zimbabwe is supportive of community seed banking. In 2010, Vice President Mrs. J. Mujuru and other senior government officials attended a seed fair at the Mabika community seed bank in Uzumba-Maramba-Pfungwe. Officials agreed that community seed banking is a strategy not only to conserve plant genetic resources but also to cope with climate change. The same year, Ms. Thandi Luphupha, a senior official from the SADC gene bank based in Lusaka, Zambia, visited Uzumba-Maramba-Pfungwe and Tsholotsho community seed banks. This visit was important as it cemented relations, links and cooperation between the community seed banks and the national and regional gene banks.

Local members of parliament, traditional leaders, government ministries and farmer organizations such as the Zimbabwe Farmers' Union are all working with seed bank committees. The SADC Plant Genetic Resources Centre in Zimbabwe has highlighted the success and relevance of community seed banks and is considering how the Zimbabwean model can be replicated in the 14 SADC member states.

Achievements and challenges

The major achievement to date is an increase in crop diversity among participating households and surrounding communities. Before the intervention, households in the district were growing an average of four crop varieties (both grains and legumes). Over the years, the number of varieties has increased to an average of eight in Uzumba-Maramba-Pfungwe, six in Tsholotsho and five in Chiredzi. The access to local germplasm desired by communities and community members has improved, and there is no longer a need to travel to far places in search of seeds. The major challenge women face is acquiring processing technology, which is usually highly priced and unaffordable for the poor. This is an area that requires more investment in terms of financial resources and research. Decline in soil fertility is also becoming a major challenge. Women are usually allocated fields with low inherent soil fertility and this affects productivity.

At least 1,500 households have directly and indirectly benefitted from seeds stored in the community seed banks (Table 38.2). Most of them are helping to conserve seed of varieties of indigenous grains and other wild crop relatives that are no longer found in most rural farming communities in Zimbabwe. Elderly farmers, who still remember some varieties that they used to grow years ago, happily make use of the seed bank. A woman farmer in her 70s commented that a long-season pearl millet variety they used to grow in the

Table 38.2 The number of farmers benefitting directly from a community seed bank in three districts

District (date of establishment)	At establishment		Currently (2013)		
	Male	Female	Male	Female	Total
Uzumba-Maramba-Pfungwe (1999)	32	65	237	474	711
Tsholotsho (2007)	3	60	52	421	473
Chiredzi (2003)	17	21	58	75	133
Total	52	146	347	970	1,317

1940s, 1950s and 1960s has been brought back thanks to the community seed bank; as she remarked, 'The seed bank is much more than a bank for money. It's a bank for life-food'.

According to local government leaders in Uzumba-Maramba-Pfungwe and CTDT staff, the community seed banks have acted as centres of excellence for sharing local knowledge and for generating new knowledge through farmer-extension worker–researcher interactions. However, farmers and field officers from CTDT have noted that there is a need to share and exchange knowledge through mechanisms, such as training provided by experts and exchanges of experience among partners at the national and regional levels. Although knowledge is shared at seed fairs and social meetings, this is mainly at a local level. Farmers feel that regional and inter-district visits would allow the exchange of knowledge among farmers from other areas who are not necessarily engaged in these activities. CTDT has signed a memorandum of understanding with the national Zimbabwe Farmers' Union to ensure adoption of the community seed bank concept on a larger scale, thus improving networking among farmers at the national level.

Access to and availability of seed has greatly increased for participating households. The community seed production initiative has filled a gap as farmers turn to growing small grains and legumes. Seed production is becoming a major source of household income. Marketing of small grains remains the biggest challenge because of low prices. Through other projects, CTDT has introduced income savings and lending clubs to improve household liquidity, and over 40 per cent of community seed bank beneficiaries are members of these clubs. All this has resulted in an increase in average household income of US$35–50 a month.

39 Brazil

Community seed banks and Brazilian laws

Juliana Santilli

Context

Over the last few years, three Brazilian states (Paraíba, Alagoas and Minas Gerais) have approved laws aimed at providing a legal framework for community seed banks created and maintained by small-scale farmers' associations with the support of nongovernmental organizations (NGOs) and sometimes local governments. In four other states (Bahia, Pernambuco, Santa Catarina and São Paulo), similar bills are being discussed in the state legislative assemblies.

The first jurisdiction to enact a law creating a community seed bank programme was Paraíba, one of smallest states in the northeast of Brazil where half the population lives in semi-arid regions. Alagoas, Bahia, Pernambuco and Minas Gerais are also (partly) located in the semi-arid region of Brazil. The main biome in this region is the caatinga (an indigenous name meaning 'clear and open forest'); it is uniquely Brazilian and occupies about 11 per cent of the country. This biome is subject to two dry seasons a year: a long period of drought followed by intermittent rain and a short drought followed by torrential rains (with intervals that can last years). Most (58 per cent) of the country's poorest people live in the semi-arid region. The Human Development Index is considered to be low (0.65) in approximately 82 per cent of the municipalities (ASA, 2014).

The Brazilian semi-arid region is characterized by sharp social inequality: water, lands and seeds have always been highly concentrated in the hands of a very small politically and economically dominant group. The development of community seed banks was part of a strategy for small-scale farmers to overcome food and seed insecurity, increase autonomy over their production systems and sustain their livelihoods. In Brazil, small-scale farmers are called family farmers, as the family is the basic unit of agricultural production. Small-scale farmers use multiple cropping systems and mainly farm-saved seed of local varieties known in the state of Paraíba as *sementes da paixão* (seeds of passion) and *sementes da resistência* (seeds of resistance). These seeds are adapted to the agro-ecological conditions of the semi-arid region and to specific social and cultural needs and demands of family farmers (see Chapter 13).

Historically, government programmes have distributed only certified seeds of a few improved varieties, and such programmes have always been accused of serving political interests, i.e. exchanging seeds for votes during elections (Dias da Silva, 2013). On the other hand, family farmers have always faced serious difficulties in buying seeds, because of high prices resulting from privatization of seed production. This reality has contributed to the loss of agro-biodiversity (Santilli, 2012).

In response, one of the main functions of community seed banks in the Brazilian semi-arid region has been to ensure access to the preferred (local) varieties, in sufficient quantities and at the right time (Dias da Silva, 2013; see also Chapter 13). Seed banks lend seed to farmers, who agree to return the same amount plus a relatively low percentage at harvesting time.

Paraíba

In Paraíba, community seed banks have been supported by a network of farmers' and community associations, small cooperatives, unions, parishes and a local NGO called Articulação do Semi-Árido Paraíbano, whose main objectives are to strengthen local biodiverse farming systems and promote social equity and local sustainable development. Currently, Paraíba has a network of more than 240 seed banks, involving 6,561 farmer families in 63 municipalities. They conserve seeds of over 300 varieties of maize, common beans, fava beans, cassava, sunflower and peanuts as well as forage and fruit species. Farmers use the banks for several purposes: food, feed, fiber and medicinal purposes (Agroecologia em Rede, 2010). The seed banks function not only as facilities for the safe storage of seeds, but also as places where local farmers' organizations can meet to discuss political issues and exchange seeds and traditional knowledge.

This network has gained political influence and one of its main achievements was the approval, in 2002, of law 7.298/2002, which established a community seed bank programme to allow Paraíba's state government to buy seeds of local varieties for distribution among farmers and seed banks. Previously, only certified seeds of improved varieties could be used for this purpose (Santos et al., 2012; Dias da Silva, 2013). This law has also allowed farmers to use seeds of local varieties to produce food and sell it (through contracts with state government agencies) to public schools and hospitals (Schmidt and Guimarães, 2008). Between 2004 and 2010, over 180t of food was produced in Paraíba using the seeds of 73 local varieties (Dias da Silva, 2013).

Before the approval of law 7.298/2002, seeds of local varieties were not recognized by the Brazilian legislation as seeds, they were considered to be mere 'grains', of low quality, and were excluded from official seed programmes.

Alagoas

On 3 January 2008, the state of Alagoas (also located in the semi-arid region, in northeast Brazil) approved law 6903/2008 establishing a community seed bank programme aimed at 'strenghtening community seed banks through public support for the rescue, multiplication, distribution and supply of seeds of local varieties'. Its objective was 'ensuring the sustainability of small-scale farming production systems'.

In Alagoas, the main seed bank networks have been managed by cooperatives of small-scale farmers, based in the regions of Alto and Médio Sertão de Alagoas. They are also supported by Articulação do Semiárido de Alagoas, a network that brings together several local organizations. Currently, Alagoas has 131 seed banks in 221 municipalities involving 3,350 farmer families and 32 local seed varieties, mainly beans, fava beans, cowpeas and maize (Almeida and Schmitt, 2010; Packer, 2010). Native species of the caatinga biome (catingueira, angico, aroeira) are also widely used and conserved by farmers on their farms.

Minais Gerais

The state of Minas Gerais passed its community seed bank law in 2009 (18374/2009). This law established, for the first time, a legal definition of a community seed bank: 'a germplasm collection of local, traditional and creole plant varieties, and landraces, administered locally by family farmers, who are responsible for the multiplication of seeds or seedlings for distribution, exchange, or trade among themselves' (see Chapter 13). According to the law, the main objectives of policies aimed at strengthening seed banks are to stimulate the recovery and conservation of plant species and varieties produced in family-farming units; to stimulate the protection of local genetic resources that are important for the sustainability of agro-ecosystems; to protect agricultural biodiversity and promote associated cultural values, as well as the conservation of natural heritage; and to promote community organization, as well as capacity building for the management of seed banks and the protection of traditional knowledge.

Federal situation

Paraíba's successful pioneering experience with community seed banks, followed by the initiatives of other Brazilian states, helped convince the national congress to allow for the use and production of local, traditional and creole seeds in the Federal Seed Law (10711/2003) approved on 5 August 2003. The inclusion of local species in this legal instrument aimed at regulating the Brazilian formal seed system was a result of strong political pressure from farmers' and civil society organizations (Articulação Nacional de Agroecologia, 2012).

According to law 10711/2003, local, traditional and creole cultivars are:

> varieties developed, adapted or produced by family farmers, agrarian reform settlers or Indigenous peoples, with well established phenotypical characteristics, that are recognized by their respective communities and

which, according to the Ministry of Agriculture, and considering also social, cultural and environmental descriptors, are not characterized as substantially similar to commercial cultivars.

This law also states that 'registration of local, traditional or creole cultivars used by family farmers, agrarian reform settlers or Indigenous peoples in the National Registry of Cultivars is not mandatory'. Such exemption recognizes the issues surrounding local varieties and the difficulty farmers have meeting the requirements of the National Registry, especially in terms of homogeneity and stability. The law also stipulates that 'family farmers, agrarian reform settlers and indigenous peoples who multiply seeds for distribution, exchange or sales among themselves do not have to be registered in the National Seed Registry'. Thus, as long as seed distribution, exchange and trade take place among family farmers, agrarian reform settlers and indigenous peoples, there is no need for registration.

References

Agroecologia em Rede (2010) 'Bancos de Sementes e as articulações em defesa das sementes da paixão,' Agroecologia em Rede, www.agroecologiaemrede.org.br/experiencias.php?experiencia=993, accessed 4 September 2014

Almeida, P. and Schmitt, C. (2010) *Construção de Conceitos e Marcos de Referência de Garantia dos Direitos dos Agricultores sobre a Biodiversidade*, Associação Agroecológica Tijupá, São Luiz, Maranhão, Brazil

Articulação Nacional de Agroecologia (2012) *Relatório da Oficina sobre Sementes Crioulas e Políticas Públicas*, Brasília, DF, 18 e 19 de setembro de 2012, Relatora: Flávia Londres

ASA (Articulação do Semi-Árido Brasileiro) (2014) 'Semiárido,' Recife, Brazil, www.asabrasil.org.br/Portal/Informacoes.asp?COD_MENU=105, accessed September 2014

Dias da Silva, E. (2013) 'Community seedbanks in the semi-arid region of Brazil,' in W. De Boef, A. Subedi, N. Peroni, M. Thijssen and E. O'Keeffe (eds) *Community Biodiversity Management: Promoting Resilience and the Conservation of Plant Genetic Resources*, Earthscan, London, UK, pp102–108

Packer, L. A. (2010) *Biodiversidade como Bem Comum: Direitos dos Agricultores, Agricultoras, Povos e Comunidades Tradicionais*, Curitiba, PR, Terra de Direitos, organização de direitos humanos

Santilli, J. (2012) *Agrobiodiversity and the Law: Regulating Genetic Resources, Food Security and Cultural Diversity*, Earthscan, London, UK, pp102–108

Santos, A., Curado, F. F., Dias da Silva, E., Petersen, P. and Londres, F. (eds) (2012) *Pesquisa e Política de Sementes no Semiárido Paraibano: Sementes da Paixão*, Embrapa Tabuleiros Costeiros, Aracaju, Sergipe, Brazil

Schmidt, C. and Guimarães, L. A. (2008) 'O mercado institucional como instrumento para o fortalecimento da agricultura familiar de base ecológica,' *Agriculturas*, vol 5, no 2, pp7–13

40 The role of community seed banks in adaptation to climate change in Mesoamerica

Gea Galluzzi, Evert Thomas, Maarten van Zonneveld, Jacob van Etten and Marleni Ramirez

In Mesoamerica, despite many successful experiences with community seed banks, some of which are described in this book (Chapters 16, 17, 26, 33), formal recognition of their important contribution to the conservation of agricultural biodiversity, food security and adaptation to climate change has yet to come. A promising advance in this direction is the recently developed *Strategic Action Plan to Strengthen Conservation and Use of Mesoamerican Plant Genetic Resources for Adapting Agricultural Systems to Climate Change* (Ramirez et al., 2014).

The plan was formulated over the course of 2012–2013 with funding from the Benefit-Sharing Fund of the International Treaty on Plant Genetic Resources for Food and Agriculture. Stakeholders from six countries in the region were involved in its development under the scientific guidance of Bioversity International's Regional Office for the Americas. The resulting plan, supported by the Central American Council of Ministers, is structured in thematic sections focussing on in-situ/on-farm and ex-situ conservation, sustainable use, policies and institutions. Each section outlines actions to be carried out over the next ten years. Community seed banks are mentioned across all sections and associated with a number of priority activities reflecting their multifaceted purposes and legitimacy as local institutions that promote community-based conservation and sustainable use.

The ex-situ section of the strategic action plan outlines activities aimed at restructuring the conservation system in the region to boost efficiency and foster synergies among actors and institutions while reducing duplication of effort. The consideration of community seed banks within this new structure is based on recognition of the role they play in linking formal conservation institutions and farmers, thereby enhancing the flow of plant genetic resources within the system, especially those with adaptive traits. The importance of fostering connections and exchanges between community seed banks, including links with farmers from local communities not served by seed banks, is also stressed. The emphasis placed on strengthening seed systems highlights the role of community seed banks as decentralized repositories of locally adapted genetic diversity and associated traditional knowledge in the hands of farmers. The plan recognizes the contribution of community seed banks to the maintenance of crops and landraces in the territories where they have acquired their distinctive features, and it suggests ways to integrate seed banks into programmes for strengthening biocultural territories and traditional food systems in the pursuit of food sovereignty, sustainability and health.

Among activities to improve the sustainable use of plant genetic resources, the plan includes the establishment of community seed banks and reserves in climate-vulnerable communities, given their capacity to respond quickly to environmental disasters and contribute to the restoration of local food security. The section on policy recognizes the importance of providing institutional support to community seed banks by formally recognizing their role in conservation and use of agricultural biodiversity, food security and climate change adaptation. This section also highlights the relevance of supporting community seed banks with implementation of farmers' rights legislation at the national level. Among the actions to strengthen capacity in the region, the plan calls for supporting further training of communities, as well as professionals in national institutions, in establishing and managing technically sound community seed banks, while strengthening their links to national and regional plant genetic resource programmes and initiatives.

The strategic action plan may be the first regional instrument to assign a formal role to community seed banks on a road map of interdisciplinary technical and policy actions centred on plant genetic resources for food and agriculture. The uptake of its recommendations by national decision-makers is the next essential step towards leveraging the role of communities in conserving, sustainably using and mobilizing the region's rich agricultural biodiversity in the wake of climate change.

Reference

Ramirez, M., Galluzzi, G., van Zonneveld, M., Thomas, E., van Etten, J., Pinzón, S., Beltrán, M., Alcázar, C., Libreros, D., Vay, L., Solano, W., Williams, D., Maselli, S., Quirós, W., Alonzo, S. and Remple, N. (2014) *Strategic Action Plan to Strengthen Conservation and Use of Mesoamerican Plant Genetic Resources for Adapting Agricultural Systems to Climate Change*, Bioversity International, Rome, Italy, www.bioversityinternational.org/news/detail/an-action-plan-to-conserve-and-use-the-diversity-of-mesoamerica/, accessed 3 September 2014

41 Nepal

Government policies and laws related to community seed banks

Pashupati Chaudhary, Rachana Devkota, Deepak Upadhyay and Kamal Khadka

Community seed banks promote collective efforts to strengthen traditional seed systems and facilitate the systematic preservation, access, availability, exchange and maintenance of high-quality seeds, especially of local varieties. In Nepal, community seed banks hold great potential for improving food security and community resilience by promoting local crop varieties. However, without government support and appropriate policies, it is difficult to manage and sustain these seed banks effectively. They continue to receive little attention from government: policies and laws are generally not supportive, although a few recent examples of positive change do exist. As a result, the traditional seed supply system is under threat from the formal system, which promotes modern varieties. Thus, it is important to review existing policies and laws, identify sources of policy constraints and suggest appropriate ways to strengthen community seed banks in the future.

After reviewing various policy documents, we identified gaps and constraints in policy, law, regulatory and legal frameworks and administrative procedures concerning community seed banks in Nepal. Looking at major regulatory documents related to seed and agro-biodiversity conservation, we identified the pros and cons of the relevant policies. The documents included are approved or draft versions of the National Seed Act (1988 and amended 2008), Seed Regulation (1997 and revised 2013), Seed Policy (1999), Plant Variety Protection Act (2004), Access and Benefit Sharing Law (2002), Seed Vision 2025, Agrobiodiversity Policy (2007, revised 2011 and revised 2014) and Community Seed Bank Guideline (2009).

In 2003, a turning point for community seed banks occurred in Nepal when the nongovernmental organization (NGO) Local Initiatives for Biodiversity, Research and Development (LI-BIRD) established a seed bank at Kachorwa, Bara. This facility, which is very active, well functioning and growing, is seen by many as an example to follow (see Chapter 34).

National Seed Act

Although policies and acts formulated and promulgated before the establishment of the Kachorwa seed bank in 2003 did not mention community seed banks proper, some of them did lead to the emergence of community initiatives in production and distribution of plant genetic resources. The first act to do with seeds, the National Seed Act (1988), has a provision for inviting two seed entrepreneurs, two seed producers and farmers to sit on a national level seed committee, a body responsible for providing advice on formulation and implementation of seed-related policies. However, although the original seed act opened the door, the amended act of 2008 has no mention of community seed banks.

Seed Regulation

In 1997, the Seed Quality Control Centre prepared a Seed Regulation, which was revised in 2013, effectively as a way to implement the National Seed Act. The regulation is in favour of promoting local varieties improved by farmers or jointly by farmers and scientists using participatory approaches. This has opened up opportunities for farmers to register their local landraces provided they meet some basic criteria, which are not very complicated. Community seed banks can play an important role in identifying promising landraces and registering them in the name of individual farmers or farmer groups. However, the Seed Quality Control Centre still has to prepare a comprehensive guideline on seed quality control to ensure that legislation is properly enacted. It would be beneficial if both community seed banks and the national gene bank were involved in this process.

Seed Policy

The Seed Policy (1999) emphasizes organization and management related to the formation of farmers' groups, revolving fund support and management, technical services and a transportation subsidy on seed with a focus on remote areas of the country. This is directly related to community seed banks, but, to date, relevant programmes have made few resources available to support them.

Plant Variety Protection Act

The Plant Variety Protection Act (2004) recognizes plant breeders' efforts and farmers' knowledge and resources used in developing new varieties. It allows farmers to register, control, reproduce and market their own varieties if they meet distinctness, uniformity and stability criteria. The act also promotes export and import of seeds of farmer-released varieties and allows farmers to secure remuneration from the sale. The act allows room for community seed bank members to test promising local varieties and release them in their own name. For instance, the Kachorwa community seed bank has been playing an instrumental role in developing and releasing new varieties.

Access and Benefit Sharing Law

As a signatory of the Convention on Biological Diversity, Nepal is obliged to pass a law on access and benefit sharing that protects the rights of local communities to indigenous knowledge and plant genetic resources and permits the fair and equitable sharing of benefits arising from their use. The first draft of the law was prepared in 2002; however, no progress has been made since then, because of controversy mainly over issues related to indigenous rights. The draft version states that indigenous knowledge concerning genetic resources belongs to the community and prior informed consent is necessary if such knowledge is used in variety development.

In 2013, community seed banks operating around the country met to form a network and discuss a strategy to secure their rights. This network could play a vital role supporting these provisions in the Access and Benefit Sharing Law before it is passed.

Seed Vision 2025

Seed Vision 2025 is the first policy document that has a clear statement about community seed banks, gene banks, community-based seed production and capacity-building among seed producers and producer groups to promote production of and access to high-quality seeds. The document also envisions identifying, mapping and developing seed production pockets within the country and emphasizes investment by the private sector. If implemented properly, this policy can make a desirable level of contribution to the growth of community seed banks in the country.

Agrobiodiversity Policy

The Agrobiodiversity Policy, first developed in 2007 and revised in 2011 and 2014, is a second policy document that gives credit to community seed banks, although implicitly. It focusses on enhancing agricultural growth and food security by conserving, promoting and sustainably using agro-biodiversity; securing and promoting farming communities' rights and welfare in terms of their indigenous knowledge, skills and techniques; and developing appropriate options for fair and equitable sharing of benefits arising from the access to and use of agricultural genetic resources and materials. It also aims to promote links among international ex-situ genetic resources, national gene banks, public and private national research institutions, seed multipliers, extension agents and farmers engaged in in-situ conservation and use. Emphasis is also placed on strengthening traditional seed production and distribution systems to protect farmer-to-farmer seed exchange and improve access to genetic resources. As there is a chance of false advertisement of the quality of seeds, the sale of spurious seeds and piracy of farmers' varieties, the policy includes penalties for fraudulent activities.

Community Seed Bank Guideline

The Community Seed Bank Guideline (2009) is a comprehensive document developed to guide appropriate planning, implementation and regular monitoring of community seed bank activities. The guideline focusses on marginalized, subsistence, indigenous peoples and war-affected households that often have poor access to seed materials. The guideline shares a clear vision and outlines strategies for coordination and collaboration with various governmental organizations and NGOs; for the complementary roles communities need to play; and for capacity-building and community empowerment plans. The guideline has been used by some government agencies to establish and support a number of community seed banks, but it has not been widely disseminated.

Key reasons for poor policy formulation and implementation

There is still lack of knowledge among agricultural scientists of the importance of agro-biodiversity conservation, in general, and the role of community seed banks, in particular. The promotion of community seed banks is still seen as an NGO activity. The government has not given it priority, except in terms of some small efforts to test a particular type of seed bank in a few districts.

Serious challenges that obstruct scientists who try to promote conservation efforts are the bureaucratic hurdles imposed by the government. It takes a long time to agree on legislation and then draft, review, revise and pass it into law, but no proper input is received from farmers and grassroots organizations before drafting of the subsequent policies. The passed laws are not clearly or transparently communicated to all levels. Their clauses, statements and articles are vague, dubious and contradicting. International treaties are signed without prior research into their relevance and without an appropriate support mechanism in place.

As a result, there is poor buy-in from the relevant government agencies and NGOs, which results in less chance of successful implementation. A high rate of turnover among leaders and managers holding key decision-making positions in government further complicates things. Although government agencies and NGOs in Nepal have cooperated in the past and continue to do so – sometimes largely based on personal contacts and friendships – a true coalition has not yet been created.

The way forward

Although several relevant policies are silent about community seed banks, they are not against farmers' rights to conserve, use and distribute plant genetic resources and to share the benefits generated from them. Farmers can exercise some rights individually, but collective efforts, such as those represented by community seed banks, remain a challenge. Strong governance and collective action by local communities in conjunction with relevant government agencies and NGOs will be instrumental in advancing community seed banks in Nepal (Plate 28). Strong and continuous functional collaboration between organizations is necessary to facilitate the fluid exchange of plant genetic resources and associated knowledge.

42 Community seed banks in Mexico

An in-situ conservation strategy

Karina Sandibel Vera Sánchez, Rosalinda González Santos and Flavio Aragón-Cuevas

Community seed banks were first established in Mexico in 2005 as part of the national strategy for in-situ conservation and to support farmers in areas exposed to natural disasters. The community seed banks in Oaxaca (Chapter 23) and those of the Red de Canasta de Semillas (the 'Seed Basket' network) were the first to be established; today there are 25 community seed banks in the country (Plate 29). Their names correspond to the community where they were established (Figure 42.1 and Plate 30). All community seed banks are integrated into the network of conservation centres of the Sistema Nacional de Recursos Fitogenéticos para la Alimentación y la Agricultura (SINAREFI, national system of plant genetic resources for food and agriculture), coordinated by the national seed inspection and certification service. Currently, seven researchers from these two institutions contribute to coordinating the operation of the banks in cooperation with 663 producers.

The main functions of the community seed banks are to:

- conserve local diversity in situ;
- select seed in the field during each agricultural cycle and guarantee seed availability for subsequent cycles;
- further seed exchanges among bank members and non-member farmers;
- produce seed of threatened or endangered varieties;
- participate in seed fairs organized at the local, state and national levels;
- participate as assistant or instructor in training events on conservation and seed reproduction;
- maintain a seed stock to guarantee recovering crops following natural disasters.

Because of the great diversity of crops in Mexico, seed banks hold a large number of species, although their emphasis is on the predominant crops of small family farms or milpas (maize, beans, squash, chilies, etc.) (Plate 31). Banks in the Seed Basket network are part of an initiative to promote organic agriculture. They work with both native and introduced horticultural crops to guarantee self-sufficiency of communities in a diversity of foods (Table 42.1). Participants are involved in improving cropping practices and productivity of the crops conserved.

Figure 42.1 Distribution of community seed banks in Mexico: 1–11 Oaxaca, 12 and 13 Chiapas, 14 and 15 Yucatán, 16 Distrito Federal, 17 Chihuahua, 18 Morelos, 19 Coahuila, 20–23 Estado de México, 24 and 25 Puebla (See also Plate 30)

Source: Prepared by authors.

Table 42.1 Main crops conserved and used in Mexico's 25 community seed banks

Community	No. of producers	No. of accessions	Main crops (varietal names)
San Agustín Amatengo	40	152	Maize (Zapalote chico), beans and squash
San Jerónimo Coatlán	40	79	Maize (Olotillo, Tepecintle, Tuxpeño, Zapalote chico), beans and squash
Santa Catarina Juquila	40	113	Maize (Conejo, Olotillo, Tuxpeño), beans and squash
San Miguel del Puerto	40	75	Maize (Comiteco, Mushito), beans and squash
San Pedro Comitancillo	40	105	Maize (Conejo, Olotillo, Pepitilla, Tepecintle, Tuxpeño), beans and squash
Santa María Jaltianguis	40	290	Maize (Bolita, Pepitilla), beans and squash
Santiago Yaitepec	40	122	Maize (Bolita, Cónico, Elotes occidentales, Nal-Tel de altura, Olotón), beans and squash

(Continued)

Table 42.1 (Continued)

Community	No. of producers	No. of accessions	Main crops (varietal names)
Santa María Peñoles	40	NA	Maize (Bolita, Chalqueño, Cónico, Elotes cónicos, Olotón, Serrano, Tepecintle, Tuxpeño), beans and squash
San Andrés Cabecera Nueva	40	NA	Maize (Chalqueño, Cónico, Elotes cónicos, Tuxpeño, Olotillo, Conejo), beans and squash
Putla Villa de Guerrero (1)	40	NA	Maize (Conejo, Olotillo, Tuxpeño), beans and squash
Chiapa de Corzo	40	85	Maize, beans and squash
Villaflores	40	60	Maize, beans and squash
Xoy	4	12	Maize (Dzit Bacal, Nal-tel), beans and squash
Yaxcaba	3	50	Maize (Dzit Bacal, Nal-tel), beans and squash
Milpa Alta	3	50	Maize (Cacahuacintle, Chalqueño)
Bocoyna	14	25	Maize (Apachito, Azul, Cristalino de Chihuahua, Gordo, Palomero)
Putla Villa de Guerrero (2)	22	22	Tomatoes, lettuce, spinach, beans, maize, carrots, peas and squash
Cuernavaca	20	21	Tomatoes, lettuce, spinach, beans, maize, carrots, peas and squash
Chiconcuautla	20	23	Tomatoes, lettuce, spinach, beans, maize, carrots, peas and squash
Ciudad Acuña	18	22	Tomatoes, lettuce, spinach, beans, maize, carrots, peas and squash
Tepetlixpa	13	41	Tomatoes, lettuce, spinach, beans, maize, carrots, peas and squash
Amecameca (San Pedro Nexapa)	6	27	Tomatoes, lettuce, spinach, beans, maize, carrots, peas and squash
Amecameca (Barrio el Rosario)	27	83	Tomatoes, lettuce, spinach, beans, maize, carrots, peas and squash
Atlacomulco	15	199	Maize (Cacahuacintle, Celaya, Chalqueño, Cónico, Reventador, Tabloncillo, Tepecintle, Toluqueño)
Xochitlán de Vicente Suárez	41	53	Squash
Total	686	1,709*	

*The number of unique varieties has not been calculated.

The seed conservation centres, established by SINAREFI, store samples of the material in the 25 community seed banks under controlled humidity and temperature. These samples are used to study diversity, morphologic characteristics, tolerance to biotic and abiotic factors and evaluation of quality.

Material transfer agreements, established by SINAREFI, are required for access and exchange of accessions. Some materials in the community seed banks are being used in participatory plant breeding processes, eliminating undesirable characteristics and focussing mainly on yield and tolerance to diseases. For example, the races Bolita and Mixteco in Oaxaca, Chalqueño and Cónico in the State of Mexico and Elotes Occidentales in Guanajuato are the result of participatory plant breeding.

Governance and management

In most cases, producers elect representatives for each bank. These representatives establish a committee in charge of managing the bank, exchanging seed, renewing the seed stock and guaranteeing sufficient reserve, scheduling work meetings and liaising with the institution directing the project. The committee decides on the criteria for use of the seed. Normally, stored seed is available not only to members, but also to farmers in the community or in neighbouring communities, but this is at the discretion of the committee. Seed is available throughout the year, but most exchanges take place just before the planting season. Administrative procedures are different for each bank, as each community has its own authority system.

Banks in the Seed Basket network include a central node, regional seed banks, community seed banks and family orchards. The central node holds samples of all materials in the family orchards and duplicate samples are maintained in SINAREFI's conservation centres. Network participants receive an initial seed stock for planting in accordance with the needs of each family and each community. This stock is enough for establishing the family's orchard and producing the first batch of seeds that goes into the bank's collection.

The amount of seed conserved in the community bank varies depending on the amount provided by each producer. In addition to the sample held by the bank, each farmer is requested to keep an amount of reserve seed of the varieties he or she plants, equivalent to the amount required for planting. If risk of loss is high, due to the frequency of such events as frosts, hail, hurricanes or drought, then the reserve will be two or three times the amount planted. Reserve seed is not consumed until the next crop has been harvested, to guarantee the immediate availability of material for planting in case of natural disaster. Most participating producers plant less than 3ha, meaning that they keep at home, on average, 20–60kg maize, 20–40kg beans and 1–2kg squash seeds. In the community seed bank, this same farmer would keep approximately 3kg maize, 2kg beans and 500g squash seeds, although these amounts vary depending on the bank. Each accession in the community seed bank has a record of data provided by the farmer, such as plant and fruit characteristics, area of adaptation, best planting dates, traditional uses and agronomic advantages.

Each year, member farmers renew their seed stock to maintain seed viability. Seed of the various crops is selected in the field, in the central part of the plot to avoid contamination with varieties of neighbouring farmers. After harvesting, seeds are dried to 10 per cent moisture content. They are then cleaned to eliminate impurities. They are then stored in hermetic containers of various sizes. All farmers participate in seed conditioning, under the guidance of the bank's committee and the supporting expert in charge.

Spreadsheets are used to record information about the seeds stored in the bank; these are prepared by the expert responsible for each community bank. Information recorded includes passport data, characteristics pointed out by farmers and morphologic characteristics observed by the experts when the materials have been characterized. Another important piece of information is the availability of seed. The passport data for material in community banks is currently being transferred to SINAREFI's Germocalli platform, which is used by the community seed banks in the national network of conservation centres.

SINAREFI and the institutions participating in activities of the community seed banks and in conservation of plant genetic resources organize local, state and national seed fairs to raise awareness about the diversity conserved by farmers in the banks. Fairs are also an opportunity for farmers to share their experience as well as materials of interest. The experts and researchers responsible for or supporting the community seed banks set up demonstration plots in farmers' fields to demonstrate the favourable characteristics of various native varieties. Training activities emphasize methods for conserving and improving seed conditioning, as well as agro-ecological practices to improve production.

A large percentage of the work of community seed banks is done by women. Women participate in seed bank activities throughout the process of selecting, conserving, exchanging and using the seed. They are also members of the administrative boards and they are more likely than men to participate in seed fairs, in preparing traditional dishes and in the training courses.

Institutional links and support

As part of the national strategy for conserving plant genetic resources, community seed banks are financed through SINAREFI's projects. Currently, Mexico's network of conservation centres is composed of five orthodox seed conservation centres (orthodox seed are those that survive drying or freezing under ex-situ conditions), three recalcitrant seed conservation centres (recalcitrant seeds do not survive drying or freezing under ex-situ conditions, e.g. seeds of avocado and mango), one base collection centre, 19 working collections centres and 25 community seed banks. The Seed Basket initiative is managed like an integrated network that is part of this strategy.

The annual budget for establishing and maintaining community seed banks is US$115,000. Each institution in charge of the projects under which the community seed banks are financed supplies personnel, infrastructure and vehicles for following up on activities with producers. In addition to this structure established in the National Action Plan for Plant Genetic Resources, legislation for conservation, management and use of genetic resources is being developed. These laws should further strengthen the link between the community banks and institutional structures.

Achievements and future work

To date, the 25 community seed banks in nine states involve and directly benefit 600 producers, mainly in areas where the risk of natural disasters is greatest. Community seed banks have been able to rescue valuable materials that are tolerant to wind, drought, pests and diseases. Some native varieties have excellent nutritional qualities for traditional or industrial use. Community seed banks in Oaxaca have increased the diversity of their seed by exchanging varieties within the community and with producers from other seed banks. Some wild species have been rescued: one example is Teocintle (*Zea mays* ssp. *parviglumis*), and others are wild relatives of beans. Banks have played a key role in raising public awareness of the importance of conserving local species. At seed fairs, bank members have been awarded prizes for the diversity and quality of their crops and of the products they prepare based on these varieties.

In addition to consolidating each of the existing community seed banks, national conservation strategies envision the creation of an electronic communications network among banks to promote the exchange of seeds and experience, at least among those responsible for the banks. Continuing to foster seed fairs at all levels is also an objective to involve and establish links among all stakeholders. Another plan is to study the feasibility of establishing new community seed banks in the country. Priority will be given to areas inhabited by indigenous groups and mestizos, as these people maintain high levels of plant diversity and threatened species, and to areas susceptible to natural disasters.

A future sustainability strategy is to raise awareness among farmers of the importance of their seed and for them to receive tangible benefits from their conservation efforts. The community seed banks also must be legally recognized. An option that could provide resources in the future to support conservation activities is the creation of producers' cooperatives to consolidate sales of traditional products based on the native varieties conserved by the network of banks.

Acknowledgements

The authors thank Dr. Luis Antonio Dzib Aguilar (Universidad Autónoma Chapingo), Ingeniero Joel Padilla Cruz (Sistema Producto de Maíz del Distrito Federal), Ingeniero Osvaldo Baldemar Pérez Cuevas (Servicio Nacional de Inspección y Certificación de Semillas–Chihuahua), Guadalupe Ortíz-Monasterio Landa (Canasta de Semillas), Ingeniero Everardo Lovera Gómez (Federación de Productores de Maíz del Estado de México) and Delia Castro Lara, MSc (Universidad Nacional Autónoma de México).

43 South Africa

A new beginning for community seed banks

Ronnie Vernooy, Bhuwon Sthapit, Mabjang Angeline Dibiloane, Nkat Lettie Maluleke, Tovhowani Mukoma and Thabo Tjikana

Complementing ex-situ with in-situ conservation

South Africa's smallholder seed systems are increasingly coming under pressure. Factors, such as drought, crop failure, difficult storage conditions and poverty, are having a negative impact on both the amount of seed and the number of plant varieties available to farmers. In addition, as a result of agricultural modernization, farmers are increasingly purchasing more seed and losing locally adapted varieties along with the associated traditional knowledge and skills in selection and seed storage.

To turn this tide, the Department of Agriculture, Forestry and Fisheries of the Government of the Republic of South Africa is considering community seed banks as a means to strengthen informal seed systems, support conservation of traditional farmer varieties and maintain seed security at district and community levels. The *Departmental Strategy on Conservation and Sustainable Use of Genetic Resources for Food and Agriculture* proposes, among other focus areas, both ex-situ and in-situ conservation of plant genetic resources for food and agriculture.

South Africa has a well developed ex-situ conservation facility, the National Plant Genetic Resources Centre (NPGRC), where accessions of plant material are maintained. The centre's mandate has recently been extended to include community seed banks as a strategy to promote on-farm management and conservation. To fulfill this mandate, NPGRC considers capacity development of its frontline staff an important step. Capacity building should empower farmers by strengthening informal seed systems, supporting the conservation of traditional farmer varieties and maintaining seed security. NPGRC has joined forces with Bioversity International to develop a national plan for the establishment and support of community seed banks. Previous efforts to establish community seed banks in two of the country's smallholder areas supported by NPGRC were not successful.

A first step was an assessment in two smallholder farming regions: Mutale in the northeastern province of Limpopo and Sterkspruit in the Eastern Cape province in the southeast (Vernooy et al., 2013). The aim of this study was to answer the following questions:

- To what extent are farmers still engaged in growing landraces?
- What are the main factors influencing the choice of crops and crop varieties?
- Is loss of diversity occurring?
- Are farmers experiencing the impact of climate change? If so, how are they responding?
- Are farmers saving seed on farm or at the community level?
- Are farmers exchanging seeds? With whom, when and how?
- Are farmers' seed-saving and exchanging practices changing, and how?
- What do farmers think about a community seed bank?

To answer these questions, the assessment team organized seed fairs (Plate 32); carried out historical analyses of crop use, four-cell analysis of crops and crop varieties and seed network mapping; and conducted a farmer survey (for details, see Sthapit et al., 2012).

Reviving local seed systems

Farmers in both regions live and work in landscapes characterized by tough conditions, including low rainfall and poor access to major markets at both sites and cold and windy weather in the mountainous areas of Eastern Cape. However, the farmers still manage to make a living. They grow food mostly for subsistence, but also succeed in producing small surpluses for marketing. Crop and varietal diversity combined with diverse animal husbandry practices (cattle, sheep and goats) is central to their farming systems and to survival. In both regions, farmers rely on combinations of a few major crops grown in large areas by most households (white and yellow maize, white sorghum and millet; and groundnut in Limpopo) and on a larger number of crops grown in small areas (pumpkin, squash, beans, cowpeas, potatoes, melon, calabash and tobacco; and many fruits and vegetables in Limpopo). Intraspecies diversity of maize, sorghum and melon is relatively high, but it is low for other crops. Farmers said they have tried a number of modern varieties of maize and cowpea, but often these modern varieties do not perform well under difficult conditions.

Traditional crops and varieties are the lifeline of farmers' livelihoods. The major reasons both women and men farmers give for maintaining diversity are good taste and nutrition (the word farmers used translates as 'powerful'), easy to use in preparation of traditional dishes, drought resistant, resistant to pests and diseases, short growing cycle, low input, long-term storage, heritage and intercropping. However, in the last few decades, several crops and crop varieties have disappeared or their seeds have become difficult to obtain. Farmers' choice of crop species is limited, and research in this area is minimal. Reasons given by farmers for the situation include increased drought, replacement of traditional varieties by modern ones (maize) and disinterest of the younger generation in farming.

The organization of seed networks varies from village to village, but traditional seed exchanges continue to predominate in both regions. However, the purchase of seeds – from other farmers, street vendors or cooperatives – on a small scale is not uncommon. In a few villages, seed networks are dynamic and strong, with many people involved in donating and receiving seeds. In most villages, however, they are weaker with fewer exchanges or exchanges between only a few farmers. Seed exchange seems to be mostly among families, friends and church members. Most take place within the same village. In Limpopo, where many men work in areas other than agriculture, women are the main participants in the seed network, whereas in Eastern Cape, men predominate. When asked about their interest in setting up a community seed bank to strengthen both conservation and exchange at village and provincial levels, the farmers at both sites responded positively (see Box 43.1).

Box 43.1 Women farmers' views

Interviews with four women farmers in Gumbu village, Limpopo, revealed that most farmers in the village grow more vegetables than grain crops. The women contend that they maintain a range of species and varieties, because they inherited them from their parents. They report that crops are consumed by the household; variety gives them satisfaction and allows them to earn some extra cash by selling part of the produce; seeds and leaves are used for decoration and cultural celebrations; and rare species are adapted to local weather and soil conditions. Crop diversity at the farm level is not high, although some farmers maintain rare varieties. According to the women, exchange takes place mainly within the family and with fellow church members. Trust is a key factor in seed exchange. However, the women say that they welcome seed exchange with farmers of different communities and cultures and they are interested in developing a conservation strategy based on a community seed bank.

A decision-support framework for moving ahead

In light of the study results, the research team developed a framework to assess the viability of community seed banks in both areas. This framework has 14 variables (Figure 43.1).

Applying this framework to the study results led to the recommendation to establish a pilot farmer-led community seed bank at each site. The research team particularly stressed the importance of farmer responsiveness, the presence of a supportive extension agency and the possibility of connecting with the Department of Agriculture, Forestry and Fisheries, the national gene bank and research agencies.

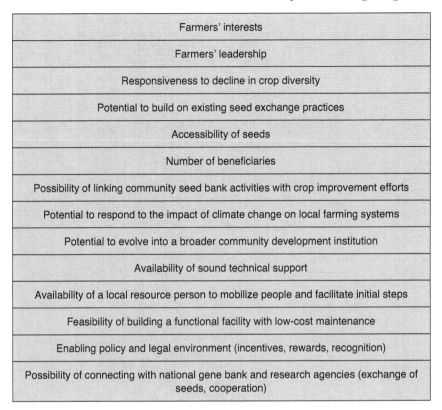

Figure 43.1 Variables involved in the decision to establish community seed banks
Source: Adapted from Vernooy et al. 2013.

It was proposed that, for each seed bank, an initial three-year management and monitoring plan be prepared and supporting activities planned to ensure that the banks are not isolated but develop as platforms of social learning and community development. Through such a platform, the government of South Africa could provide incentives, such as awarding farmers for the greatest efforts to maintain traditional crop and variety diversity; supporting diversity fairs to bring together seed holders and seed seekers from the various sources, such as municipality, villages, other provinces and the national gene bank; and delivering improved seed management and production kits.

References

Sthapit, B., Shrestha, P. and Upadhyay, M. (eds) (2012) *On-farm Management of Agricultural Biodiversity in Nepal: Good Practices*, Bioversity International, Rome, Italy, Local Initiative for Biodiversity, Research and Development, Pokhara, Nepal, and Nepal Agricultural Research Council, Khumaltar, Nepal

Vernooy, R., Sthapit, B., Tjikana, T., Dibiloane, A., Maluleke, N. and Mukoma, T. (2013) *Embracing Diversity: Inputs for a Strategy to Support Community Seedbanks in South Africa's Smallholder Farming Areas*, Bioversity International, Rome, Italy, and Department of Agriculture, Forestry and Fisheries, Republic of South Africa, Pretoria, Republic of South Africa, www.bioversityinternational.org/uploads/tx_news/Embracing_diversity_inputs_for_a_strategy_to_support_community_seedbanks_in_South_Africa%E2%80%99s_smallholder_farming_areas_1698_02.pdf, accessed 3 September 2014

44 Epilogue
Visions of the future

*Ronnie Vernooy, Bhuwon Sthapit
and Pitambar Shrestha*

In this book, we have recognized and applauded the major achievements of 30 years of community seed banking around the world. We have also identified a number of common weaknesses and challenges and offered some critical thoughts about the way forward. To conclude, we present three broad possible scenarios for the future development of community seed banks as input for reflection – and action.

More of the same

The first scenario depicts a development path that consists of more of the same. Community seed banks would come and go, perhaps increase in number in countries where they have made a recent start, but decrease in countries where strong growth occurred earlier. Support from external agencies would remain an important driver, although dwindling international development funds would most likely put the brakes on current levels of support. This could lead to supporting organizations not spending sufficient time to understand the local context and to build social and human capital according to the needs and interests of the community. Community seed banks would be faced with the challenge of generating funds locally (for example, through community-based management funds) or obtaining financial resources from donor agencies. A few 'new' countries would develop a strategy for institutional support through a specific policy clause or a national conservation strategy. In a few countries, existing or emerging networks would be consolidated. Other such initiatives would be difficult because of lack of recognition, weak financial and technical support and difficulties in establishing effective collaboration with other actors, such as research agencies and national gene banks. Community seed banks around the world would remain largely disconnected from each other.

Institutionalization

The second scenario represents a strong institutionalization path. Elements of this scenario are already being explored by various community seed banks highlighted in this book. Community-based frameworks for the conservation of agricultural biodiversity would gain ground in many countries and internationally. Building on these processes, community seed banks, with the technical support of external agencies, would pursue interactions with national and even international gene banks to set up robust, dynamic and well-funded national systems that are well connected to the international level. Through this system, community seed banks would become part of a global system of conservation and exchange, receive institutional recognition and benefit from adequate, long-term technical and financial support. Community seed banks would form an international 'confederation' to share knowledge and experience and speak with a common voice. Community seed banks would take an active part in this system, not only in terms of seed management, but also concerning questions related to seed research and development, seed policies and laws and farmers' rights. The system would be based on agreed rules and regulations about providing and accessing seeds and related knowledge as well as concerning the sharing of non-monetary and monetary benefits. The system at large would operate in an enabling policy and legal environment at national levels and under international agreements, such as the International Treaty on Plant Genetic Resources for Food and Agriculture and the Convention on Biological Diversity's Nagoya Protocol. Community seed banks would embody the concrete practices that would make local access and benefit sharing a reality, as intended by international agreement.

Towards open-source seed systems

The third scenario would lead to the establishment and expansion of open-source seed systems around the world. This is a more speculative scenario; although the idea of open-source seed systems is not new (e.g. see Kloppenburg, 2010), the actual practice is. (In 2014, the Open Source Seed Initiative in Minnesota, USA, began operations on a small scale; see www.opensource seedinitiative.org/about/).

For a global open-source seed system to become a reality, well-functioning connectivity of community seed banks with each other and with other seed actors would be required. Another condition would be the creation of a supportive, or at least non-obstructive, policy and legal environment. An open-source seed system would be based on the principle that benefits can be maximized if no access and use restrictions exist based, in particular, on (private) monopolistic property rights. The underlying logic is that farmers are both users and innovators of technology, i.e. seeds in this case. Such a system aims to promote experimentation, innovation, sharing, exchanging, using or reusing seeds.

An open-source system would not necessarily mean free for all, but rather access and use could be regulated through licensing under a creative commons, open-source license (OSL) or general public license (GPL) agreement. The open-source model could be applied to the development of plant varieties or any other product used in farming, agro-machinery and sharing of information and knowledge. For example, in plant breeding, any existing or newly developed variety could be made available under an OSL/GPL or a similar document explicitly outlining rights and claims.

To implement such a model, community seed banks would have to be empowered and could serve as coordinating or nodal agencies bringing together farmers, plant breeders, gene bank managers and others in the following areas:

- legitimization of community seed banks as local organizations for the conservation of agricultural biodiversity, the organization of seed fairs, participatory seed exchanges and community seed production and distribution;
- conservation and revival of existing varieties by providing access to and availability of rare and unique local varieties;
- participatory varietal selection to generate added value for cultivation and use of existing varieties;
- participatory plant breeding to develop newer varieties and provide options for access to new diversity to cope with adversity and strengthen farmers' skills in selection.

This scenario would be supported by significant local resource mobilization because of increased levels of awareness of and concerns about the need to safeguard agricultural biodiversity. International benefit-sharing funds would be strong supporters of community seed banks, and this might further influence government policies in support of community seed banks.

Reference

Kloppenburg, J. (2010) 'Seed sovereignty: the promise of open source biology,' in H. Wittman, A. A. Desmarais and A. Wiebe (eds) *Food Sovereignty: Reconnecting Food, Nature and Community*, Fernwood, Halifax, Canada, pp152–167

Index

Page numbers in *italics* denotes a table/figure